DARK TO LIGHT

Volume 2
Ancient Codes of Kabbalah, Zohar & Torah

By
DR. STEWART A. SWERDLOW
*Rabbi Shalom Chaim ben Baer-El
HaRav HaAkravim*
WITH JANET DIANE MOURGLIA-SWERDLOW

Expansions Publishing Company, Inc.
Saint Joseph, Michigan
USA

Copyright © 2023 Expansions Publishing Company, Inc.

Published by: Expansions Publishing Company, Inc.
                P.O. Box 12
                Saint Joseph Michigan 49085 USA
                269-519-8036
                Skype: eventsatexpansions
                customersupport@expansions.com
                www.expansions.com

ISBN: 978-1-7349281-9-8

Cover Photo by Jonathan J. Swerdlow
www.jonathanswerdlow.com

All rights reserved. Printed in the United States of America. No parts of this book may be used or reproduced in any manner whatsoever without written permission except in the case of brief quotations embodied in critical articles and reviews.

Medical Disclaimer

The information provided in this publication is not an attempt to attempt to practice medicine or provide specific medical advice, nor is it a substitute for medical care.

We always recommend consulting with a healthcare professional before starting any diet, exercise, supplementation, or medication program.

You assume full responsibility for using any information provided and agree that we are not responsible or liable for any claim resulting from its use by you or any user.

Dedication

When I look back on all of the books I have written in the last decades, I have thanked just about everyone I ever knew that has inspired me in my life. The most important one of all is my wife, Janet. Without her, no books would ever have been written by me.

She is also the only one who has the patience and courage to edit my writings, knowing how I react to changes. She is a brave lass and a Woman of Valor.

In addition to all of this, a great inspiration and source of advice, has been the 7th Lubavitcher Rebbe, Menachem Mendel Schneerson, may his name be blessed in heaven. Although he left the Earth in 1994, he is still with us and guides me daily. I have been blessed to have met him twice in my lifetime.

I am grateful to the Chabad movement and the knowledge of Chassidut, which will enable this troubled world to move forward from End of Days to Messianic Times.

May You Be Blessed with God's Grace and Mercy.

Amen!

Books by Stewart A. Swerdlow & Janet Diane Mourglia-Swerdlow

13-Cubed: Case Studies in Mind-Control & Programming

13-Cubed Squared: More Case Studies in Mind-Control & Programming

1099 Daily Affirmations for Self-Change

Alternative Medical Apocrypha: Body-Mind Correlations

Blue Blood, True Blood: Conflict & Creation

Dark to Light Volume 1: Ancient Codes of Torah, Kabbalah & Zohar

Dark to Light Volume 2: Ancient Codes of Torah, Kabbalah & Zohar

Dark to Light Volume 3: Ancient Codes of Torah, Kabbalah & Zohar

Dark to Light Volume 4: Ancient Codes of Torah, Kabbalah & Zohar

Decoding Your Life: An Experiential Course in Self-Reintegration

Healer's Handbook: A Journey Into Hyperspace

Healing Archetypes and Symbols

Heights of Deprogramming

Heights of Health

Heights of Relationships

Heights of Spirituality

Heights of Wealth

Hyperspace Helper

Hyperspace Plus

Keys to Success

King Bee, Queen Bee

Light Shines in Darkness

Little Fluffs Children's Series

Miracles in Motion

Montauk: Alien Connection

Revelations of Time & Space, History and God

Stewart Says…

Template of God-Mind

True Reality of Sexuality

True World History: Humanity's Saga

Unlocking New Perspectives

White Owl Legends: An Archetypal Story of Creation

Table of Contents

Introduction 11

Hebrew Holidays 13

Spiritual Fulfillment 31

Age of Aquarius 45

Miracles 55

Inner Consciousness 65

Rectification 77

Judgments 91

Gratitude & Devotion 103

Hebrew History 115

Noahides 127

Cosmic Code 139

End of Days 149

Thoughts Create Reality 159

Protection 167

Eliminating Chaos 179

Choose Elevation 189

Trust God 195

Soul Growth 205

Deeper Levels 215

Healing Light 225

Addendums

King Solomon 236
Tale of Two Talmuds: Jerusalem and Babylonian 242
Dan: The Tevet Personality 247
The History of Yiddish 252
The Story of "Oy Vey" 256
What Does "Maccabee" Mean? 259
Lighting Shabbat Candles 262
The Hanukkah Story 266
Bereishit: The World Needs a King 268
How to Pray for Happiness 273
What is Sigd? 277
Tzom Gedaliah 278
A Guide to Jewish Acronyms and Abbreviations 280
Hebrew Letter Vowels 285
What Is Gematria? 293
Hoshana Rabbah 297
Jewish Death and Mourning 101 300
5782: Numbers and Meanings for the New Year 303
Elul: The Month of Self-Discovery 315
9 Jewish Things About Pomegranates 324
Funny Jewish and Yiddish Sayings 327
Jewish Views on Cremation 332
Jews and Guns 336
What Is Idolatry? 341
Judaism and Sex: Questions and Answers 345

What Is Midrash? 352

The Noahide Laws 354

Ask the Expert: Kosher Pig 359

How to Acquire the Right Mental State for Prayer 361

Quick Reference For Hebrew Terms 366

7 Reasons to Observe Shabbat 370

Translation of The Shema 373

What is Shemini Atzeret? 376

How the Sounds of the Shofar Rectify Our Psyche 378

Ask the Expert: Slanted Mezuzah 383

What Is the Talmud? 385

Unetaneh Tokef: Do We Control Our Fate? 388

Witches & Witchcraft 391

The Making of a Torah Scroll 396

Yom Kippur Info/Services 400

Glossary 410

Index 416

Introduction

This book continues the journey that you began in ***Dark to Light Volume 1*** and is based on my *Dark to Light* webinars Sessions 7-11. There is so much information to introduce that while these books barely scratch the surface, they are comprehensive enough to propel you deep into your own inner Light. The more you explore within, the more you understand what a vast resource you already contain. Working through the homework, exercises and visualizations allow you to explore your inner depths and open up new pathways of knowledge. I have included comprehensive Addendums so you can easily research some of these topics at your own pace. All of this information is extremely multi-layered and multifaceted. Torah, Kabbalah, and Zohar are exciting additions to your Hyperspace/Oversoul tools and techniques. Be sure that you have the following books in your Personal Library to strengthen Body, Mind, and Soul as you move forward into these *End of Days*.

*** King Bee, Queen Bee***

Template of God-Mind

Revelations of Time & Space, History and God

Heights of Spirituality

Miracles in Motion

Light Shines in Darkness

You chose to be here for a reason. You are part of the solution so it is important that you fulfill your function and mission. You are important to the process of changing **Dark to Light** on this planet that we all share.

May God Bless You!

Amen!

Hebrew Holidays

E lul is the Hebrew month that is a time for repentance and precedes the Hebrew Holiday Rosh Hashanah. Elul correlates to the astrological sign of Virgo. According to the Zohar, during Elul you are supposed to go back in time to correct the errors of what you have done in the past, not only in this lifetime but in all of your existence. This means you reincarnate to correct the negativities that you have created and experienced.

The month of Elul also contains the frequency that allows you to control your life. Remember that the Gematria of a Hebrew word reveals layers of meaning. Letters are also permutated or rearranged, to reveal more layers of meaning, including reversing the letters to read the word backward. When the letters of Elul are reversed and read backward, Elul becomes the Hebrew word lulav. Lulav is a palm tree that is symbolic of releasing. The tall trunk of a palm tree with the palm leaves at the top represent a phallic symbol of ejaculating, referring to release and creating.

Interestingly, *Name of God Frequency #1 Time Travel*, Vav Hey Vav, from the *72 Names of God*, is about Teshuva, which means repentance. The Hebrew root letters also mean returning, so you literally return to whatever you did in order to correct it. When you deal with darkness all you have to do is turn on the light to make the darkness disappear. The Zohar says that the letter Vav represents the phallic symbol of the staff, rod, and the power of the Sword of God. Knowing this, Vav can be used to bring the Shekinah, the female energy of the God-Mind Energy, down to Earth. You can combine this with *Name of God Frequency #5 Healing*, Mem Hey Shin, to go back in time to the point where you have negatively erred so you can make the correction. This is done during the month of Elul which correlates to the month of August.

The Zohar says that Israel, or the location of Israel, is the center of energy for the entire world. Israel is essentially the Pineal Gland of the world and for this reason, maintains the peace of the world. You may question this due to the difficulties that have arisen because of the existence of Israel. However, without Israel, the world would have even worse troubles. For example, before Israel existed, the Soviet Empire and Nazi Empire created and enacted horrible atrocities.

Remember the books of the Zohar are in Aramaic, not Hebrew. When you translate to your language the words may not make very much sense to you because, in addition to the codes, some words are not easily translatable Hebrew is the language of the nonphysical universe of God, Creation, and spoken by the Hebrew Priests. Hebrew was used for religious and spiritual energetic purposes, not in daily conversation. Aramaic is the language of the physical universe spoken by the people. Both languages use the same letters but are different in the same way that French and Italian are different languages even though they use the same letters. In addition, the Zohar is a mathematical formula. The Zohar was written in Aramaic instead of Hebrew because it states that the Evil Ones do not understand Aramaic, therefore the Zohar confuses them. Simply scanning the Zohar in Aramaic removes evil. Aramaic had many different dialects and was used throughout the known world in Ancient times. Even the

Babylonians spoke Aramaic as well as the Phoenicians and Ancient Hebrews.

Torah Covers Codes

The Zohar says that the Torah is like a garment that covers the codes. In a Synagogue or Jewish Temple, the Torah is kept in the very front within a cabinet that is covered by a curtain. The cabinet is called an Ark. When the Torah is to be removed from the Ark, the curtains are opened and the congregants must stand. This is because the Torah represents the Presence of God. As the Torah is removed from the Ark, there is a specific prayer that is recited in Aramaic called the *B'rich Sh'mei*. Hebrew was the original language from which Aramaic developed. B'rich Sh'mei means the *Blessings of the Name*. In Hebrew, it would be *Barukh She'amot*, which is very similar. You can say the *B'rich Sh'mei Prayer*, or simply scan it with your eyes, before you use *72 Names of God Frequency #1 Time Travel*. In the Holy Temple, you would also have a Torah in front of you, so if you can say this in the presence of a Torah in your home or synagogue, that would be a plus.

B'rich Sh'mei (Aramaic)

Transliteration

La Al E'nash Re'chitz'na Ve'La Al Bar E'la'hin Sa'mich'na, E'la Beh'E'la'ha Di'Shma'ya, De'Hu E'la'ha Ke'shot. Ve'O'rai'teh Ke'shot, U'Ne'vi'o'hi Ke'shot, U'Mas'ge Le'Me'bad Tav'van U'Ke'shot. Bay A'na Ra'chitz, Ve'Li'Shmei Ka'di'sha Ya'ki'ra A'na Ei'mar Tush'be'chan. Ye'hai Ra'a'va Ko'da'mach De'Tif'tach Li'ba'i Be'O'rai'ta, Ve'Tash'lim Mish'a'lin De'li'ba'i Ve'Li'ba De'Chol A'mach Yis'ra'el, Le'Tav U'Le'Cha'yin Ve'LiSh'lam.

Translation

> I do not at any time put my trust in man, nor do I place my reliance on an angel, but only on the God of Heaven Who is the true God, whose Torah is truth, whose prophets are true, and

who performs numerous deeds of goodness and truth. I put my trust in Him, and I utter praises to His holy and glorious Name. May it be Your will to open my heart to the Torah, and to fulfill the desires of my heart and the hearts of all your people of Israel for good, for life, and peace. https://rsa.fau.edu/brich-shmei

From Aramaic, Arabic developed along with Farsi and Turkish. When spoken, these languages sound very similar to Hebrew. Even though Aramaic is related to Hebrew it's a different language that is more connected to European languages and Arabic. Translations of certain words and numbers are almost identical to Hebrew as well. Ethiopians speak Amharic which has its origins in the Middle East. Of course, the Emperor of Ethiopia called himself the *Lion of Judah*. Aramaic is the basis of many of the modern Middle Eastern languages now.

According to the Zohar, the Five Books of Moses, or the Torah/Bible, contain the solution for all problems. This means you need to know the codes. Each word has 70 layers of meaning. Some say there are 600,000 layers of meaning. Each word has a Gematria, or numerical, value. You can rearrange, or permutate, the letters of a word to understand the different energies and layers. The Torah is a comprehensive, complicated formulate that could take lifetimes to comprehend in its entirety. Always remember that the Torah is the surface, the Kabbalah is the codes and Zohar is the formula for the codes. Ultimately, the Torah is already within; You are the Torah. Understanding of Torah means understanding Self.

The Torah contains all universes within its codes. The Zohar, says your Soul travels to 250,000 different planets for reincarnation and to work on its Tikkun. The Zohar also says that parallel universes exist within you at all times. The Hebrew letters are the seeds of Creation and they are purposefully written in a specific way in the Torah scroll to affect its energy. The Torah is a formula, written in columns with all letters the same size. There are exceptions in various places where a letter will be exceptionally large or small; sometimes a letter is missing from a word or there is an additional letter added to a word. Sometimes there is even a dot in a seemingly odd place that indicates a connection to the intelligence of the God-Mind and you should look at the higher levels of meaning of that word and the letter above which it appears. Large letters may be a placeholder for another word. Some letters are always written with crowns whose meanings are said to be revealed when the Messiah comes. The Sages say that these are all hidden codes to be interpreted. The Torah stories are all codes and when correctly interpreted are a mirror for what is going on in your life today.

Shofar Blowing (K'Tiot) Meditation

The sound of the Shofar connects to the God Mind and destroys Satanic energies. The four types of tones that are used are as follows:

Tekiyah/Blast: Blast of sound.

Shevarim: 3 undulating noises or waves of tones.

Teruah: Staccato undulating tones, such as ta ta ta ta, nine times three.

Tekiyah/Blast Gedola/Big: Big long blast; the final sound.

According to the Zohar written 4,000 years ago, the four different sounds of the Shofar act like a vaccine against the Covid virus. The following chart shows you the sequences of the blasts. Trump encoded these sounds in the Covid-19 vaccines which is why he pushed the vaccines. The vaccine is like getting a Shofar blast in your body and energy field to remove demons. As previously stated in Volume 1, the vaccine has nothing to do with the virus, absolutely nothing, because there was no virus, but rather an artificial parasite. People get sick and die from the vaccines because they are possessed by demons and Satan. The Shofar blasts in the vaccine remove them. Then the body has a problem after decades of being inhabited by Satan.

Each sound of the Shofar correlates to one of the Holy Fathers, plus David who was the father of King Solomon.

Tekiyah: Avraham/Abraham	Removes Idol Worshipping
Shevarim: Yitzchak/Isaac	Removes Incest
Teruah: Ya'akov/Jacob	Removes Bloodshed
Tekiyah Gedokla: David/David	Removes Evil Speech

Each of these Shofar blasts works on the right, left, and central columns of your Sephirot to balance and remove these negativities from your person and energy field. Before you do or listen to each sound, concentrate on the corresponding names to boost the effects of the Shofar on you. These names represent the energies that remove evil from this planet. In addition, Isaac and David represent negative energies; Abraham and Jacob represent positive energies. They also represent the four protein bases of the DNA. Even thousands of years ago before they had microscopes and scientific knowledge supposedly, they knew about DNA, they knew there were 4 protein bases and they knew what the codes were from the Zohar that told them these things.

Tekiyah means smooth flow. Shevarim comes from the root word of shaver, which means to break. Teruah comes from the root word Teruh, which means to cut or separate. This means that the sound of the Shofar breaks and removes Satanic energies, separating them from you. The Shofar destroys negativity, injecting positive consciousness via sound. When the Israelites surrounded the walls of Jericho, they blasted the Shofar and the walls came tumbling down. It's a frequency. Sound/tone makes things move. Think of the sounds of wind, water, earthquakes, helicopters and planes. These are all tones that make things move and shake.

Listening to the Shofar is like taking the Covid-19 vaccine. But because most people are not going to listen to the Shofar, or even know what that is, the vaccine is being pushed to remove demonic entities. The Zohar calls these spiritual missiles, meaning that the vaccines are spiritual missiles against Satan. People who have the most negative effects from the vaccines are the ones most possessed by demons. If the people that you love and care about got sick from the vaccines, this is because they were connected to demonic energies. It is almost more common for someone to be connected to these negative energies than not to be at this point.

Words and Codes

In Aramaic, the word for the Zodiac sign of Libra is Mozna'aim. The root is ozen, which means ears. Therefore Libra has to do with ears and represents the planet Venus. Libra also has to do with scales that weigh because this Zodiac sign is in the month of Tishrei, the month of trials and hearings. This is why Rosh Hashanah is also in the month of Tishrei. The spiritual energy of this time is about going to your personal hearing to review what you did and how you are going to correct it.

Adam, the first human was created on Rosh Hashanah. Adam was androgynous, both male and female, meaning the positive and negative aspects of Light. Adam does not refer to a person, but rather to the energy of Light. The Zohar, thousands of years ago, states that technology will never solve problems; only the mind can do this. The Zohar also says that the normal life span of a human is 1000 years. In Atlantean times, people lived for 1100 to 1200 years. The Zohar says when you help someone, give in such a way that it makes them independent. If you give too much the person has no motivation to do something on his/her own. Read **Heights of Wealth** and **Light Shines in Darkness** to understand how to give without hurting people.

The Zohar very specifically states that every Holiday exists for all of humanity on this planet, not just for the Hebrew people. Most people, including Jewish people, don't understand the significance of the Hebrew Holidays. Holidays are not about religion but rather remembering to use specific energies that peak at specific times. These unique Holiday energy frequencies can be used to improve your Self and remove negative energies such as chaos, pain, illness, and death not only from Self but from the entire world. Conventionally, days are 24 hours long from midnight to midnight. Jews consider a day from sundown to sundown. This means the length of a Jewish day varies depending upon the season. This also means that you may get up in the morning thinking that the holiday begins that day but it does not begin until the sun sets.

The first Hebrew Holiday is Rosh Hashanah known as the Jewish New Year. Rosh Hashanah connects to the internal energy that is revealed throughout the universe. In other words, it's not just Rosh Hashanah on Earth, it's Rosh Hashanah throughout the Universe at the same time. In Hebrew, Rosh means the head, which in humans, and all intelligent creatures control life. When a fetus develops in utero the first thing that develops is the head followed by the brain and nervous system. This is why the New Year is the head of the year because if you are developing a new life and new directions with new mind-patterns you are like a new fetus in development. Rosh Hashanah this year starts September 6 which in the United States interestingly enough is also Labor Day, which is the first time that's ever happened. Usually, Rosh Hashanah is later in September, sometimes even October. This means that big, sharp changes can be expected after that first weekend in September as well as within the various subcultures of Judaism.

What's interesting is that Rosh Hashanah is not the head of the year because it is in Tishrei, the 7th month of the year on the Hebrew calendar. This is because in the first month of the Hebrew calendar Creation was made but not activated. The Zohar also says that nothing was activated on Earth until humanity appeared. This happened during the 7th month because 7 is the number of completion. Rosh Hashanah usually occurs at the end of September or early October in the Western calendar. Tishrei is in the sign of Libra which is about balance. Rosh Hashanah is about balancing the negative and positives as well as neutralizing all negative outcomes.

On the morning of Rosh Hashanah, keeping in mind that the Holiday does not start until sundown, there is a widespread Jewish custom to perform a Kaparot Ceremony. Kaparot means atonements, just as Yom Kippur means Day of Atonement. Before dawn, you are to get a white chicken, pick it up humanely and swing it 3 times around your head. While it swings above your head, it is supposed to be taking in all your sins. If you are a male, you are supposed to use a rooster; females use hens. If the woman is pregnant and doesn't know the sex of her baby, she is to use 2 hens, one for herself and a possible female child as well as a rooster for the possible male child she is carrying. If you can only afford one chicken then it should be a rooster for the man of the household, representing the entire family. Then, the chicken is kosher slaughtered and given to poor people to eat. If chickens or kosher slaughter are not available, you can perform the Kaparot Ceremony with money, giving the money to charity.

According to the Zohar, on the two days of Rosh Hashana, your Soul energy and all your actions from the previous year are reviewed to determine your repercussions. On the first day, your most serious transgressions are reviewed. On the second day, wearing a new clean garment represents a new holy aspect of your Self as your lessor infractions are reviewed. The second day is considered the new fruit of the year. A long prayer called Shekhecheyanu is said while eating the new fruit of the season. First, females light the candles and make a blessing, called a Kiddush, over the candles. Then males make a Kiddush over the wine. The Bible also talks a lot about wine and milk because these are symbols of the Torah. Milk represents the nourishment that the Torah provides for your Soul. Wine alters your consciousness.

Yom Kippur

Yom Kippur, meaning Day of Atonement, comes 10 days after Rosh Hashanah. These 10 days is a time of repentance. You can use *Name Frequency #1 Time Travel* and *Name Frequency #5 Healing* from the *72 Names of God* to go back in time, repent and correct your past so that when you are judged your past transgressions are cleared. The Sephira of Binah is revealed on Yom Kippur. Binah removes uncertainty and reveals light. Darkness is an expression of negativity. Darkness is not evil or bad, it's simply the lack of Light, which also serves a purpose in Creation. If Light was all that existed in Creation, you would not have the motivation to do other things. Darkness motivates you to go forward and become more powerful.

On Yom Kippur, there are five prohibitions. You are not allowed to eat or drink; bathe for pleasure; use oils, lotions, or cosmetics; wear leather shoes; or have sexual activity. These activities are prohibited because by restricting these activities you learn to do things for your Self as well as do things for others. In ancient times, on Yom Kippur, the priests sent two male goats into the wilderness to influence or remove the sins of the people. One goat represented God and the other Satan. Animals absorb energy, so the priests would place their right hand on the head of the goat, confess and infuse the sins of Israel into the goats before they were released into the wilderness. This symbolizes that you must confess your sins to God and take responsibility for what you have done. On Yom Kippur, you can change the entire year ahead of you by releasing your negativity. Judgment for the people was based upon which goat survived. Subsequent chapters will discuss Rosh Hashanah and Yom Kippur in greater detail.

Some animals specifically come into the world to be sacrificed. No animal should be killed unless there is a reason for it. Sacrificing allows the animals to share and reach a higher universal level. When you ingest an animal or plant, you're raising its vibration to a higher level. The reason you eat plants and animals is to raise their frequency by digesting them and assimilating their energy into your own. In this way, the animal or plant frequency is elevated. Studying Kabbalah is said to elevate the subhuman nature which can be worse than animals.

In the very beginning, there was only Adam HaRishon, the first human who did not eat animals. In those days, the animals were quite intelligent with the ability to speak and communicate. Animals were very much like humans. But, the sin of Adam HaRishon caused the animals to lose their higher level frequency because animals existed to serve humans. When humans became contaminated so did the animals. Because humans caused the downfall of animals it became the responsibility of humans from this point forward to rectify this situation. Eating is a form of punishment because, before the sin of Adam Ha Rishon, humans did not have to eat much.

Kabbalah says that humans must even eat dirt and dust because some human Souls are punished by being attached to soil due to evil things that they did. Ingesting dirt and dust helps to raise them to another frequency level. Of course, in general, people don't eat dirt. But sometimes there may be a speck of dirt on your food or a piece of dirt/dust gets blown into your mouth. One person I knew craved certain dirt from a specific area when she was pregnant. This person had a friend dig the dirt and send it to her. Some people eat clay for digestive issues. There are countries where people are so poor that they eat cakes made from dirt. When sanitation is lacking people sometimes ingest dirt, dust, and even small rocks.

Torah Protection

Reading the Torah creates protective energy around you. Simply looking at the words even without understanding protects you. This is why it is commanded that the Torah be read every Saturday. In addition, whatever you read is appropriate for that year and specific time. This emphasizes that time and space are only an illusion. By reading a story that happened thousands of years ago, you become part of that scenario which still reflects something in your life at this moment that relates to what is going on inside of you. When you read a section of the Torah on a specific day, you then interpret the symbolism as it applies to some level of your life.

70 Nations

The Zohar says that there are 70 Nations on the Earth, meaning 70 genetic strains on this planet, each with an overseeing Angel. So there's An angel for each of the 70 frequencies of humanity. The Zohar says you should speak to them. Angels can be in multiple locations simultaneously because they're Messengers without a wide range of functions. Each Angelic frequency is programmed by the Mind of God to perform a specific function. The Angelic frequency doesn't have a choice; it does not have the free choice that you have. This means that you have more power than an Angel. Angels bring news, but your mind-pattern filters and judges it as good or bad when in reality it is simply news.

The Zohar also says that reading Deuteronomy in the Old Testament opens up the technology of antimatter, going into your consciousness to remove chaos. All physical universes are twins; the physical universe and the antimatter universe. The buffer between these twin universes is the String Theory of quantum physics. Matter and antimatter keep each other alive. All this is stated in the Zohar which was written thousands of years ago.

Homework

Go online and listen to the 4 sounds of Shofar: Tekiyah, Shevarim, Teruah, and Tekiyah Gedola. Remember that there are two different kinds of Shofar horns. The Yemeni one is a long curved horn that is not the ram's horn Shofar that is used for the Torah. Be sure you listen to the sounds of the ram's horn Shofar.

Observe how you feel when you recite, mentally read, or scan with your eyes the *B'rich Sh'mei* prayer in Aramaic.

Jewish and Yiddish Sayings

If the rich could hire the poor to die for them, the poor would make a very nice living.

If he were twice as smart, he'd be an idiot.

Homework Review

Comment: I listened to the B'rich Sh'mei prayer and saw myself in the body of someone singing the words of the Torah in front of a Torah scroll. I also saw myself writing a Torah scroll in calligraphy as the sun beamed onto it. When I listened to the Shofar it at first made me uncomfortable.

Response: You went back in time. You most likely felt uncomfortable listening to the Shofar because it purges negativity from the energy field.

Comment: The prayer is a good reminder of truth and to trust in God.

Response: That's a very significant statement because everybody has their own interpretations. That doesn't necessarily mean what they write is the absolute truth. Remember that there are 70 meanings to each of the words and lines.

Comment: I wonder if the Torah ever refers to God as a woman.

Response: No, but it does refer to the Shekinah, which is the feminine aspect of God. The Torah speaks of the Original Souls that came out of the God-Mind as having both male and female aspects. When you get to that level the way you think of males and females is going to be different with nothing to do with gender. Rather it is about frequency and the positive/negative charges. Remember that the Sefirot has one column that is a positive, one column that is a negative and the middle column is neutral. You have to rise above what you have been imprinted with by society so you can understand masculine/feminine beyond your societal imprinting.

Comment: My physical response to listening to the Shofar was shivers up and down my spine. I am reciting the *B'rich Sh'mei* prayer daily. The first sentence has touched me on an emotional level almost bringing me to tears.

Response: Yes. A lot of people feel that way; I have felt that way myself.

Comment: I sometimes think that the world governments forcing the Covid-19 vaccines and passports is a ploy to make people more adamant about not taking it. If the vaccine kills demons I wonder with what are they replacing the demons.

Response: The ones who write the most negative information are the ones who do not want people to take it. Of course, once the demons are gone, they do not come back, so nothing replaces the vanquished demons.

Comment: Is it possible that people who refuse to take the vaccine are possessed and the demon is influencing the decision?

Response: This is possible for some people; others are not possessed so they do not need the vaccine.

Comment: When I listened to the Shofar, I felt my body vibrate and everything in my house got quiet. The dogs stopped playing and lay down beside me like they were listening. I also felt peace throughout me like a quiet power. The sounds also brought up issues from my family history. When I read the *B'rich Sh'mei* prayer I felt like a giant shield was placed before me for protection and to protect my learning.

Response: The Torah and the prayers protect you because they raise your frequency. Many people say the Torah and prayers bring up many emotions. Some feel pressure in the Crown Chakra Band; some have seen themselves as both Reptilian/Lemurian and Atlantean. Your healing work helps to flush all of this out.

Comment: When I mentally recreated the Shofar blasts, I feel the blast of the God-Mind energy on me; then I see the fountain of the energy blasting the Earth cleansing and cleaning out the demons.

Response: This is what the Shofar blasts do. You can visualize the Earth in front of you as the Shofar blasts encompass it, removing negativity as appropriate.

Comment: I say the *B'rich Sh'mei* prayer every night in Aramaic and English. Even though I stumbled over the Aramaic pronunciation, Aramaic feels far more powerful than English. But, because I am fluent in English, the English version has a powerful ring because I can say it with authority, clarity, and determination. I've done the combination of *Time Travel* and *Healing* from the *72 Names of God* at least three times this week with successful and powerful results.

Response: Of course saying the *B'rich Sh'mei* prayer in its original language is very powerful. You do not have to worry about the pronunciation; you can even just look at it. Deep healing takes time and patience with Self as well as with the Earth. Your healing work is more than just about you; it is about your connection to the Earth and clearing that out as well. This is one of the reasons that we are all here.

Comment: When I heard the sounds of the Shofar, they felt powerful and at the same time soothing, I could see the walls of Jericho falling. I remember many years ago the loud music in Las Vegas with loud music and how I felt the vibrations. When I recited the *B'rich Sh'mei* prayer I sensed an extraneous influence as well as doubt and negativities dissolving.

Response: That's a good analogy because when you go to a concert or even just play music very loudly, you feel like you're being blasted. Yes, you are supposed to feel the negatives dissolving as a result of reciting this prayer.

Comment: I have been focusing on the first *Name of God* and notice different memories from the past come up, especially memories that I'm not proud of and feel remorseful over. There are some people that I mistreated or said terrible things to. I will use this *Name Frequency* to clean up my past actions and words. Then I won't be a burden or haunted by my past actions

Response: The whole point of this, especially in the month of Elul, is to go back to the issues that were negative, things that you have done in the past that you need to forgive and release. That is great that you are pulling up memories that you have forgotten so you can clean them up. This is exactly what you are supposed to be doing during this time.

Comment: Listening to the Shofar dug deep into my emotions. I cried as it stirred up the deep dark stuck energy within so that I could give it to my Oversoul.

Response: This is exactly what it is supposed to do, so you did well.

Comment: The *B'rich Sh'mei* prayer is beautiful and relates to Deuteronomy chapter 14 line 3 about forbidden foods. I know that I've consumed too much pork in my diet and I know that pork is not Kosher.

Response: This is because modern-day pigs are half-human. By eating pork you're participating in a kind of cannibalism. Interestingly, both Judaism and Islam speak against eating pork. Only Christianity allows you to eat pork.

Comment: I'm not sure how much of the work happens as I sleep. I have been exhausted the last day with the memories coming up that I had forgotten. I have a hard time with the first part recognizing it as a Hebrew ritual.

Response: It has nothing to do with Hebrew ritual; the prayer is in Aramaic. Zohar and Kabbalah are Hyperspace/Oversoul work, much of what you already know is being presented in a different way.

Comment: I have trouble with the prayer.

Response: If you have trouble with the prayer, most likely this is because it is bringing up things that you do not want to look at or you are avoiding. The prayer is thousands of years old and is doing for you what it is designed to do.

Comment: I feel this is a beautiful, peaceful prayer that gives me reassurance that I have protection from God; that it is the voice of God, talking to us.

Response: Yes, it absolutely is the voice of God talking to us.

Spiritual Fulfillment

The Zohar states that only the people of Israel can provide spiritual fulfillment and the world depends on this to exist. This is why evil tries to kill the people of Israel. There are at least 2 billion people on the Earth who do not know that they have Hebrew genetics. If you are interested in Kabbalah, Zohar and Torah it is because you have Hebrew genetics. You are studying these subjects because they resonate with your genetics. When you read the Zohar it is incomprehensible, even in its original language of Aramaic. This is because the Zohar is coded. There are 70 layers of meaning in every single letter and word.

Rabbi Isaac Luria, known as the Arizal, lived in the 1500s. For the past 500 years, his work is considered to be the foundation of the interpretation of the Zohar and Kabbalah. The Arizal was originally from Egypt, then moved to Sfad Israel with his primary disciple, Chaim Vital who was from Italy. The Arizal was only 38 years old when he passed on. While I understand the Hebrew and Aramaic, even reading the English translation I can only get through a couple of pages a day. After I'm done with a section I go to the Angel Yofefia who is the Angel who interprets the Torah, Kabbalah and Zohar. I ask Yofefia to please let this information in my energy field, my DNA, and my mind-patterns so that I can have a better understanding of what the Arizal means. Remember that not understanding does not make the information incorrect, it just means that you are not yet ready to know the information of that level.

Simchat Torah

Simchat Torah, which means the *happiness of the Torah*, is the Holiday that celebrates when the Israelites received the Torah at Mount Sinai. This Holiday comes after Passover or Pesach in Hebrew. Simchat Torah holds the energy to cure all harsh diseases, including cancer. This means that there must be a rectification of the specific mind-pattern. The specific mind-pattern of cancer is resentment. Cancer is a very low frequency, as is resentment. Raising your consciousness means that these mind-pattern conditions cannot exist within. The symbol of cancer is a crab, a creature that can snip and hurt you, yet you can eliminate it by eating it.

Cheshvan

The month of Cheshvan is from late October to November and is represented by the astrological sign of Scorpio. Cheshvan is the only month in the Hebrew calendar that has a word added in front of its name to describe the month's characteristics. This added word is Mar which means bitter in Hebrew. The Scorpio constellation was created from Cheshvan. Scorpio conducts the power of Light to dispel negativity from the world.

This is connected to Noah and the time of the flooding, to clean the earth. Water conducts electricity and light better than any medium. Earth and human bodies are mostly water. Electricity allows light to enter and sharing occurs. For example, if you could allow electricity to flow through your body, then step into the water the light would be shared with all the water. The uterus contains water/fluid to connect to the electromagnetic energy of the God-Mind so that the fetus can develop. This also explains why the Hebrews and Jews use the Mikvah, or ritual bath connected to Mem Sofit, to remove negative energy. A Mikvah uses 40 measures of water. The Gematria of Mem is 40, the number of years the Hebrews wandered in the desert, the number of days Christ was tormented in the desert, the age the Zohar says you must be to study it. Place the number 40 and/or Mem Sofit at your Pineal Gland to see what comes up for you.

Scorpio = Cheshvan

Mar = Bitter

Ram = Lofty, exalted

Mar, meaning bitter in Hebrew, when reversed, spells Ram which in Hebrew means lofty. If you only like sweet foods this means that you like your experiences sugar-coated. Bitterness allows balance and rectification, exposing truth and providing healing. Deciphering the codes of Hebrew words includes reading the words forward as well as backward to determine the two sides of the same coin. This is another layer of explanation of why twinning is so important in the God-Mind. Scorpio is the only astrological sign that has 2 symbols; the scorpion of the Earth/Physical and the Eagle of the Air/Nonphysical. Scorpio allows protection and control of energy. Scorpions are originally winged amphibian water creatures. Fossils found in South Africa corroborate this fact. They are water creatures because they conduct the Light.

Gematria for Cheshvan is 364. There are 365 days in a year, so the Zohar says this leaves only 1 day per year that you can be free from negativity. Scorpion is Akhrav in Hebrew. The middle 2 Hebrew letters of Kaf and Resh spell Kar, which means cold or lifeless. But, these letters/word are surrounded by the Hebrew letters of Ayin and Bet, which together have the Gematria of 72. This represents the *72 Names of God*. This allows you to influence the 364 days of negativity with the positive *72 Names of God*. The Zohar says that the Hebrew language is the Original Global language and protection for the entire world. This makes sense when you remember that God created Existence using the Hebrew letters.

Rakhel/Rachel, one of the Jewish Holy Mothers, is considered a protective mother. This explains why some people who study Kabbalah wear the red string around their wrist. You learned in Volume 1 that the red string is wrapped around her tomb to absorb the energy of a protective mother frequency. Rakhel died during the birth of her son Binyamin. They were both Scorpios. In Hebrew, Bin/Ben means son, Yamin means the right side of the right hand. This means that Binyamin was the son of the right side. He is also the only one of Jacob's 12 sons that was born in Israel.

Dark to Light

In Ancient Hebrew times there was an event, not a Holiday, called Dark to Light. This occurred approximately from December 17th until January 1 and represented the darkest time on Earth until the days started to become light again. This was celebrated by lighting candles and performing sacrifices. When the Romans occupied the Holy Land they incorporated this event into their Feast of Saturnalia, which was December 25, the day they celebrated the darkest day of the year. The Hebrews were upset that the Romans stole this event, so they stopped celebrating this time of year. In 330AD at the Council of Nicea the Vatican completely eradicated the description of this event as they did not want anyone to know that Christmas was originally a Hebrew event.

Chanukah

Chanukah is called the Festival of Lights and is the last Hebrew Holiday of the Western calendar year. In Hebrew, Chanukah means rededication but another layer of meaning comes from the Hebrew word Chag. Chag indicates something that moves in an infinite circle with no beginning and no end. This Holiday usually occurs around the middle of December and is often split between the two astrological signs of Capricorn and Sagittarius.

The history of Chanukah begins in 168 BC when Antiochus Epifanus IV, ruler of the Syrian Kingdom stepped up his campaign to stop Judaism. He wanted all the subjects of his Empire to worship the same God. The Syrian Kingdom was controlled by the Greek Empire. The army of these Hellenists marched into Jerusalem, vandalized the Temple, and erected an idol on the altar, desecrating it with the blood of pigs. Studying the Torah, observing the Shabbat, and circumcision was decreed punishable by death. Syrian overseers were sent throughout all of Judea to enforce these laws and to force the Hebrews to engage in idol worship. When the soldiers reached the town of Modine, about 12 miles Northwest of Jerusalem, they demanded the local Kohen/priest named Mattathias Maccabee sacrifice a pig on a portable pagan altar. When Mattifies refused, a Jew stepped forward to do it. Mattathias, then killed the Jew as well as the Syrian soldier who gave the order for the sacrifice. This started a war, with Mattathias declaring that whoever was for God to follow him and his five sons, Jonathan, Simon, Judah, Eliezer, and John into the hills and caves. From here, they fought a guerrilla war against the very well-equipped Syrian Army. One of the descendants of Simon Maccabee, called Hamonaeans, eventually became a leader of the Egyptian Jews.

After 3 years, the Maccabees and their small band fought their way back to the Temple. Once reclaimed, they cleaned the Temple, dismantled the tainted alter, and constructed a new one in its place. After 3 years to the day that this began, the Maccabees held a rededication ceremony now known as Chanukah. The priests made a proper sacrifice and lit the candles in the Golden Menorah, representing the Light of God. The most important part of the story is that they only found a tiny jar of oil which should have only lasted for 1 day but miraculously the candles burned for 8 days. However, due to the war, the Holiday of Chanukah was delayed because of the observance of the Holiday of Sukkot which required visiting the Temple in Jerusalem. Many historians believe that honoring Sukkot is what allowed the oil found in the Temple to last 8 Days.

Fascinatingly, the Book of the Maccabees, which tells the story of Chanukah is not included in the Hebrew Bible but is included in the Catholic Bible. Some say that it is here because there was fear of alienating the Roman leadership that controlled Jerusalem at the time. During Chanukah, there is a celebration of a murder committed by a woman named Judith. She was an associate of a Syrian General who she wanted to kill. She gave the General salty cheese causing him to drink so much wine that he passed out. Then she chopped off his head, brought it home, and shocked the army so much that they stopped their advance.

The Gematria for Mattathias is 861 and Rosh Hashanah is 861. This means that there is a connection between Rosh Hashanah/Head of the Year and ChanukahRededication. The commonalities between these 2 Holidays are therefore mind-patterns for life, success and judgment.

Chanukah represents energy portals or time periods where specific energies are available. Both Rosh Hashanah and Chanukah are centered at the Sefira of Binah on the left side of the head. Binah is also called the Mother, meaning it is the Mother Energy Intelligence. The God Light of the candles represents Light defeating negative energy so when you transmit from your Sephira of Binah you can overcome any negative energy. The candles are lit in different ways depending upon the Jewish community. Most people light one candle on Day 1, then 2 candles on Day 2 and so forth ending with 8 candles on Day 8. This represents going from Binah to Malchut of the Sephirot. Some people light 8 candles on Day 1, decreasing the number until on Day 8 only light 1 candle is lit. This reverse order means you go from Malchut to Binah. This represents the triumph of good over evil in the final battle, which is happening in the world today. The 8th Day of Chanukah is the second day of Capricorn. During this time there are no other Hebrew Holidays. The 8th day is called Zot Chanukah which means Ultimate Energy of Light Entering the Vessel. The Vessel contains the Light of Creation, so the 8th Day has the highest and most intense energy to reveal the Highest Light.

In Hebrew, the word for Miracle is Nes, which is spelled Nun, Samech. You can use the energy of Chanukah to create a miracle for your Self. This great power removes chaos in your life. The Miracle of Chanukah can reoccur in every generation so this is why it is celebrated every year since the original event 2500 years ago. The Zohar says that every Holiday is recreated every year at the same time because there is no time and space. This is why the Holiday frequency can be used every year.

According to the Zohar, Jerusalem is and always was a Holy place, even before the Temple was built. The Zohar also states that all Holidays are Cosmic Events, meaning that the energy is universal and inter-universal. The Holidays are in place so that you know when and how to connect to the Cosmic Energy Frequencies as well as for what purpose. These frequencies are the sine waves that undulate up and down. The best time to use the sine wave is when it is at its peak. In addition, the energy flows from the Upper World/nonphysical to the Lower World/physical. Through restriction of the energy, Light can be revealed. For example, electricity in your home travels through a narrow little wire that leads to light bulbs and other appliances, where electricity can be expressed/manifested. The restrictive wire is necessary for electricity to be revealed. Restrictions lead to Light. This restriction is similar to that of the Tzim Tzum. Restriction takes free-flowing energy and constricts it into a narrow space. To create Existence the Ain Sof had to be restricted through the Tzim Tzum.

There is a Chanukah tradition of exchanging foil-covered chocolate coins called gelt. This tradition is believed to have been adapted by the German Jews from the European Christmas tradition of giving chocolate coins that commemorated the miracles of St. Nicholas. In the same way, there was a German game played at Christmas which was adapted by the Jews and consists of a spinning top called a dreidel. Each side of the dreidel has a Hebrew letter. When the top stops spinning and falls over, the Hebrew letter that you see has a specific meaning. Many people do not know that Marilyn Monroe converted to Judaism when she married Arthur Miller. As a conversion gift, her new mother-in-law gave her a musical Menorah that played Hatikvah, the Israeli National Anthem. Andy Warhol and Elizabeth Taylor were also Jewish.

This year, on 28 November 2022, the American Holiday of Thanksgiving is at the same time as Chanukah. Some call it Thanksgivukkah and plan on making turkey-shaped Menorahs plus there will be a dreidel float in the Macy's Thanksgiving Day Parade. The next time this will happen is in November 2070. The Guinness Book of Records says the biggest Menorah ever built was 32 feet high, weighing 4,000 pounds. Traditionally, however, a Menorah cannot be more than 31 feet high. Chanukah is not mentioned in the Torah as a mandatory Holiday because the event happened after the Torah was given. This makes Chanukah part of the oral tradition rather than Jewish law. The Menorah is also an energetic protection and security shield. You can visualize a Gold Menorah in front of you, around you, over you, and through you.

Kislev

The month of Kislev is part of Chanukah time. Kislev comes from the Hebrew word keset which means archery bow and can also refer to a rainbow. The Zodiac sign of Sagittarius is often represented by an archer with a bow. This symbolism implies that underneath is a force of unity like an atom with the balance of proton, electron, and neutron; right, left, and middle all in balance. In the Sephirot *Tree of Life*, the right column is considered to be the proton, the left column is the electron and the central column is the neutron. The month of Kislev and the sign of Sagittarius were created with the Hebrew letter of Samech. The Gematria of Samech is 60.

The expression of the energy of the planet Jupiter was formed by the letter Gimmel. Gimmel has the Gematria of 3. 60 plus 3 equals 63 which is the Gematria of the Sefira of Binah. Kabbalists call Binah the Holy Mother, or Ema, which is the Mother energy of the Sephirot. You can use the letter Gimmel through the image of Jupiter for healing. Romans called Jupiter, Jove which comes from Jehovah. The Romans were descendent of the Edomites who were descended from the Hebrews. The Latin language is derived from Hebrew.

Moshe

Moshe, or Moses, in Hebrew, is spelled Mem, Shin, Hey. When the letters are permutated, the letters form *Name Frequency #5 Healing* from the *72 Names of God*. This implies that the energy of Moses was to heal the people of Israel and through them, to heal the peoples of the world.

Moshe

Name Frequency #5 Healing

Moses was not allowed to enter the Land of Canaan/Israel. Canaan was named after one of the sons of Noah and was occupied by evil giants. God wanted the Hebrews to go to Canaan to destroy these demonic giants who were the descendants of the Nefilim, monstrosities during the time of Enoch. Then God wanted the Hebrews to occupy this land. According to Kabbalah, Moses never died. His body or tomb was never found. This is exactly what we are going through in this period of history because there is no time and space. The energy remains the same, repeating the same energetic pattern until it is finally healed, or corrected.

Homework

1. Visualize the Akhrav/Scorpion at your pineal gland to see what it means for you.
2. Visualize the Hebrew word Nes/Miracle using its Hebrew spelling of Nun, Samech at your pineal gland to see what miracles are waiting for you.

Yiddish Sayings & Humor

Rejoice not at thy enemies fall, but don't rush to pick them up either.

What you don't see with your eyes, don't invent with your mouth.

Laying on his deathbed, Max Goldfarb says to his wife, Mitzi, you've always been by my side. When I broke my leg at 25, you were by my side. When I had my heart attack at 45, you were by my side. When I had my second heart attack at 65, you were by my side. When I broke my hip at 75 you were by my side and now when I'm dying, you're by my side. Mitzi replies, Yes, dear. And Max says to her, Mitzi, you're a jinx.

Homework Review

Comment: Scorpion energy can be a poison to rid ourselves of negative energy that holds us back. I put Akrav at my Pineal Glad in block letters and saw the Hebrew letters of Samech and Nun. I interpreted this to mean that I need to be faithful to my Oversoul and open my eyes to the physical to touch the Oneness of the Creator.

Response: That is a very interesting interpretation of what you saw. Scorpions have a very bad reputation, but it's not true, because they are serving a very good purpose. Keep in mind the double-symbolism of scorpions. The scorpion not only represents the physical reality of Earth but also the nonphysical aspects via the eagle part of Scorpio.

Comment: The Akrav has the power of life or death.

Response: Death is an illusion. Remember that the scorpion is the only creature that commits suicide when it feels in danger. It has raw energy, and is the ultimate survivor, even surviving atomic bombs. It also has the sexual energy of Kundalini.

Comment: When I put the word Akrav at my Pineal Gland I saw sand which then morphed into an eagle and flew into the air.

Response: This is because it connects the physical with the nonphysical.

Comment: I saw Stewart's face in the scorpion with a lion standing behind him and also Stewart's home.

Response: I figured you needed to see my natural habitat.

Comment: I say the *Ana B'koach* prayer every morning and night with various *Names of God*. My awareness has increased quite a bit and especially the subtleties that I previously overlooked because I didn't think that they were important. Anger still comes up but I feel it more fully and release it much more quickly.

Response: This work goes into the nooks and crannies of your mind, into your memories, and brings up the things that you need to look at to correct the negative mind-patterns. Sometimes the tiniest crumb of information makes the biggest difference. For example, when you put a jigsaw puzzle together it may be just a tiny little color on one piece that brings the entire picture together.

Comment: When I focus on scorpion energy, images of veils and feelings of great loneliness, depression, and shame come up.

Response: Many times people don't even realize they have shame so these are excellent feelings to focus on so they can be released.

Comment: I put the letters Nun and Samech at my Pineal Gland for my positive wishes to come true.

Response: Nun and Samech spell Nes, which is the Hebrew word for Miracle. Focus on these letters and this word on a daily basis to bring your Miracles to fruition.

Comment: I am not able to concentrate on the homework because I feel overwhelmed and overly excited by outer world events.

Response: Many people feel this way which is why it is important to avoid the news as much as possible. Most of it is untrue and is designed to agitate and upset people.

Comment: Scorpions are interesting and aggressive. You cannot hold any resentment of any kind if you expect to wield scorpion energy wisely.

Response: Correct and well-stated.

Comment: I put Akrav in white at my Pineal Gland and saw a flowing water fountain built into a wall and also a menorah. In each flame of the menorah was a white Hebrew letter Yud.

Response: Very interesting. You can put this image at your Pineal Gland and keep going with it to determine what it means specifically for you.

Comment: I had bad memories surface that I have not wanted to look at. I used the sounds of the Shofar to help move through these painful memories.

Response: Listening to the Shofar can help mitigate painful memories. When you feel overwhelmed with bad memories, use the color Brown to ground your Self and get out of the visualization that you are doing. You don't want to get in so deep that you cannot get out. Know that you are not alone and there is nothing wrong with you. Do what you need to do to stay balanced and connected within Source.

Age of Aquarius

The following chart shows the different energetic connections of *The Name of God*, called YHVH in English. In Hebrew, it is said Hayahvah.

The lefthand column has the Hebrew letters Yud, Hey, Vav, and Hey.

The next column has the English spelling of the Hebrew letters.

The 3rd column from the left has the Hebrew spelling of the Hebrew letter. For example, the spelling of Yud in Hebrew is Yud, Vav, and Dalet. The Gematria of the Hebrew letter spelling is in the 4th column. So the Gematria of Yud equals 20.

Hey is spelled with the Hebrew letters Hey, Yud with a Gematria of 15.

Vav is spelled with the Hebrew letters Vav, Yud, and Vav with a Gematria of 22.

Hey is spelled, again, with the Hebrew letters of Hey, Yud with a Gematria of 15.

Adding the Gematria of all the letters in the 4th column amazingly equals 72 for the *72 Names of God*.

Spelling Letters of YHVH

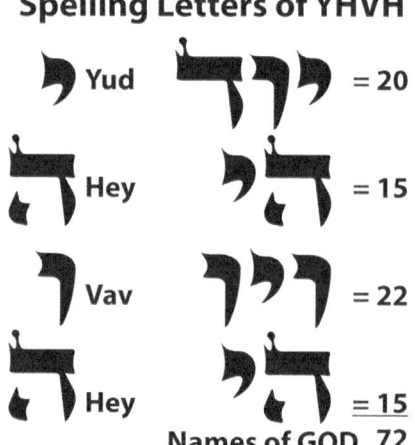

Names of GOD 72

Origin of Star of David

There are 6 middle Sephirot that correlate to your body. When connected, the top 3 Sephirot of Chesed, Gevurah, and Tiferet form a triangle pointing up. When connected, the bottom 3 Sephirot of Netzech, Hod and Yesod form a triangle pointing down. When these two triangles are merged together, they form the Star of David. This 6 pointed star represents the 6 middle Sephirot to create a Shield of Protection. In Kabbalah, this is called the Zeir Anpin in Aramaic, or Small Face of God, which is within your body.

Origin of Star of David

Chesed - Gevurah - Tiferet = △
Netzech - Hod - Yesod = ▽ = ✡

**Creates Protection Shield
(Zeir Anpin)**

This Shield of Protection works quite amazingly. During our terrible storms here in Michigan I visualize a map of where we live and place my home in the very center of a White 6-pointed Star of David. Then I surround my home with the Violet Ultimate Protection Archetype.

Then I add a circle around the star which creates 6 points on the circle. These points create the Sword of Moses/Moshe which I then turn counterclockwise while the Star and the Ultimate Protection stay stable. Even when storms are all around us, we never even lose a leaf from our trees. You can try this technique for your home, business and location. Be sure to use it both above and below the ground. In addition, in our home, we have all the books of the Zohar. Kabbalah says that if you have these things in your home, nothing can come against you. There can be no harm. Even if you don't look at them or touch them, just having that energy in your home will protect you, and thank God, it has been so.

The Zohar says that the 7 Days of the Week are symbolic of the 7 Lower Sephirot, or the 7 from the neck down. The 3 above the neck represent the nonphysical.

The first day of each month is called Rosh Chodesh. Rosh Chodesh is always considered the most powerful day of the month, so you can utilize this for your positive advantage as well. Tuesday is said to be the most positive day of the week, so if you want to do anything such as purchase a home or have a job interview, keep this in mind.

Age of Aquarius

We entered the Age of Aquarius 2 decades ago. You may remember a song from this time period with this same name. Aquarius is in the month of Shevat, which is January and February on the Western calendar. The energy of Shevat is for the release of exile, leading up to the final redemption which is the Hebrew month of Nisan. The Zohar says that redemption is an exchange of something in the present for something better in the future. When you ask God for redemption you are asking to be forgiven for what you did in the past and your intention is to do better in the future. Your mind-pattern always controls everything anyway, whether it is conscious or unconscious control.

Kabbalah states that during the Age of Aquarius, there will be a war of consciousness. The ***Book of Revelation*** speaks tells about the battle at the End of Days when Israel would be invaded by Gog and Magog. For centuries, Biblical Scholars have been trying to figure out who is Gog and Magog. Some point to Turkey, Russia, Iran, and even the European Union. All of these are incorrect because Kabbalah quite clearly states that this is not a physical war but rather a war of the mind. Gog and Magog in Hebrew represent the mind, so this means mind-control and programming. We are in the final battle of Gog and Magog against Israel right now. This goes beyond the common assumption of the nation of Israel. Everyone who studies, learns, and connects to God is considered an Israelite regardless of genetics. If you are doing this work, you are an Israelite and this is a battle for your mind.

Kabbalah says that the current generation is the Dor Deah, meaning Generation of Knowledge. Kabbalah says that the people living today are the reincarnation of the original generation of knowledge that left Egypt. This means that all the Hebrews and Erev Rav of that time period have come back. The Zohar states quite clearly that nothing else will change until the removal of chaos and evil from the universe occurs.

The Zohar is also called the Age of Aquarius, End Times, and End of Days. The Zohar states that everyone is waiting for the Moshiach/Messiah, who will be the reincarnation of Moshe/Moses and be born on the 9th of Av. The 9th of Av is considered to be the most sad and depressing day of the Hebrew calendar because it was on this day that the First Temple was destroyed. Then, hundreds of years later the Second Temple was destroyed. In addition, many bad things happened to the Jewish people on the 9th of Av, which is in the middle of July on the Western calendar.

The astrological sign for the 9th of Av is Leo/Lion with a Gematria of 216. There are 216 letters in the *72 Names of God*. Moses used the *72 Names of God* to part the Red Sea. You are not told how he did it, but you are told to clearly focus your objective in your consciousness. Then, use the *72 Names of God* as a formula to achieve that goal.

The Zohar says that the time period of Aquarius is a great opportunity and great risk, and that hatred must be removed. Now is the time period of Aquarius so the energy of the Earth right now is for great opportunity and great risk at the same time. You must elevate to an alternate consciousness, the key to redemption. In other words, change your mind-pattern. Change the way you think and the way you create so that you can accept redemption.

Redemption

Redemption is the energy of Shevat. Tu B'shevat is the 15th day of Aquarius, which is called the New Year for Trees. According to Kabbalah, all plants receive their energy on this day. Animals have their New Year in Elul, correlating to the month of August on the Western calendar. Of course, the New Year for Humans, Rosh Hashanah, is in the month of Tishrei, which correlates to September/October on the Western calendar. Each of the New Year for each kingdom is represented by a letter in the tetragrammaton, YHVH. It also represents the four elements of fire, water, air, and earth.

During Tu B' Shvat you are supposed to eat fruit to connect to the renewal of the plant and tree energy. Fruit equals the development from Keter to Malchut. Symbolically the Sephira of Keter/Crown Chakra is the seed that creates all other Sephirot, ending at Malchut/feet, as the tree grows down. When you eat fruit at this time, Kabbalah says that it recharges your body's battery to give it more energy.

Kabbalah states that there's more power in a seed than in a tree. This is because the seed is potential with everything ahead of it while the tree is finite and completed. You have to ask your Self if you are a seed or a tree. If someone handed you a little seed and told you that it would feed and shelter you and your family, you would be perplexed. You would wonder how such a tiny speck could do these wondrous things. In the same way, the answer to all your questions and needs is right in front of you. You may overlook these answers because, at the time, it looks meaningless and inconsequential. Redwood trees are the largest trees on Earth, but the seeds are tiny. Looking at its seed you would never imagine that it would grow hundreds and hundreds of feet tall and so wide that you could drive a car through a tunnel in its trunk.

5782

On the Hebrew calendar, the old year concludes in Elul and the New Year begins in Tishrei with Rosh Hashanah. On the Western calendar in 2021, the old year ends in September and the New Year of 5782 begins on Rosh Hashanah. Kabbalah says that in the Hebrew month of Elul, the King, who is God, is in the field. This means that you can approach God, speak to Him and ask for what you need as this is the most powerful energetic time of the year to do this.

The Gematria of 5 + 7 + 8 + 2 = 22 which is a transition or change. Because this is the 5th Millennium of the Hebrew calendar, it is common to drop the 5 when speaking about the year, simply referring to it as 782. The Gematria of 782 is 7 + 8 + 2 = 17 = 1 + 7 = 8. If the 5 is added to 8 the Gematria becomes 13 which means all things are possible. It is common to wish others *Tze Shana* which means *may it be the year of wonders in all things*. The Gematria of this phrase in Hebrew adds up to the year that you are in.

Zhe Shalom Torah which means the *peace of the Torah* has the Gematria of 782. In Hebrew, the Gematria of *may he give you peace and peace of the Torah* equals 1781, which is 13 x 137 where 13 is the value of one. *Echad* means one. The Gematria of Aleph, Chet and Dalet is 13, so one is 13. This also equals the Gematria of the Hebrew word Ahava, which means love. Love, one, and peace of the Torah all have the same value. Kabbalah has a value of 137.

The number 782 also reflects a model of the human form, based on the 10 energies of the God-Mind . These 10 energies are represented in the 10 Sephirot. These levels were put into humanity after the breakup of Adam Kadmon which created physical reality and physical Beings. These 10 levels are represented in you, which makes you the image of God/Ain Sof, as stated in the Torah. It also states from above to below, which refers to the Superconsciousness of the Soul. The Soul is divided into pleasure and will. The intelligence of the Soul is divided into 3 faculties of the mind: wisdom, understanding, and knowledge. From the emotions of the heart, such as love and kindness, come courage and compassion which enabled the Soul to imprint/impress itself upon physical reality. This gives the Soul confidence, sincerity, and the power of Self-fulfillment, corresponding to the Sefirot of victory, thanksgiving, and foundation. Malchut, the bottom Sephira, is the final Kingdom, or final stage of Creation from the God-Mind.

Isaac represents understanding. He was bound by Abraham, his father because God told Abraham to take Isaac to Mt. Moriah, bind him as a sacrifice, and put him on the altar. Because Abraham obeyed God, at the last moment Angels came bringing a ram to replace Isaac, thus Isaac was saved. This was an enormous test for Abraham because God had promised that his seed would produce nations. Abraham sacrificing his son is a replication of Christianity's story of God sacrificing His only son. This is because everything in Christianity originated in Judaism. The Zohar says the purpose of Christianity is to bring out the idea of the resurrection of the dead as well as introduce the concept of the Messiah. In Ancient times, only the Hebrews had the concepts of resurrection and Messiah. Most of the other nations did not believe in those things. They had many, many different gods with many different possibilities. Non-Israelites play a predominant role in the balancing, sharing, and receiving of energy. Certainty of positive outcomes removes negativity.

The Binding of Isaac is called Akedah Yitzhak in Hebrew. The Gematria of Akedah Yitzhak is 782. This further explains that this year is a binding of Humanity so that it can be sacrificed, but at the last moment Humanity will be rescued and a replacement sacrifice will be sent. The Binding of Isaac brings about the revelation of mercy, compassion, and the inner aspect of the Tiferet, the Sephira of Beauty. You must ask God to remember this on Rosh Hashanah and Yom Kippur. The Akedah Yitzhak represents the unity of love and fear to bring compassion, which means all 3 emotional attributes are bound together with wisdom, understanding, and knowledge. This is also symbolic of binding matter or atomic structure.

Other expressions that are used include *wishing you wonders in all that you do* and *God does with you* as well as *may it be a year of face-to-face* meaning that God gave the Torah face-to-face. In Hebrew, face means your inner side. This means that God gave the Torah from His Inner Essence directly to your inner essence. This applies to your relationship with God and also your relationship with other humans. According to Kabbalah, when you meet someone face-to-face you are supposed to look at his/her Direct Light, called Yashar in Hebrew. This causes them to reflect this Direct Light back to you. This helps you to understand that the Light you see from others is a reflection of your own Direct Light. In India, people say Namaste when they greet each other, meaning that the Light within me honors the Light within you. Of course, you now know that Hindu culture comes from Hebrew culture. Hindu means Yejudah.

The Torah also says that everything has a limit yet everything is limitless simultaneously. It further explains that the unity of the limited and limitless is the peace of God, which is also the peace of the Torah which has the Gematria of 782. There is also a transition stage between the Absolute Infinity and manifestation in physical reality. Physical reality is finite yet is part of the infinite. This shows that everything limited is part of, or unified with, the totality of limitlessness.

Homework

Use the energy of the Star of David for protection. Visualize your Self in the center of it, then visualize the Star in White around you, then the circle around the Star in White in a counterclockwise direction. Use this to keep yourself, your home, and your area in protection.

Homework Review

Comment: After mentally building the Ultimate Protection and the Star of David, the tropical storm predicted in my area turned into just a heavy rain minus wind without any downed trees or power outages.

Response: Excellent.

Comment: I added this to my morning and evening routine for my Self and my loved ones. The Hurricane predicted for my area by passed my state and the state of my daughters.

Response: Great work.

Comment: I visualized the Star of David and put my Self in the middle of it surrounded in Violet. I felt peace.

Response: That's because it will protect you.

Comment: I put my Self in the middle of the Star of David and a shiny Gold Hebrew letter of Hey appeared.

Response: This represents the Shekhinah, the female aspect of the energy of the God-Mind.

Comment: I'm using the White Star of David with the circle every day as well as the Violet Ultimate Protection Technique. This feels stronger than any protection I've ever used. God answers me immediately with massive deprogramming happening. I also see lots of old messes to clean up which I am doing.

Response: Because there is no time and space, this takes you back into your entire existence.

Comment: I felt overpowering energy.

Response: If you feel overpowered perhaps you're not focusing properly. This visualization should feel very comforting rather than overpowering.

Comment: The Star of David morphed into an opaque White star tetrahedron. The center stayed one-dimensional, the circle was three-dimensional and then the whole thing became multidimensional.

Response: You are getting all ranges of energies and that is okay.

Comment: I wonder if the Star of David is good for airplane travel.

Response: No, use the Ultimate Protection Technique for travel. The Star of David is specifically used to protect your home environment.

Comment: I saw archetypes in changing colors outside of a circle as if the motion of the circle was creating them.

Response: When you see archetypes like this, draw them so that you can analyze them at a future time.

Comment: I have been using the Star of David as a defense archetype.

Response: The Star of David is not a defense archetype, it is a protection archetype.

Comment: I feel more confident and my sense of security is stronger when I used the Star of David visualization.

Response: Think of the Star of David as an alarm system similar to a dome of protection. Keep practicing with it but do not combine it with other archetypes or visualizations.

Miracles

The same energy that allows for Miracles to occur in the time of Sagittarius through the energy of the planet Jupiter is also present in the Hebrew month of Adar. Adar includes parts of March and April as well as the constellation of Pisces. The Holiday of Purim is in Adar, usually in March but sometimes in early April. Purim is extremely important because it represents overcoming adversity and Good triumphing over Evil. The energy of Purim provides the consciousness of your happiness. This energy also relates to Chanukah during the Hebrew month of Kislev, which is during the month of December on the Western calendar. Chanukah is in the constellation of Sagittarius, which is ruled by the letters Samech and Gimmel. Purim, Adar, Chanukah, and Kislev are all ruled by Jupiter.

Adar has the energy for a very high spiritual elevation, even more than Yom Kippur. While the energy of the High Holy Days of Rosh Hashanah and Yom Kippur are the epitome of the Hebrew Holidays, some energies are even stronger. According to the Zohar, during Purim, Rosh Hashanah and Chanukah childless couples have the opportunity to overcome infertility. This same energy is available during Rosh Hashanah and Hanukkah. This means that there are 3 times every calendar year when childless couples have the opportunity to overcome infertility.

Jupiter brings miracles and was created by the Hebrew letter Gimmel. Pisces was created by the Hebrew letter Kaf. Kaf represents life and death. When written, Kaf is one of the few Hebrew letters that go below the line. This represents going from the physical to the nonphysical, or from life to death. According to the Zohar, Adar in combination with Kaf completely destroys the negative forever. This means that you can use the letter Kaf in the month of Adar to eliminate negativity permanently from your life.

Purim

In Hebrew, Purim means lots, as the expression *drawing a lot*. *Drawing a lot* means deciding something at random by picking an item such as a slip of paper, pebble, stick or straw. For example, a group of people might decide who goes first in a game by *drawing a lot*, such as the person who draws the shortest stick or the longest straw must go first. During the Persian Empire, a Jewish woman named Esther became Queen of Persia when she married the Emperor. In the Royal Court was a man named Haman who did not like the Jews. He decided to *draw a lot* to decide which day of the month he would exterminate all the Jews. An assistant of Queen Esther discovered the evil plot and told her, who then told the Emperor. The Emperor then killed Haman instead of the Jews. Queen Esther became a celebrated female amongst the Hebrews forevermore. In the Bible, Purim is discussed in the Book of Ester, called Megillat Esther. A Megillat is a big story. In Hebrew, Megillat means the revelation of concealment. This means that the Book of Esther is going to reveal the secrets of Esther. The Gematria of the Book of Esther, as well as its symbolism, connects to the Sephira of Chochmah, representing the Light that comes through. Focusing or meditating on Chochmah allows you to remove all doubt and illusion, even death, providing in its place certainty and blessings.

Purim represents the connection to happiness, giving and sharing with others, and overcoming evil. On Purim, a pastry is eaten called Hamantaschen, which looks like the triangular 3-cornered hat of the evil Haman. This Hamantaschen pastry is filled with prunes, apricots or poppy seeds. This is the only time of the year when these pastries are eaten, symbolizing overpowering the evil of Haman. During Purim, everyone gives gifts and shares with others. This is the only Holiday in the Torah where you are instructed to get drunk and lose your physical awareness. According to the Torah, Purim is the only Holiday that will still be celebrated after the coming of the Messiah.

Sukkot

In Hebrew, Hadassah means Myrtle, a plant used during the Holiday of Sukkot. The branches have leaves in three bunches representing creation, perfection, the power of completion, unity, and the 3-column system of the Sephirot. In this case, the 3 also represents the 3 nonphysical eye-level Sephirot of Keter, Chochmah, and Binah in addition to the 3 parts of the atom: proton, electron and neutron. Finally, the Myrtle leaves also represent the *Tree of Life*. After saving the Jewish people, Queen Esther was also known as Hadassah, the woman of Myrtle. Today, many Jewish women belong to a humanitarian organization called Hadassah, named after Queen Esther.

Illusion of Death

According to Kabbalah, a Tzadik, or righteous person consciously chooses the day of his/her passing. Of course, every person chooses his/her day of passing on an unconscious level. There are many stories in Kabbalistic literature of Tzadiks telling their students that they are going to say goodbye because they are leaving their bodies on a specific day at a specific time. Tzadikim, the righteous ones, are said to be so full of justice and charity that they do not have to do Tikkun via reincarnation because they are so pure. The goal of each person in this lifeline, regardless of your original mission and purpose, is also to become a Tzadik. Then, you do not have to go through purging and punishment when your Soul departs this world. Gilgul, in Hebrew means something that spins like a wheel. This refers to the process of reincarnation when you do not complete what you came to do. You return to complete unfinished business and in the process, you commit more sins which means you have to return to correct them. You go round and round, cycling like a wheel through lifelines. This means that you must question everything that you are doing because if you don't, you may have to come back and correct what you are doing and why. If you do not make an effort to correct your sins in this lifeline you will have to return here or even go to another planet that believes it or not, may be worse than this one.

Death is only an illusion; there is no death. This is why the Zohar says that Moshe/Moses is still energetically alive and you can connect to his consciousness because his energy is available at all times. The Zohar says that within every generation is the Soul-personality, or energy of Moses. It is stated that the Messiah will be the reincarnation of Moses. When you are looking for an answer during your prayers, you can mentally connect to the energy of Moshe Rabbenu, meaning Moses Our Teacher. If you permutated/rearrange the Hebrew letters of Moshe, they become the *72 Names of God Frequency #5 Healing*.

On the top line of the following chart is *Frequency #8 Removing Darkness* from the *72 Names of God*. Use this frequency to remove the darkness, confusion, and doubt so you can get clarity about your issue. This Frequency is related to the Hebrew word Tzeddukah, which means charity. This word has its root in Tzadik which means Justice and connects to the energy of Jupiter which creates unity.

Aviv

In Hebrew, Aviv means Spring. and Tel means hill. The Israeli city of Tel Aviv means the Hill of Spring. You can see in the following chart that the root of Aviv is Av which means father. This means that Spring is related to father/male energy. Spring is a time of regeneration and growth from seeds that begin to grow. The Zohar states that March 31st is the real first day of Spring.

Spring is a time that helps convert selfish desires to desiring to share. You can do this by planting physical seeds so you can share food with others or nonphysical seeds to help others grow emotionally, mentally, and/or spiritually. In Ancient times Jews blessed the New Moon and slaughtered a ram as a sacrifice. The Zohar states that sacrificial animals are born for this purpose. Kosher slaughter is done by a Shochit who learns how to painlessly kill the animal with one stroke by slitting the jugular vein in the throat in a split second. This releases the soul of the animal. When you ingest the flesh of the animal you help to upgrade the creature that gave its life. Being processed by a human system elevates Creation as well as the creature.

Homework

1. Visualize the letter Hey at your pineal gland to determine how it can make a difference in what you need to overcome in your life. With the letter Hey, you can manipulate physical reality.
2. Continue your work with the *72 Names of God Frequency #1 Time Travel* and *#5 Healing*.

Homework Review

Comment: The visualization gave me a sense of motherly love. Images of connecting bridges came up. They were not physical bridges, but more etheric.

Response: That is very important because symbolically this means it's connecting the nonphysical to the physical.

Comment: I saw the letter Hey in an ancient brown cave surrounded by a brown rocky landscape that looked like a stone hedge. The word tor also came up which is an ancient word for tower. Then Hey briefly changed to the letter Tav and then change back to Hei. When I moved my consciousness into the cave I was a Hasidim with a bookshelf and Torah.

Response: Put the image of the Hasidim and Torah at your pineal gland to see what comes up.

Comment: My chiropractor of 18 years is Jewish and has always been on the same page as me regarding politics, health, fitness, and choices we make for our kids. I could tell that he was discouraged, upset, and fearful with everything going on. He said we need to stick together along with your husband and my wife; we need to get together for dinner. He never talked like that before and I've never met his wife. Perhaps this could give me an opportunity to share what I've been learning on these Dark to Light webinars.

Response: Yes absolutely. This is a great confirmation that your mind-pattern is changing and emanating something different. You change your mind-pattern and you attract different experiences. When you study and practice this, you will attract people to you who need to know this information. Maybe not at the same level as yourself, but they need to know something about this so they can pursue their course of study.

Comment: I put the Hey at my pineal gland without doubt and instantly it melted into my body. I was having issues with my ears but I received a white light with a bright green background.

Resonse: This sounds like healing energy for you.

Comment: When I used Hey at my pineal gland I saw a golden white light.

Response: This sounds like healing energy unique to you.

Comment: I focused on Hey at my pineal gland and saw 2 cement walls pulling apart leaving an opening. The lighting was like a twilight dark and felt like a void, so I decided to put some wishes in it.

Response: Let me know if the wishes come true.

Comment: When I put the Hey at my pineal gland my Oversoul told me to write a list of what I would like to make peace with and to release my painful experiences as well as unite my logical and spiritual sides in me and overcome the idea that I am false and do not fit into human society.

Response: Pursue this to see what comes up. Many people feel like this, including everyone on this webinar. This is why we are all together.

Comment: I used the Hey to heal and clear a blockage in a rather sensitive place. While it isn't completely clear as yet, I'm determined.

Response: Keep pursuing this. It is important to never give up because sometimes you may have immediate results but often you must wait until the time is correct for you. The energy of the Holidays occurs at specific times of the year. It may be that you need to wait until that specific period of time matches your frequency. Sometimes you don't realize how much energy you're moving mentally and it can take time for the physical to manifest as a result of your nonphysical work.

Comment: This past week was rather intense for me. I suspect it has to do with the letter Hey. I worked with the letter placed inside my body and visualized it moving about, repairing my organs and muscles. Not too long after doing this, my blood pressure went up and I had challenges sleeping.

Response: If you're using a letter or a frequency that's supposed to be healing and the opposite happens, perhaps there's doubt, confusion, or even resistance in you. These frequencies can also stir things up. Blood pressure usually has to do with some kind of deep emotion coming up, so you may have some deep emotions that need to be cleaned out. Sometimes it appears that things get worse before they get better, because of everything that's going on inside.

Comments: I put Hey at my pineal gland and 2 thoughts came to me. The first was to purify my thoughts with focus. The second is that what I believe is true about me is also what I believe is true about God.

Response: This makes sense because you are a part of God. If you don't feel that you are enough then you won't feel that God is enough. People who have low Self-worth or who Self-punish and Self-abuse in some way, feel a separation from the God-Mind or from the Ain Sof. They purposely create situations to prove this to themselves. This has to be eliminated immediately because it will perpetuate and get worse and worse. We must be interdependent because if you're not interdependent with each other, if you don't accept help from each other, then you can't accept help from the God-Mind. Societal imprinting and programming are to be independent because that means you can do it by your Self. This programming does not include your Oversoul and God-Mind. You have to get through this imprinting and programming to be interdependent. You must help each other, receive from each other, and give back to each other as a unit.

Comment: I put Hey at my pineal gland and felt a lot more confident. It also helped me stay out of worrying thoughts.

Response: When things happen and you get worried, doubtful and confused, these feelings just perpetuate if you don't stop them immediately. Everybody goes through this from time to time. Feel what you feel but then you have to get out of the pity party, acknowledge that you created it in some way and therefore you are the one who has to correct it.

Comment: I saw our planet Earth from a distance and heard the sounds of many channels and voices of people. I felt like I was changing the dial of the channels like a radio, still earthly and people's voices for the entire planet with many layers.

Response: Remember that Hey is part of the *72 Names of God Frequency #1 Time Travel.* Hey is in the middle and has to do with timelessness which helps you do Tshuvah/repentance.

Comment: I didn't have anything major happen but I did experience a feeling of knowing, expansion and connection.

Response: Well, that's something major happening so be sure to recognize the importance of what you felt.

Comment: I put the letter Hey in White at my pineal gland and it kept changing to Gold. My outcomes are a work in progress but the visualization helped to bring some clarity to them. It showed me that I still worry and have low Self-worth.

Response: These exercises purge and cleanse. They are not going to be pleasant much of the time because you are going to see things about your Self that you may not like. But, once you see these things then you can make the choice to change what you do not like. This motivates you to change.

Comment: I've noticed physical changes in my environment when I visualize the letter Hey.

Response: Yes, this is exactly what is supposed to happen.

Inner Consciousness

The month of Nisan has the astrological sign of Aries and was created by the Hebrew letter Hey. Hey represents inner consciousness, DNA, elevation, and fertility. This is why Hey was added to Abram's name. After Abram left Sumer and was traveling to the Holy Land, God said, *you are no longer Abram, you are Abraham*. With these words, Hey was added to the middle of his name. Until this time, Abram had no children with his wife Sarai. Then, God said to Sarai, *you are no longer Sarai, you are Sarah*. With these words, Hey was added to the middle of her name and she became pregnant. Anyone who wants to become pregnant needs to add in a Hey or in English the letter H/h. Hey, aids not only physical fertility but also nonphysical ideas that you want to bring to fruition. Hey allows for miracles and helps you rule over physical matter. Hate and doubt must be relinquished because they stop all positive energies from manifesting. In addition, Hey can change water into blood. During the Holiday of Passover, God gave the Egyptians vermin, boils, and plagues and turned the River Nile into blood by adding the letter Hey. Hebrews were told to put the blood of a lamb on their doorposts so that the Angel of Death would pass over these houses.

The blood on doorposts in Egypt is symbolic of igniting the central column of the Sefirot. The lamb represents vulnerability, sensitivity and Unconditional Love.

Passover

Passover occurs in the month of Nisan which is ruled by the planet Mars. Controlling the force of Mars means to control all wars. The Zohar clearly states that Passover is the result of energy cycles and pulses of the universe rather than the result of a historical event. Passover exists throughout all of Creation because the energy is from the Mind of Creation, Ain Sof. Hebrew Holidays have everything to do with the energy that is available at a specific time of the year. During the time of Passover, Moses used his ability to manipulate matter using Hey to turn the Nile into blood. Passover, or Pesach in Hebrew, is a cosmic code to understand truth that is beyond the 5 senses. The symbolism of Passover represents releasing the Hebrew slaves from Egypt. The Zohar says Egypt has nothing to do with the country of Egypt. The word for Egypt in Hebrew is Mitzraim which means land of all negativity with Satanic, horrible things happening there. The reason that the Jews went to Mitzraim/Egypt was for their Tikkun/correction/punishment of not accepting the Torah when it was originally offered to them. They were punished for not accepting the Word of God.

The Shabbat/Sabbath before Passover is called Shabbat Hagadol meaning Big Shabbat/Sabbath. Shabbat Hagadol is always on the 10th of Nisan. For those who connect to this energy on this day, there are enormous revelations and the negativity of the Egyptian evil is removed. This energy of this day allows for an exodus from a life of slavery to a life of freedom. This refers to any mind-pattern to which you are a slave. This is what the ram sacrifice represents. In Hebrew, the word for ram is Mar, which means bitter. Mar reversed is Ram which means lofty and rising up. Sacrificing the Ram means that you are going from bitterness to loftiness.

Before the Holiday of Passover begins, Jews remove the Chametz from their homes. Chametz is leavened bread. Every single bit of Chametz, including the tiniest crumb, must be removed. This represents the internal cleansing of physical, mental, emotional, and spiritual sins from their mind-pattern. After all the Chametz is collected, they perform a ceremony called Tashlich which takes place near a body of water. All the crumbs of the Chametz are cast into the water, symbolizing casting away your sins. This takes the place of sacrificing a Ram, which was done during the days of the Holy Temple. At that time, the Tashlich ceremony was performed followed by sending Rams into the desert after the sins of the Hebrew people were put into the heads of the goats.

A Seder is held during the first 2 nights of Passover. Seder means order, so this indicates that there are specific ceremonies and rituals that need to be followed, one step after another. The Seder represents creating order out of Chaos. The Seder ritual changes the pattern for the year, transporting you to a parallel universe where all judgments are erased. This means that the purpose of Passover is to erase negative judgments. In your Hyperspace/Oversoul work, you can compare this to merging with alternate realities or alternate selves where only positive exists using the Brown Merger/Self-Integration Archetype. This is what Passover is about. Every event in the universe is the result of human action. All of these energies are to help the intelligence of humanity and all creatures that are on this level. This helps to change the script from negative to positive outcomes.

The Seder Plate contains the following items with its symbolism:

Beitzah/egg represents the mind-pattern of desire.

Maror/bitter herbs represent death because in Ancient Egypt the Angel of Death passed over all the homes, taking the lives of the first born son unless the doorframe was pined with the blood of a lamb.

Charosset/fruit blend represents sweetness in life.

Karpass/parsley represents oppression.

Chazaret/lettuce represents mercy.

Z'roa/shank bone represents removing negative mind-patterns.

The Passover Seder table also includes 3 pieces of Matzah/unleavened flatbread representing the 3 columns of the Sephirot: right, left, and central columns. This also represents the sacrifice of the Ram which is about the balance of your own 3 Sephirot columns and mind-pattern correction. After the prayers are said, the plate is passed so that each person eats a bit of everything on a piece of Matzah. Matzah is unleavened bread which represents restricting your desire to receive. Matzah is a cracker that could have become bread but did not. This symbolizes what you could have been but did not. Passover is an opportunity to open a new page in your life as you leave your slavery of the past and venture forward into a more positive life.

Iyar

Taurus is the constellation in the Hebrew month of Iyar, which is about the revelation of both destruction and healing. The Hebrew letters Peh and Vav are responsible for all the events during this month. Peh created the planet Venus and the Light of the Creator comes through. During this time is an event called Counting of the Omer which remembers the time when 24,000 students of the Holy Rabbi Akiva were killed because of a plague. During the Counting of the Omar people do not get married, start anything new or sign contracts. However, on the 33rd day of Counting the Omar, there is a transmission of intense positive energy so many people get married, start new businesses, and sign contracts.

Yirah / Rayeh

In the following chart, the Hebrew word Yirah is often translated as the word fear. But Yirah means awe. The next Hebrew word is Rayeh which means vision or to see. English translations of the Bible usually say that you should fear God, but when these 2 words are put together it means that you should see God and be in awe of God; to see the energy and power of God.

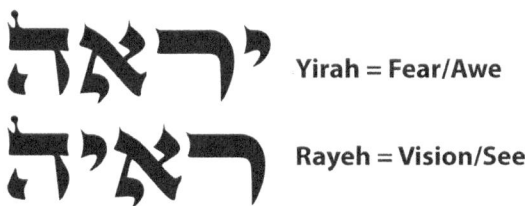

Yirah = Fear/Awe

Rayeh = Vision/See

Numerical Gem of the Torah

The Bible says that God will be King over the entire world. When this happens, on that day God and His Name will be One. These words symbolize the flow of the Sephirot as the powers of the Soul unite with God as One Being. The following 3 verse blessing, called the *Numerical Gem of the Torah*, was given by the priests in the Holy Temple:

May God bless and guard you.

May God shine his countenance upon you and give you grace.

May God lift His countenance upon you and give you peace.

Most people know that the Hebrew word for peace is Shalom. But Shalom is a very profound word that means much more including consummating perfection or soundness, having good health, and to have anything that needs to be completed in peace. The Torah has the power to make peace between opposites. This is why Creation is comprised of opposites such as matter/antimatter, male/female, positive/negative, and Angels/demons. Everything in Creation has an opposite to balance and neutralize each other. This means that the 2 opposites are 1. The Torah makes peace between people that express opposite opinions. Kabbalah says that Love is in the end meaning that opposite opinions are clarified through the study of Torah, Kabbalah and Zohar. Keter, the crown symbolizes that all people are actually one and the same within and under the Divine Essence. This shows that every person is part of the whole even those with opposite opinions.

Book of Kings

King Solomon, in the ***Book of Kings***, says God has chosen to dwell in a mist. The first time mist appears in the Bible is when Moses goes up the mountain to receive the Torah. The Bible says that Moses approached the mist in which God was. The word mist appears in the Torah 3 times and 15 times in the Bible. Interestingly, the Hebrew word for mist, Arafael, has a root of 4 letters instead of 3. These letters are Ayin, Resh, Peh, Lamed, from right to left. This is extremely uncommon in the Hebrew language as each word normally has a root of 3 letters.

King Solomon said that the secret of the Holy Temple is that the purpose of All Creation and the entire world is to become a dwelling place for God. Lishvon b'arafel are the Hebrew words that mean to live in the mist. The Gematria of this phrase is 782 which equals the year (5)782, indicating that this is going to be a powerful year. The first letter of each of these words is Lamed, Bet which in Hebrew spells heart.

In Hebrew, the word for mist can also mean uncertainty, yet God is certain. The Torah is certain that God chooses to dwell in the uncertain or the mist. The exact translation in English would be closer to fog or condensation which determines the thickness of the fog/mist. Condensation is the vapor of the mist creating fog which is comprised of droplets of water. These droplets of water fall to the ground to become part of the firmament.

Light represents the Infinite. Everything is made of Light. Vessels come into Existence from the Light. Uncertainty exists between the two definite states of being. Uncertainty is a relative state of nothingness. When the water becomes part of the firmament and part of the vessel that holds the Light, there is an exact metamorphosis. For example, think of all your issues being a mist/fog with God being a part of this mist/fog. When you concentrate on the God-part of the mist/fog, this coalesces into condensation or droplets of water. These droplets of water fall into the Earth/you, watering your seeds of potential. Even when you feel confused in your personal mist/fog, there is a certainty that will happen. Kabbalah says that the world has to go through transition so that it can undergo condensation. This represents the changes in the world as the mist/fog is condensing into water droplets.

Forget Sin

Kabbalah teaches to reverse words to get deeper layers of meaning. For example:

C O V I D

D I V O C

Remember in the Hebrew AlephBeit that Bet with a dagesh/dot is pronounced like the English letter B. This means that COVID can turn into DIBOC which is the Hebrew word dybbuk. Dybbuk is an evil spirit. This is another layer of proof that the vaccinations are removing evil spirits and demonic attachments from people. This is why there are so many negative reactions to the vaccinations, including death. When a person is completely controlled and then the evil spirit/demon leaves, the body dies because there is no soul left. The original Soul-personality of the person is long gone.

Kabbalah says that Torah study is a labor in life that makes you forget to sin as study removes sin. In other words, when you are busy studying Holiness you are not thinking of sin. Of course, the light shining in the darkness brings up whatever needs to go so that evil and darkness will not exist in the same way anymore. Kabbalah also says that toiling over the Torah makes one forget sin because studying the Torah takes strength and toil breaks the body, thus nullifying the person's evil inclination. Another result is that Torah study increases your love for other humans and teaches them to do the same by your example. You must expend great effort to constantly engage in helping others both materially and spiritually. You must have compassion, restraint, and loving kindness in your approach to all other Beings. With this attitude, you cannot sin and evil has no hold over you.

Truth Within Opposites

The ultimate objective of Truth is to sustain a paradox. To know Truth, you must know both sides to every single thing. Truth is concealed until you know both sides. For example, the Gematria of the Messiah equals 358. The Gematria of the Hebrew word Nachash, meaning snake, is 358. These words are opposite with the same value. This is because you have a choice of which opposite to choose: the way of the Messiah/Holiness or the way of the snake/personification of negative intelligence.

Homework

Visualize all of your challenges, doubts, and confusions as mist/fog around you. Then allow the mist/fog to condensate into water droplets. Watch the water droplets watering the ground that is filled with your seeds of potential for the next stage of your life. Observe what happens.

Homework Review

Comment: When I visualized my issues as a mist around me, I saw them condensing into droplets, then falling to the ground. As this happened I heard the sound of coins falling like at a casino. Then plants similar to tall young corn plants immediately grew around me to the height of my shoulders and were a bright medium green color.

Response: This is very symbolic because it means that your creative efforts are now coalescing and growing in a positive way, showing how you can creatively turn your issues into something positive

Comment: I am wondering if this visualization actually affects reality.

Response: This visualization is a status report of your creativity.

Comment: I went into the visualization with the question of what is the most important thing to do next. Then the foggy clouds turned to dark black clouds changing to a deep, gray fog that fell endlessly, turning into heavy rain with images of violent flooding all over the Earth. At the end, I saw a clear star with bright stars followed by the morning sun rising in a clear blue sky.

Response: This tells you that your emotions must be grounded and cleared for you to see what you need to do next. The key to your solution is to work on healing hurt emotions relating, to feminine energies.

Comment: During this very powerful visualization I mentally blew all my problems away in a blast of gold white light but instead of allowing them to fall gently to the ground, I called them back. I put them all into one larger bubble of gold white light and sent everything to my Oversoul.

Response: You combined several different visualizations instead of the one you were given. You are mixing too many things so you need to do it again in the format it was given.

Comment: I have the most confusion and uncertainty with my career path. I am always questioning and second-guessing myself. I feel the most certain with my career choice. I am finally at peace knowing I'm in the right place at the right time for the right reasons. It's taken me this long to finally realize it deeply, especially in the midst of this pandemic.

Response: That's excellent, I'm so glad to hear that you think to that conclusion.

Comment: I tried this numerous times. Each time I saw my problems melt with the mist with the message that my problems are temporary.

Response: Yes, of course, all the problems on this Earth are a temporary illusion anyway designed to help you learn major lessons.

Comment: I love the visualization of putting all my issues around me in a fog and seeing them turn to water droplets falling to the ground. Everything turned from gray to Springtime. Everything was lush, green, and beautiful with the sun shining brightly above me. As I turned my face toward the sun, I knew I was looking into the face of God.

Response: That sounds like a very beautiful experience.

Comment: I did the Tikkun Hanefesh after skimming, the *72 Names of God,* and the *Ana B'koach* prayer. I felt like the dark forces in the world are propelling people forward so they can progress with new beginnings. I feel like there will be lots of miracles as the clean-out without means people will clean out within.

Response: That's a very good perspective because you have to remember that whatever you see in the outside world, even the terrible things, is a reflection of something inside of each person. This means that you cannot condemn it because ultimately the people created it. You have to continually look inside to determine what the reflection is so you can correct Self. Only in this way can society be corrected.

Comment: When I did the visualization I saw myself walking through a thick fog. Then the fog changed into a mist that slowly traveled up above me forming a large covering tent above my head. Next, it changed into droplets that fell on and around me. The droplets that fell on the ground produced a fig tree, rose bush, and an olive branch.

Response: This is highly significant. The fig tree represents fertility and creative abilities. The rosebush represents emotions that can be thorny or involves love with conditions. The olive branch represents peace. These are all issues that are within you that need to be analyzed.

Comment: This visualization definitely clears the air. I feel more certain about seeing programming. I recognized other emotions that tried to jump in to create doubt.

Response: Programming that is activated within can create imagery that blocks you, keeping you doubtful and confused. Be sure that you keep up with your deprogramming techniques.

Comment: When I started my visualization, I was going to address my health and work concerns, but instead I was shown to place the Earth in the fog. When I did this, the fog condensed and the droplets went into the ground. Then a renewed Earth showed up without the current chaos. I was told this is a way to share healing with the world.

Response: When you do this visualization rather than stating specific issues that you want to be addressed, allow whatever issues that need to be addressed to surface on their own. Of course, the Earth can represent you and your need for a renewed life without your current chaos. Healing Self helps the entire world heal; this is how you share healing with the world.

Rectification

The following graphic shows the Hebrew word for Mist. The root of Mist is Darkness. You know that each Hebrew word has a root comprised of 3 letters and in rare instances, 4 letters. These letters are permutated/manipulated to create 13 letters with a Gematria of 841. Interestingly, the Holy Temple called Beit Hamikdash in Hebrew, and Rosh Hashanah both have a Gematria of 841. This means that the Mist/Darkness, Beit Hamikdash, and Rosh Hashanah are all connected with common energy. You can transform this by adding a Resh to the word which then means beauty of speech.

Holy Fathers

The Gematria of Abraham, Isaac, and Jacob equals 782 which is the same Gematria of the 3 emotive faculties of the heart. This means that when you look at the Sephira of the heart or Heart Chakra Band, you are looking at the 3 energies of Abraham, Isaac and Jacob. All 3 faculties are part of your heart energy which is related to Rosh Hashanah.

Abraham = Wisdom

Isaac = Understanding

Jacob = Knowledge

Rosh Hashanah begins a sequence of Hebrew Holidays that are all part of the Jewish New Year. Next comes Yom Kippur, then Sukkot and ends with Simchat Torah, which is when the Hebrews accepted the Torah from God on Mt. Sinai. The 2 days of Rosh Hashanah are considered one long day.

On the first day of Rosh Hashanah, the Shofar is blown 100 times in various combinations. The first one, Tekiyah, is one long blast. The next is Shivarim which is a trio of undulating sounds. Teruah is a staccato of 9 short blasts. The sounds are to correlate God as King of the Universe with a call to repentance. When Abraham was told by God to bind his son Isaac and sacrifice him on the altar. Because Abraham obeyed, God sent a ram to take Isaac's place. This is the original story of God sacrificing his only son for humanity. This energy continues to repeat.

Listening to the Shofar on Rosh Hashanah is considered a Mitzvah that rectifies your Soul. Mitzvah is sometimes translated as a commandment, but the true translation is connection. This means that doing a Mitzvah connects your Soul to God. The Shofar reminds you that the world was created, and considered to be, very good, even the things you perceive as bad. You must dig deeper into the bad to find the good within it. The sound of the Shofar is equal to a voice that carries an intimate message that rectifies the root of the Soul even if the listener does not understand the meaning of the message. Listening to the Shofar goes into the deepest part of your Soul to cleanse it of its sins. From the root of the Soul, the voice of the Shofar reaches into the superconscious mind giving the listener the power of faith called emnuah in Hebrew. The sound also gives ta'anug which means pleasure in Hebrew as well as ratzon which means will in Hebrew.

Tziddikim, or Holy people, say that everyone can strengthen their emnuah/faith by studying Torah because even if you do not understand everything, your Soul understands. Torah penetrates the Being, strengthening pure and simple faith in God. Ta'anug/pleasure comes from listening to the Song of the Shofar because the song goes from the crown to the root, awakening and revealing the simple pleasure of the Soul which is its connection to God. God wants you to be completely happy and pleasured at all times just as God was pleasured in the manifestation of Creation. Ratzon/will gives balance and potency so you can achieve your goals by completely actualizing them. The Soul plays a role in the Stage of Creation, actualizing the will of God. Listening to the Shofar balances this, and helps you center, prioritize goals and accomplish them.

The intellectual powers of the Soul are in the Sephirot of Chochmah/Wisdom and Binah/Understanding as well as Da'at/Balance. Da'at is not a Sephira but is located in what Hyperspace/Oversoul work calls the T-Bar Archetype at the pineal gland. Da'at gives you balance between the superconscious mind and the left side/ego part of the brain. The sound of the Shofar awakens the powers that direct behavior for the entire year so that you can evaluate your life and enliven your insight which is part of the Chochmah Sephira. This leads to Binah which is the feminine part of the Sephirot on the left side and brings you to repentance/Teshuva/return

The Shofar reminds you through the Sephira of Gevurah to be in awe of God and fear nothing as a courageous, and tireless soldier in God's army that dares to turn the world upside down to bring redemption. The Sephira of Tiferet in the heart area responds to the Shofar by unifying all the people who study this information, making the Souls of each person equal. The Shofar penetrates the behavioral powers of the Soul in Netzach/Victory, Hod/Acknowledgment, Yesod/Foundation, and Malchut/Kingdom, energizing them all together to give them focus and cause the listener to advance toward the very essence of God. Malchut, at the bottom of all the Sephirot, is reflected Light. If someone attempts to reproach another and the words are not accepted, the words return to the speaker as reflective Light.

Remember that everyone reflects each other so this creates the opportunity for the speaker to find the correct words to penetrate the Soul of the listener as direct and inner Light. In the same way, when you do not understand the content of the sound of the Shofar, the light of the Shofar is reflected back to heaven. Then, you can draw that energy back down into you. In Ancient times, an injury to the ear was life-threatening because hearing relates to the life force of the person. Hearing the Shofar awakens in the Soul with the power to serve God with vitality and exuberance. Simply listening to the Shofar is extremely important. The Zohar says all of these thousands of years ago. You can listen to the Shofar online and then try to keep the sound in your mind to continue to positively influence your Being on all levels.

Rosh Hashanah, the day of judgment, is called Head of the Year. God is called Father, not Mother as well as King and not Queen. While Rosh Hashanah may appear patriarchal, Judaism declares that Rosh Hashanah is the birth of the world. Men don't give birth, so Rosh Rosh Hashanah is a feminine day. There's always a balance in Judaism. Rosh Hashanah is the day that God created the Human Being, male and female. Yet Rosh Hashanah is not about male energy or female energy. Rather this Holiday is about the unification and dynamics between male and female. The Hebrew Bible/Tenakh, Kabbalah, and Zohar all say that the relationship between man and woman is the most common metaphor for the relationship of Human Beings with God. Humanity as well as physical reality are all considered to be the feminine aspect of God, called the Shekhinah.

The Torah is the Mother Matrix of all Creativity and is the blueprint of the Cosmos. The written Torah comes down from Heaven as a Divine Monologue. The Oral Torah is the dialogue between Human Beings and God as well as the struggle to apply God's words to life situations. Herein lay many challenges as interpretation is often subjective rather than objective. Rabbinical law arises from these interpretations leading to a lot of rules. A common saying is that if you ask 5 Rabbis a question you will get 10 answers.

The Zohar constantly discusses energy striking each other, stating that creativity emerges not from any single origin, but out of a collision of forces running in opposite directions and that is God in the explosion. Then the energy of the strike reflects back to the Original Source which is the energy of the God-Mind in Creation. The Zohar says that the ending is before the beginning because this process is a circle. The reception and the feedback it delivers reach before the beginning of thought, to a place where the speaker and the listener are not separate, but fused as one. From here, the most creative ideas emerge. This describes unity where everyone is all one, then everyone is split into opposites so you can see both sides of any given situation and then come to a single conclusion. This is the masculine and feminine forces of Creation. The command chain or initial origin of the energy is male/masculine energy but the feedback loop where Creation takes place is female/feminine energy. Neither is dominant because both energies are necessary for Creation in Balance. The ultimate Female is Planet Earth. The male/masculine energies are the initiators but the female/feminine brings the energy to fruition. This is why there are male and female genders.

Kabbalah says that the night of Rosh Hashanah is the nesirah/sundering apart of Adam and Eve who were initially created as one single androgynous Human Being. They were taken apart so they could meet each other face-to-face. This represents knowing what is inside of you. Kabbalah explains that the creative process begins when God decides that He is going to make a universe of 2 opposing but complementary energies comprised of the energy of transcendence/male/descending Light and eminence/female/returning/ascending Light. Out of this union merges Existence, Life and the meaning of all things. When King Solomon in his Song of Songs wrote about two lovers, it was really about God and Creation; the Holy One and the Shekhinah; the presence of God in the world.

The Name of God YHVH refers to God Creating from the top down. Elohim is the Name of God that is used when He interacts with His Creation. The Mitzvah/connection is to return these 2 energies back to their original state of perfect union because the world only needs to see one of them, not two. Therefore, they need to be merged into one. Kabbalah quotes Moses as saying *Know this is clear as day in heaven and beyond the earth beneath, there's nothing else.* There is only All One.

Malchut, the 10th Sephira, is equal to royalty, the point beneath the foundation of Creation and feminine energy. Kabbalah says that during the Messianic Time, when the Messiah comes the feminine will transcend the masculine to fulfill the commandment that a woman of valor is the crown of her husband. This means that Malchut will rise up to Keter and they will unite as one. The Essence of God will be true Oneness. The feminine is not absorbed within the masculine nor does the feminine absorb the masculine. When the two energies are at their peak of fulfillment, there is exquisite harmony between them that ultimately emerges as Light.

This helps explain Rosh Hashanah because you depend on God as Judge and Father. God chooses to depend on Humanity to complete the story because Humanity is the feminine aspect of Creation while God chooses to be the King of All Creation. Because God provides dominance to the feminine energy embodied by Humanity, the Universe receives each year a deeper hidden origin coming forth to all people of Creation.

This further explains why Rosh Hashanah is called the first day of your world meaning God's work as well as the birth of the world because Rosh Hashanah is the day of first Human Being was created. Tishrei, the month of Rosh Hashanah, is not the first month of the year, it's the seventh month. God created everything in the first month but it wasn't activated until the feminine energy, or feedback loop to Creation, allowed everything to manifest. Humanity is the female of Creation and therefore the point where all begins. Kabbalah describes femininity as the capacity to be receptive to others, drawing out their inner power in the womb of life with healing waters and becoming a gateway back to God.

Humans are called Adam from the Hebrew word Adamah, meaning the ground or soil. Adam is also the Hebrew word for Humanity because the soil is common to everyone. There is a Hebrew saying *let my life be as fertile soil from which many others may flourish.* This means you need to use your energies to help others grow and create within Existence, know life from within and nurture empathy. Learn to properly appreciate the opposite of dominant power and transcendence to balance the two as harmony between male and female as well as Earth, Universe and Creator. This further explains the purpose of Rosh Hashanah.

Unetanah Tokef is a very important prayer that is recited on Rosh Hashanah and Yom Kippur. This prayer helps with repentance and means *let us proclaim.* This prayer is a very dramatic way of describing in imagery the *Book of Life* and what will be inscribed in the coming year for each person. On Yom Kippur, the *Book of Life* is sealed and cannot be altered. Here is part of the prayer:

On Rosh Hashanah, it is inscribed, and on Yom Kippur it is sealed - how many shall pass away and how many shall be born, who shall live and who shall die, who in good time, and who by an untimely death, who by water and who by fire, who by sword and who by wild beast, who by famine and who by thirst, who by earthquake and who by plague, who by strangulation and who by lapidation, who shall have rest and who wander, who shall be at peace and who pursued, who shall be serene and who tormented, who shall become impoverished and who wealthy, who shall be debased, and who exalted. But repentance, prayer and righteousness avert the severity of the decree.

The idea of this prayer is to acknowledge that your time on Earth is limited and your life is precious. You must ask not who shall live, but how shall you live. You perform Teshuva/repentance not to appease God but to remind Self of the value to one another and to strengthen your relationships. You give Tzedakah/charity to help the lives of others. This is a very powerful prayer.

Yom Kippur

When you enter the Temple for Yom Kippur, you need to be dressed appropriately. For females, this means a long dress or skirt with a conservative top. Married women cover their hair. Males cover their head usually with a yarmulke/kippah and after Bar Mitzvah wear a prayer shawl called a Tallit draped over their shoulders. On Yom Kippur, males wear the Tallit for the entire duration of the service. In many synagogues, especially Conservative and Orthodox, males and females do not sit together. Males are usually on the right/right brain and females on the left/left brain. Many people wear white clothing and/or a white robe called a Kittel because you are like an Angel that is devoted to praising God. The Kittel symbolizes a shroud, reminding you that all life on Earth comes to an end so now your old life is dead and you are born into another life of goodness and better quality. Angels do not eat, so on Yom Kippur, you fast to symbolize becoming Angelic.

In front of the area where you sit is a large cabinet with a curtain draped over it called the Ark, Aron Ha-Kodesh in Hebrew, where the Torah and Torah scrolls are kept. Whenever the Ark is opened and the Torah is exposed, you must stand. Then the prayers are led by a Cantor, Chazzan in Hebrew who sings the prayers, beginning and ending each paragraph in Hebrew. The Yom Kippur prayer book is called Machzor which has all the prayers and Torah readings for the entire day. You don't have to say anything in Hebrew. You can pray in your own language because God knows all languages.

On the eve of Yom Kippur there are 3 parts to the service:

Kol Nidre = All Vows

Ma'ariv = Evening Prayer

Selichot = Forgiveness

Kol Nidre

The Ark is opened and 3 Torahs are removed. Kol Nidre is a formal declaration stating that any vows made unintentionally during the coming year should be considered null and void. You also tell Self and God that you regret your distancing from God due to the incorrect decisions that you made as a Human Being.

Ma'ariv

Ma'ariv is the evening prayer, which is recited every evening. This begins with the most central of Jewish prayers, the Shema Israel which says that God is One and you owe your loyalty to God. Then you whisper Baruch HaShem, which means Blessed is the Name. You whisper because this pronouncement is so Holy that it belongs to the Angels and since you are like an Angel, you whisper for all to hear. Next is the Amidah is a silent standing prayer. Facing the front of the synagogue with feet together, the words are whispered so only the person praying hears. This prayer is said 5 times during the 25 hours of Yom Kippur.

Selichot

Yom Kippur ends with an extensive confession and expression of regrets by listing your sins for the past year beginning with each letter of the Hebrew alphabet. As you enumerate each sin you strike your heart with your right hand symbolizing that you are punishing your Self for the sin. Then you confess any sin you failed to include during your confession. If you harmed anyone, you must make amends by writing the wrong and asking the offended party for forgiveness. The Selichot prayer for forgiveness is said toward the end of the service to ask God to forgive you on this day. The entire service concludes with the Avinu Malkeinu, a very beautiful prayer that means Our Father, Our King:

Our Father, our King, we have sinned before You.

Our Father, our King, we have no King but You.

Our Father, our King, act [benevolently] with us for the sake of Your Name.

Our Father, our King, renew for us (on fast days: bless us with) a good year.

Our Father, our King, a good year.

Our Father, our King, remove from us all harsh decrees.

Our Father, our King, annul the intentions of our enemies.

Our Father, our King, foil the plans of our foes.

Our Father, our King, wipe out every oppressor and adversary from against us.

Our Father, our King, close the mouths of our adversaries and accusers.

Our Father, our King, remove pestilence, sword, famine, captivity, and destruction from the members of Your covenant.

Our Father, our King, withhold the plague from Your inheritance.

Our Father, our King, pardon and forgive all our iniquities.

Our Father, our King, blot out and remove our transgressions from before Your eyes.

Our Father, our King, erase in Your abounding mercies all the records of our debts [sins].

Our Father, our King, bring us back to You in wholehearted repentance.

Our Father, our King, send a complete healing to the sick of Your people.

Our Father, our King, rend the evil [aspect] of the verdict decreed against us.

Our Father, our King, remember us with a favorable remembrance before You. Our Father, our King, inscribe us in the book of good life.

Our Father, our King, inscribe us in the book of redemption and deliverance.

Our Father, our King, inscribe us in the book of livelihood and sustenance.

Our Father, our King, inscribe us in the book of merits.

Our Father, our King, inscribe us in the book of pardon and forgiveness.

Our Father, our King, cause deliverance to flourish for us soon.

Our Father, our King, exalt the glory of Israel Your people.

Our Father, our King, exalt the glory of Your anointed one.

Our Father, our King, fill our hands with Your blessings.

Our Father, our King, fill our storehouses with plenty.

Our Father, our King, hear our voice, have pity and compassion upon us.

Our Father, our King, accept our prayer with mercy and with favor.

Our Father, our King, open the gates of heaven to our prayer.

Our Father, our King, let it be remembered that we are but dust.

Our Father, our King, we beseech You, do not turn us away from You empty-handed.

Our Father, our King, may this hour be an hour of mercy and a time of favor before You.

Our Father, our King, have compassion upon us, and upon our infants and children.

Our Father, our King, do it for the sake of those who were slain for Your holy Name.

Our Father, our King, do it for the sake of those who were slaughtered for Your Oneness.

Our Father, our King, do it for the sake of those who went through fire and water for the sanctification of Your Name.

Our Father, our King, avenge the spilled blood of Your servants.

Our Father, our King, do it for Your sake, if not for ours.

Our Father, our King, do it for Your sake, and deliver us.

Our Father, our King, do it for the sake of Your abounding mercies.

Our Father, our King, do it for the sake of Your great, mighty and awesome Name which is proclaimed over us.

Our Father, our King, be gracious to us and answer us, for we have no meritorious deeds; deal charitably and kindly with us and deliver us.

Day of Yom Kippur

The morning service begins with hymns, followed by the Shema Israel and the Amidah. This is followed by a reading of the Haftorah, which is a portion of the Torah about the prophets. Next is the Yizkor which is a Prayer for the Dead. If your parents are alive, you cannot stay for the prayer. If one or both have passed on, you remain for the prayer. Then there are a series of men who are called to the bimah/reading table to say the blessings over the Torah. Being called to the Torah is called an Aliyah. Aliyah means rising up and going above your current stage in life. Interestingly, Jews who move to Israel say they are making an Aliyah because going to Israel is compared to being called up to the Torah. Musaf, is a second silent prayer and then Unetanah

Tokef from the previous evening is recited. Some people get down on their hands and knees, prostrating on the ground when they read a part of the prayer that says *We bend the knee, we bow down, and offer praise before the Supreme King*. Muslims also do this because Muslims are basically like Jews.

Avodah is the next prayer that took place in the Holy Temple when the Kohen/High Priest performed the Temple services. This is also when the Kohen sacrificed one goat on the altar and released the second goat into the desert to symbolically release the sins of the Hebrew people. The High Priest also addressed God with His Sacred Name that no one else could say. Now, the priestly blessing is called Birkat Kohanim and can only be given by the descendants of Aaron, the High Priest who was the brother of Moses. The Kohanim wash their hands before making the blessing and cover their upper bodies with their prayer shawls. It is customary for all males to cover their heads with their prayer shawls and for small children to stand beneath the tallit of their father. Then the Priest blesses the congregation with prosperity, Divine favor, and peace using an ancient formula written in the Torah.

The afternoon service is called Minchah, consisting of a Torah reading and the Amidah prayer. The *Book of Jonah*, the smallest book in the Bible is read, tells how to overcome life's challenges. Neilah, which means closing, is the final prayer. Neilah is said as the sun is setting and the Gates of Heaven are closing, God's decisions are made and your fate is sealed for the coming year. There is one long Shofar blast called Tekiah Gedolah, which concludes Yom Kippur. Everyone returns home to break their 25-hour fast, usually with very light food. Then, it is customary for every observant Jews to start building their Sukkah.

Judgments

Tzom Gedaliah is a Hebrew Holiday that is observed immediately after Rosh Hashanah on the 3rd of Tishrei from sunrise to sundown, unlike other Holidays that are observed from sundown to sundown. Tzom is the Hebrew word for fast; Gedaliah is the Hebrew word for observance. This day is observed with a minor fast, commemorating the assassination of a man named Gedaliah. Gedaliah was a Jewish liaison employed as an official for the Babylonians who occupied the Holy Land of Judea. He was in charge of administering the Jewish population following the destruction of the Temple and the exile in 586/587 BC. The Romans did the same thing. After occupying a country, they employed a local person as an administrative liaison.

Gedaliah was a good person who did his best to mitigate the rules that the Babylonians imposed upon Judea. Because Gedaliah was working with the enemy, he was considered an enemy by the Jewish people, so they assassinated him. The Babylonian Talmud references Gedaliah and as does the Book of Zechariah, Chapter 7, verses 5, 8, and 19. These verses refer to this month of observance although not the specific date. The Rabbis ruled this a fast day designated to commemorate the death of a righteous man that they say was just as tragic as the burning of the Temple. Fasting on this day is not obligatory.

Sukkot

The Holiday of Sukkot is 4 days after Yom Kippur; 4 represents the DNA. Sukkot means the Feast of Booths, like a little building. Rosh Hashanah includes the 4 Shofar blasts and Sukkot also incorporates 4 items:

Lulav = Palm Frond

Aravah = Leaves from a willow tree

Hadassim = Leaves from a myrtle tree

Etrog = Fruit of the citron tree

The Lulav, Aravah, and Hadassim are held in the right hand. The Etrog is held in the left hand. These 4 items represent the 4 protein bases in your DNA. They also represent the 4 letters of the Tetragrammaton, YHVH. These 4 items are shaken in the 6 directions of east, west, north, south, up, and down which also represent the 6 points of the Star of David. The Star of David represents the middle 6 Sephirot of Chesed, Gevurah, Tiferet, Hod, Netzach and Yesod.

There's a reason why Holidays last a certain number of days. Sukkot lasts for 7 days, representing the 7 lower Sephirot. The top of the Sukkah, or booth, is called the s'chach, which means a covering. This roof must be a natural covering such as branches or grass but must allow light to come through in the day and starlight to come through at night. This represents that there is always Light. Even if it is raining, cold, and snowing and you can remain fairly comfortable and eat without your food getting ruined, you must stay in the Sukkah. Males are supposed to stay in the Skukkah even if they are cold or uncomfortable but females are allowed to go inside. You are supposed to make kreplach which is a square dumpling filled with meat that is folded into a triangle because a triangle represents creation and perfection.

Sukkah is spelled Samech, Vav, Kuf, and Hey with a Gematria of 91 which equals the Gematria of Amen which means it is done. Sukkah is equal to Amen because Elul, Rosh Hashanah, Yom Kippur, and Sukkot comprise a 4 word sentence which is essentially a formula. You are purified, judged and now it is done. This makes perfect energetic and Spiritual sense. No human created this.

On Sukkot, judgments are pronounced with respect to water, a precious resource, especially in the desert in ancient times when even merchandise could even be purchased with water. Water is included as a judgment 4 times during the year: Rosh Hashanah, Sukkot, Passover, and Shavuot. Shavuot means weeks, so Shavuot would have been when the exiles left Egypt, journeyed through the desert, and after 50 days received the Torah on Mount Sinai. On Sukkot, the people are judged regarding how much rain will fall in the coming year. In Ancient times the people planted crops in the winter so they would have crops by spring, so rain in the winter was extremely important. The Zohar says that there is to be rejoicing in water everywhere. Water can be drawn from a river or stream and sprinkled at the base of the altar. Wellbeing and economy are dependent upon bountiful rainfall. Even Christians revere water in their rituals, such as baptisms and sprinkling Holy Water during their services.

Water is symbolic of kindness. Chasidim, or Chasidic righteous people, are known for their kindness and rejoicing. The Zohar says that happy are the righteous who are not afraid of judgment, neither in this world or in the world to come, but the righteous are as confident as the young Lion. The righteous shall inherit the Earth. This quote is sometimes misinterpreted to say the meek shall inherit the Earth but the Zohar says the righteous shall inherit the Earth. How you interact with the energy of the Holidays determines how the energy of the forthcoming year carries you forward.

A stiff-necked person stubbornly believes in the certainty of uncertainty. The Zohar says this is why humans have the small indentation in the back of the neck, called Oreph in Hebrew, spelled

Ayin, Resh, Peh Sofit from right to left. The Zohar says that if you look at a caterpillar it is almost unimaginable that it can go from a worm to a beautiful creature. Our current times are like the worm. You must have certainty that eventually the world will become a beautiful butterfly. Even though the current world situation looks ugly it will not stay like this.

As you know, Moses was punished by God who forbid him to enter the Holy Land. When the Hebrews needed water, God told Moses to speak to a specific rock to bring water forth. But Moses was angry because the people were yelling and screaming at him for water, so instead of speaking to the rock, he hit it with his staff. Instead of gushing, the water only trickled out. Because Moses was impatient and allowed his emotions to rule him, God only allowed him to see the Holy Land from the mountain but not enter it.

The Torah says that there are two mountains when entering the Holy Land from Jordon, Mount Eival and Mount Grizim. Blessings were given on Mount Grizim and curses were given on Mount Eival. The Torah says that Mount Eival is more necessary than Mount Grizim because knowing that everything is for the good transforms curses into blessings. This means that even bad things are really good because they lead you in the direction of change. Solomon's Temple had 2 pillars, which are also seen now in Masonic temples, symbolizing these 2 mountains. These 2 pillars also represent Self-confidence and sincerity as well as the 2 feet and 2 legs of the Soul that walk into physical reality. This means that these mountains also represent the Sephirot of Netzach and Hod. When the Hebrews entered the Holy Land they were commanded to go to the town of Shechem, located between these 2 mountains. Shechem represents the pineal gland. Now, Shecham is a Palestinian town on the West Bank called Nablus. This year 5782 is about putting your mind between these two mountains and returning symbolically to Shechem by balancing the left and right brain. The Zohar says this is a mirror of God's creation.

Hoshana Rabbah

Hoshana Rabbah is the 7th day of Sukkot and is considered to be the final day of the Divine Judgment in which the fate of the New Year is determined. This is the day when the verdict that was issued on Rosh Hashanah and Yom Kippur is finalized. Most people believe that Yom Kippur is the day your judgment is finalized but the Midrash says that if you do not attain atonement on Yom Kippur it will be given on Hoshana Rabbah. The word Rabbah means big or great, so Hoshanah Rabbah means the bigger or great salvation. The word Hashanah is connected to Yeshua which means salvation or rescue. And of course, Yeshua is another name for Jesus.

The Midrash is a Rabbinical interpretation of Ancient commentaries of scriptures and texts. The Midrash says that God told Abraham that if atonement is not granted to your children on Rosh Hashanah then it will be granted on Yom Kippur. If they do not attain it on Yom Kippur then it will be given on Hoshana Rabbah. This applies to you as well.

On Hoshanah Rabbah a ceremony is performed called the Taking of the Willow which originated during the time of the Holy Temple. Large 18-foot willow branches are placed around the altar and remain there during Sukkot. People hold the branches, circling the altar 7 times representing the 7 lower Sephirot of physical reality. The top 3 Sephirot represent the nonphysical. 7 is the number of completion which is why there are 7 days in a week. Then a bundle of 5 willow branches is used to strike the ground 5 times. This symbolizes the tempering of the 5 measures of harshness, or levels of punishment that could be meted, from the least to the most harsh. Men, women and even small children do this symbolizing beating your bad energy into the ground. You never use the willow bundle of another person because it is considered contaminated with their negative issues. After this ceremony, there is joyous dancing because you are now rid of your terrible issues.

The Torah Scrolls are removed from the Ark. Hebrew stories pertinent to the Holiday are read including the entire Book of Deuteronomy where the precepts of love and aw of God are expounded in length. The Zohar says that when the Book of Deuteronomy is ready, it creates an inter-dimensional vortex around you. After midnight the entire Book of Psalms is read. The next morning, the Shofar is sounded for repentance followed by more prayers. Finally, the Rabbi distributes Lekach/honey cake which you also eat before Yom Kippur. Then you have a festive meal inside the Sukkah where you dip the bread and honey one last time.

Simchat Torah

Following Sukkot is the Holiday of Simchat Torah which means the Happiness of the Torah. Simchat Torah is the day that celebrates the final reading of the complete Torah for the year so that you can start over again. The Zohar says that the Torah is an advisor because it contains the answer to every single problem, issue or challenge that you have. Sometimes, all you have to do is open it and point to find your answer. The Messiah is called the wondrous advisor which has the same Gematria as doctor. According to the Zohar, every doctor should be a wondrous advisor.

The root of advice and advisor in Hebrew is the Hebrew letters Ayin and Tzaddi. Together they spell Eyts which means tree as well as concentrated energy or power that can be used inter-dimensionally. This also refers the Sephirot's *Tree of Life*, inferring that the *Tree of Life* is a center of inter-dimensional power that advises. Another level of Eyts takes the meaning of Ayin/eye and Tzaddi/Holy or righteous person. This tells you that another level of Eyts means the eye of a righteous person and that trees are Holy. This is why there are Jewish organizations that ask for donations to plant a tree in someone's name in Israel. This is not to create a forest but to create the Eye of a Holy Person.

Kabbalah says that when you deal with an advisor, whether it is the Torah or a person, you must use the principle of Mind Over the Heart before you act. This means do not allow your emotions to cloud your judgment or actions. Use your Mind instead of your Heart. When someone tells you to follow your Heart, they are telling you to allow your emotions to cloud your judgment. You must balance your Mind to determine the correct action.

The Hebrew Bible says that every male is an image of God and every female is a likeness of God. The Hebrew word for likeness has feminine energy. Likeness is the ability to receive, so it is a commandment, or connection, for the female to receive and reflect Godliness into the world as a state of Being. Females represent physical reality and are therefore the connection between the physical and nonphysical. Without feminine energy, there would be no Creation because females are responsible for the manifestation of Creation. The Zohar says that females have more positive energy than males, which is why they are the ones who bear children.

Tzelem is the Hebrew word for image and represents a Tzaddik or righteous person who is the foundation of the world. Tzelem has masculine energy. Males represent the nonphysical so while they are supposed to reflect Godliness it is not a commandment because they do not have the same connection to the physical as females.

Homework

1. Do a visualization of the Hebrew word eyts, spelled Ayin, Tzaddi, right to left.
2. Do a visualization of the Hebrew word Tzelem for male energy and Tzaddi for female energy.
3. Look at the difference between the words image/projection and likeness/reflection.

Homework Review

Comment: When I visualized Ayin and Tzaddi Sofit, I didn't see any images or pictures. I get certain thoughts or revelations that surface. This is how all my mental work and visualizations are. I never see images or pictures like others do.

Response: This is because you are more centered in your logical mind. People who work in the left brain/logical mind, see different perspectives. If you daydream, you can visualize. When you try too hard you block the images from coming up. This is very common. Sometimes you are afraid of what you are going to see. Everyone processes things differently; there is no right or wrong way, only the information.

Comment: What came to my mind is how we are all one from the same tree, split off into branches, experiencing different aspects of this reality. We are all exposed to evil and good.

Response: That is absolutely correct. That's a good description of how our actuality is.

Comment: Evil is in our faces 24/7 on television, social media, and even in some of our family or friends. The good is hidden. Our job is to uncover and expose the good as well as the evil.

Response: Yes, shine your Light so others reflect theirs back.

Comment: Black Lives Matter represents evil. They are fighting against vaccine mandates in New York City, stating that the mandates are racist and they are threatening to riot.

Response: Ironically, evil is fighting against evil. Evil is turning against itself. Yes, that's the plan. It's working perfectly and that is why we are experiencing what we are experiencing now. The whole purpose is to turn evil against itself.

Comment: I saw a big green leafy feminine tree. I was teaching when I did the visualization and saw that I am more important to my students than I thought. How I teach will matter to them and their adulthood.

Response: There are male and female trees. Male trees are preferred in cities because female trees drop seeds all over the street. The seeds of the female trees are said to add to allergy issues. You are absolutely correct; even to this day, I think about some of the teachers whose words are still in my mind.

Comment: This was a difficult assignment. I had to relisten three times just to make it easy on myself. I meditated on words, images, and likeness. Sorry if this is not what you wanted.

Response: The homework is not about what I want, it's about what you need. I gave direction and you do what you need to do with it.

Comment: With the image, I got a stronger feeling that it was closer to God and was a strong male energy. Likeness was weaker than image but still was a strong female energy. Both had the power of creation.

Response: That's exactly correct. Both are necessary. One is not more important than the other.

Comment: I saw an image of God behind an immense palace surrounded by light with a vast area of water in front of it. The water had a reflection of the inner Earth with elements such as fire, air, water, and earth. The palace was the image and the water was the likeness with its ability to receive God's light. It seemed to parallel Heaven on Earth.

Response: That's correct. Malchut or the lowest Sephira represents where we are now. Physical reality is a reflection of the Sephirot above it that coagulate into this one final step.

Comment: The image of Ayin and Tzaddi Sofit and likeness merged to reveal righteous actions as projections to vanquish plagues. I came up with 7 new righteous actions:

1. What you reject in others as you discard needs rejoining with the glue of compassion and mercy.
2. Review before you speak about others so you only reveal spirituality.
3. When speaking and exposing truth, use the Light of Justice to bring a balanced perspective.
4. Godliness is always revealed when we create Chesad actions.
5. Call into Creation, peace, and harmony while balancing ego and price with Self-esteem, value and power.
6. Reveal God's praise by praising and credit the ideas and manifestations of others.
7. Reveal your abundance by letting your desires be the springboard for you to sing the praises of and celebrate with others.

Response: When you see the success of others, this is a reflection of your own success. Always feel what you feel, pass your feelings up to your Oversoul, and keep moving forward.

Comment: I saw my Self living in a house with a woman and a man. The woman has made things beautiful by creating a home.

Response: The woman represents your reflection and the man represents your projection of your Self. Malchut is the feminine energy that manifests Creation. God-Mind is the projection of Creation; Creation and humanity are the reflection.

Comment: Keter had an impact just looking at this Sephira on the *Tree of Life*. The area of the third eye was like a huge expanding ball of pressure.

Response: Da'at is the energy between Binah and Chochmah. It's not a Sephira but it is the lower energy of the Keter. Your perspective is correct.

Comment: When I visualized Ayin and Tzaddi Sofit, drops of water appeared, and then heavy rain appeared.

Response: The drops of water represent your emotions; heavy rain is the intensity of the emotions. Now, visualize the water/emotions evaporating and clear up.

Comment: I saw Moses, his staff, and a spinal column.

Response: This represents the central column of the Sephirot and balance. This means you need to balance your energies because you are leaning one way or the other which is keeping things in your life from coming to a conclusion.

Comment: I saw a tree, which is eyts in Hebrew, and a symbolic connection between Earth and Heaven

Response: Every tree has roots that go below the earth and branches rising up into the sky, so you are correct that trees connect Heaven and Earth.

Comment: Zeir Anpin, the male aspect is the giver. Zeir Anpin represents the 6 Sephirot below the 3 top ones, but above Malchut. It is the female aspect of Malchut which receives everything it has; Malchut has nothing of its own except what is received. Malchut is commanded to give in order to manifest blessings into the world. Giving is what makes us righteous. Giving makes us become like God who is the ultimate carer.

Response: Absolutely correct. That's the whole purpose of what we're supposed to be doing. We are to receive the energy of the God-Mind, manifest it, and transmit it. We receive information and send it out. If you hold onto it, then you cannot send it out and you clog up the entire system. To give, you must open up and receive. You must open completely and unconditionally surrender so you receive abundantly until your cup overflows. In this way, you give to the world by manifesting and bringing blessings into Existence. This is a perfect way to describe it.

Gratitude & Devotion

The last day of Sukkot is called Shmini Atzeret. Technically Hoshanah Rabbah is the last day of Sukkot but the Rabbis decided to treat Shmini Atzeret and Simchat Torah as part of Sukkot because of their significance. Shmini means the eighth time in Hebrew. There are references in the Torah in the *Books of Leviticus* and Numbers where God commands that Shmini/Eighth Day, referring to Sukkot, is to be a sacred occasion. In Hebrew, Atzeret means solemn gathering. Therefore Atzeret Shmini is defined by its textual context which implies that it is a deliberate extension of the prior 7 days.

The Talmud states that the Eighth Day is a Holiday in its own right. At the same time, the Talmud tries to separate Shmini Atzeret from Sukkot, saying that 70 Temple sacrifices are made throughout Sukkot and only one on Shmini Atzeret. The Talmud then says that on this Eighth Day and final celebration you must store up the sentiments of gratitude and devotion acquired throughout the entire Fall Holiday season. There are 4 significant differences between Shmini Atzeret and Sukkot. The first is that on Shmini you do not shake the lulav and Etrog. The second is that while you still eat and recite the Kiddush in the Sukkah, the blessing to sanctify the commandment to dwell in it.

This means you do not have to be in the Sukkah on the Eighth Day as you did in the previous 7 days. The third difference is that after the Torah reading in the synagogue the Yizkor, prayer for the dead is recited. The fourth difference is that Geshem, a special prayer for rain, is recited. This is added to the evening prayer, beginning a period of an additional call for rain which lasts to Passover. Remember that in the Middle East it is dry and warm from approximately February until October. Only from November to the first part of March does the rain come, which is needed for crops and their water supply, so it is very important to pray for rain. From a Hyperspace perspective, the number 8 signifies Oversoul, abundance, prosperity, Infinity, and spiritual connection. From Shmini until the next Holiday in December is a highly spiritual time. The interim period between Holidays is called Hamad.

Sivan

Sivan is a month in the astrological sign of Gemini. During this time period is the Holiday of Shavuot which some Christians call Pentecost. In Hebrew Shavuot means weeks. That is the time period after Passover when the Hebrews wandered in the desert for 7 weeks or 49 days. On the 50th day, Moses received the Scrolls of the Torah. On the night of Shavuot, you are supposed to stay awake all night studying the Torah. Doing this ensures that you will receive 4 months free of chaos and negativity, which takes you to Rosh Hashanah. Then you are supposed to be granted life for the coming year. The Zohar says that during this time, go into the moonlight during a full moon. If you see your shadow, you will live through the following year. This is because, in Hebrew, Tzelem means shadow which represents the image of God and the unity of all Creation. Another layer of meaning of Tzelem in physical reality is the DNA that creates your cells.

Gemini represents twins, so there are 2 aspects of the same thing. Just like the 2 Golden Angels with wing tips touching on the Ark of the Covenant. Among other things, they represent twin souls or two parts of one soul. Every soul is part male and part female. Souls are androgynous and only when the Soul enters physical reality does it break into male and female components. The Zohar takes this concept one step further to say that the soul cannot be considered an androgynous Being like Adam Kadmon. In actuality the soul is split into male and female parts meaning the soul has both positive and negative energy, but the soul is not necessarily androgynous.

In physical reality the positive and negative energy has become sexualized, meaning that all focus is on genitalia. On the soul level, the positive and negative energy is more like a battery. You need both positive and negative working in the correct position to attain the correct results. According to the Zohar, usually, the female or male part incarnates separately. This means that all parts of your soul won't necessarily all be in a body at the same time. When people want to change their gender, this can mean many things. It is possible that the whole soul incarnated in one body at the same time, so because obviously, the body is either male or female there is confusion about what that soul wants to be. It is also possible that the person was of different gender in a previous lifeline. Or it is possible that programming is activated that includes a variety of genders within that person. **Heights of Health** discusses in detail the physical structure of males and females and why changing the outside does not change the truth of what the body is. Shavuot is always on the 6th day of the month of Sivan, connecting you to the consciousness of certainty and unity. Even though there are male and female splits you must create certainty and unity.

In the month of Sivan you can also connect to immortality because the giving of the Torah removes death. The Zohar says that Immortality means creating life from Death because in Actuality there is no Death. Immortality means that you have realized that there is no Death, but only Life. This upgrades your perspective of the Totality of Existence. This was the whole purpose of Moses going up on Mt. Sinai but instead, when he brought the Torah down he found the people worshiping the Golden Calf. Because of this great sin, the connection to immortality was removed. People who worship false idols cannot attain immortality. Counting the Omer starting from the 2nd night of Passover until the day before the holiday of Shavuot builds the energy to accept the power of Shavuot and represents another step to immortality. In this way, you receive the energy without it being so powerful that it damages you.

During this month you can also elevate your consciousness with inner truths by using the Hebrew letters of Resh and Zayin as channels of communication to connect to the Light of the Torah. Meditate and visualize these letters to elevate your consciousness so you can receive inner truths and enhance your ability to communicate.

Tammuz

The month of Tammuz is part of the astrological sign of Cancer and occurs in mid-summer in the Northern Hemisphere. This is controlled by the energy of the moon. The Hebrew letter Tav created the moon and Chet created the sign of Cancer.

Regardless of when it is diagnosed, the disease of Cancer always starts in the month of Tammuz. In Hebrew, the word Sartan means both cancer and crab.

Sartan = Cancer/Crab

Sar = Remove, eliminate, clean

Tan = Chaos, hatred

Sartpin = Removing sorrow

Sar means to remove, eliminate or clean. Tan means chaos and hatred. So Sartan is about removing sorrow. The illness of cancer is a mind-pattern of held resentment over a long period of time. Resentment is connected to sorrow because when you resent something you feel sad. These are the negative emotions that feed the disease of cancer.

10 months of the year are controlled by only 5 planets, each planet controlling 2 months.

1. Saturn

2. Jupiter

3. Mars

4. Venus

5. Mercury

The month of Tammuz controls the Moon. It was the 17th of Tammuz when Moses brought the two tablets down to the Israelites. In Hebrew, Tov means good with a Gematria of 17. The letter Q in the Western alphabet also has the numerical value of 17. This means that on the 17th of Tammuz, Moses was connected to the energy to bring good into the world, but instead found the people worshiping the Golden Calf which brought sadness and creates cancer. The Zohar says that depression is a result of the desire to receive for Self alone. When you feel sorry for your Self this is because you desire something that you are not receiving. Zahar says that if you are depressed and feeling sorry Self, that is a sin and of course, as just stated, this can lead to the disease of cancer.

The month of Tammuz is a revelation of the Hebrews letters Vav and Zayin. Meditate on these letters to receive more inner revelations.

Av

The month of Av controls the Sun and is in the constellation of Leo which controls destiny and removes chaos. The Hebrew letter Khaf created the sun. The astrological sign of Leo was created by the Hebrew letter Tet.

Khaf = כ **Created Sun**   **Tet =** ט **Created Leo**

The Hebrew word for Leon is Ariyeh which means lion and has the Gematria of 216. The 72 Names of God are each comprised of 3 letters; 3x72 = 216. This tells you that the 72 Names of God are connected to Ariyeh the lion. This is why in ancient times the lion was a symbol of Judaism. The Ethiopians called their Emporer Haile Selassie, the Lion of Judah.

Tisha B'av

Both Holy Temples were destroyed on the Tisha B'Av which means the 9th of Av. This day is considered the saddest day in Hebrew history. The 9th of Av is energetically connected to the Sephirah of Yesod, the genital area of the body. There is a period of mourning called the Three Weeks which begins on the 17th of Tammuz and ends on the 9th of Av. During this time period there are various layers of restrictions from fasting to bathing, depending upon the day. In general, you are not allowed to marry, start a business or buy property. On more rigid days you are not allowed to eat, drink wear, leather shoes, have sexual relationships, or bathe for pleasure. These restrictions are designed to allow for more light once the restrictions are lifted. The Zohar says that what an Israelite does or does not do affects the entire world.

If you are studying this material, according to the Zohar, you are an Israelite, so keep in mind that whatever you do and think affects this world. Make the conscious choice to affect it in a way that elevates and uplifts all. The Zohar also states that whatever happens to Israel also happens to the world.

The Zohar says that the Holy Temple was never destroyed. You just can't see it, but it's there in an alternate reality. Everything already exists. If you want to build a house, for example, the house already exists. You simply bring the materials to bring it from the nonphysical to the physical.

Tu B'Av

Tu B'Av is the 15th day of Av with a Gematria of 15. The 15th of every Hebrew month, which is different than the 15th on a Western calendar, is always an excellent time for a new beginning. But especially on Tu B'Av, you are supposed to choose a mate, give to the poor and create new beginnings because this day allows the full force of the Sun and begins a union with the Sun and Moon.

The Hebrew letter Tav created the Moon and Kaf created the Sun. Remember that God used Hebrew letters to create Existence. Kaf, Tav from right to left, spells sect, a group of people with similar beliefs. This means that these letters take you from Light to dark because sects are considered to distort the truth. When you reverse the spelling to Tav, Khaf from right to left, because Khaf is at the end it is now Khaf Sofit. Tav, Khaf spells stitch. When you stitch something together you are connecting and completing it, so this word means you are going from dark to light.

Tav + Khaf
Moon + Sun } ת כ = Sect
(Light to Dark)

ת ך = Stitch (Light to Dark)

This means that you can connect to the Light with little or no effort on Tu B'Av, which is connected to the Sephira of Binah. This Light can remove all sins and is symbolized by a vineyard, a perfect expression for the world of truth because it is a code for the consciousness of the middle 6 Sephirot called Zeir Anpin, meaning the revealed aspect of God.

Shemesh

In Hebrew the word for Sun is Shemesh. Shem means name and esh means fire. This means to name fire, which is God, the symbol of the sun. In Hebrew the word for Moon is Yirach. Yir means city. Rach can mean brother or noise. This means that the Moon can be a city of brothers or a city of noise; it can be unified or chaos, depending upon how its energy is used.

Fire is a projection of energy, which is male. Noise is a reflection of energy, which is female.

Homework

Visualize each of the following at your Pineal Glad to see what comes up for you:

1. Tav that created the Moon
2. Chet for the sign of Cancer
3. Khaf that created the Sun
4. Tet that created Leo

Homework Review

Comment: The first time I put Tav and Chet at my pineal, I felt shock and saw lightning flash. The next time I heard the words constraint, difficult and harsh. These felt like undercurrent frequencies that are always present yet unseen.

Response: Exactly. Many people have similar reactions.

Comment: When I visualized Tav I experienced the color Black with huge feelings of speed to the degree that it was almost scary.

Response: Well Tav did create the Moon. It is possible that your frequency zoomed toward the Moom since that was your focus.

Comment: I focused on the Chet sign of Cancer. I felt like a black hole or snake looking for something. When I visualized Khaf that created the Sun, she felt like she needed to keep her eyes shut because the Light was so intense.

Response: Very good work with very close associations to the frequencies.

Comment: I visualized the four Hebrew letters and didn't get anything immediately. But interestingly all of this study of the Kabbalah and ancient Hebrew teachings has attracted outer confirmations. Recently I attended a wedding and sat next to a woman who studies Hebrew. It was nice to have a discussion about the Hebrew letters, their meanings, and how it links to our existence. She was a stranger who I never met before. Another man who also sat at my table was talking about the scamdemic. He was telling me things that I already knew, but it was nice to hear it from a stranger who was not buying into the narrative.

Response: All of these experiences that you have are connected to this work and you are attracting people who are within your range of vibration/frequency.

Comment: I was driving my car in heavy traffic when all of a sudden information started flowing into me.

Response: When you focus, you are constricting your energy; when you let go then things can come into your head. This even happens with your dreams. This is why it is important to not be discouraged when something doesn't come into your head immediately. Things are stirring up inside and when the time is correct all the information will come flooding into your conscious mind. One person here had a flood in her basement. She was working on her mental and Spiritual foundation, stirred things up within and the result was the cleansing of the foundation of her physical home. These are blessings in disguise. This is rewarding, albeit not necessarily fun, but at least you understand what is happening and why.

Comment: When I visualized the Tav, the word Silver came up along with the word death.

Response: This could be a connection to the Moon and/or the Oversoul. You need to put this at your Pineal Gland and keep going. Some people get visuals, some people get words, and some people attract experiences. There is no right or wrong way to get information. The information comes in the way that is most appropriate for you to learn and assimilate it.

Comment: Chet made me feel very close to the Sun as bright beautiful Light started to penetrate my body. I felt a Divine energy within.

Response: The Sun represents the Father/Son in the Solar System, transmitting through to the Foundation Stone.

Comment: I saw a clear glass oval-shaped table with a base of pyramid-shaped crystals. On one side were spices for medicinal purposes in different colored jars. Another side had water pitchers filled with Gold liquid and Silver mixing bowls. I also saw a banquet with beautiful food.

Response: This tells you that whichever side you feed from is good. You will perceive the images that you need to feed your energy and your Soul-personality.

Comment: I put the letters at my Pineal Gland and they became a huge circle containing All That Is.

Response: That is absolutely correct.

Comment: This class makes things in my life make sense. I feel taller with more acute vision.

Response: Yes, you can feel physical enhancements as a result of this work.

Comment: Tav felt like deep water emotions, deep into my psyche.

Response: There is a lot of emotional stuff that comes up with this work because it disconnects you from the physical so the first layer you feel is emotional. If you stay with this, the emotional energy then goes to a mental capacity and then into pure mind-pattern. This means that whenever you feel emotions, stay with them for a bit until you go higher into the mental level where you will receive even more information.

Comment: Janet often discusses being comfortable with feeling uncomfortable. My visualization of Tav and Chet feels like this. The emotions in a programmed person as well as the process of the programming is uncomfortable, but it is a safeguard. Discomfort alerts the person to a problem. Without that discomfort, the person could easily be lulled into a false numbness. Discomfort is an alert, a light, and a gift.

Response: This is true. If you sit in a comfortable chair without anything bothering you then you are not going to move. But when someone starts poking you and you feel uncomfortable then you have the motivation to move.

Comment: I visualized the letter Tet and saw the Lion of Judah as a Mighty Warrior. The Lion of Judah is a frequency that means the time is now to get on that frequency for the true Second Coming The Lion of God is always there when you call him.

Response: This is similar to the Temple that was destroyed. According to the Zohar, the Temple is still there but you cannot see it unless you tune into that frequency. In the same way, the Lion of God is still there. Everything that you strive for, everything that you seek as a goal is already there. You simply have to connect to it to manifest it.

Comment: I saw a key opening that is hidden. I saw infinite rows of files.

Response: This is most likely your own personal information.

Comment: I saw Chet as a gateway, an eye of the needle, or a camel, which is Biblical terminology. I saw humility being stripped bare to enter through a narrow way. Khaf was more focused energy with the ability to bend light.

Response: This is very appropriate because when you bend light you can become invisible. This is what cloaking is about in military terminology. When you bend or refract light from hitting something you can't see the object. This could mean that you are not seeing what you should be seeing or you might be protecting something that should not be seen.

Comment: I saw that Tav is truth that always expands into Infinity. Chet means that life is eternal and only ego perceives life as finite. Khaf means balance. Worshiping the Creator allows us to bend with experiences rather than break. Tet means long life that comes from searching for the hidden goodness in life experiences.

Response: Great work.

Hebrew History

There is a difference between Jews, Hebrews, and Israelites. Jew was a religious designation as well as nationality. Jews were called Yehudim. There was a time after King Solomon when the Kingdom of Israel split into twin kingdoms. The Northern Kingdom was the Kingdom of Israel. The Southern Kingdom was the Kingdom of Judah. When the Assyrians invaded in 587- 586 BC and destroyed the first Temple, they dispersed the Kingdom of Israel. These people went to the north and became the Scythians, Parthians and Khazars. But the Kingdom of Judah remained intact until the Babylonian Invasion. The people of Judah were called Judean which eventually became Yehudah(singular) and Yehudim(plural). This became Yid. In German Jews is Jude. A Jew traces his/her origins to the Kingdom of Judah, not to the Kingdom of Israel. Over time, the people of the Kingdom of Israel dispersed leaving only the Judeans. The Judeans eventually split with some becoming Samaritans who lived on what is now referred to as the West Bank in Sumeria. The tribe of Judah is said to be the Tribe that will bring in the Messiah.

Hebrew means one who has crossed over. In Ancient times, Hebrew was a nationality and eventually became an umbrella nationality that designated an Israelite or Judean. According to the Zohar, even if you're not a descendant of the Kingdom of Judah or the Kingdom of Israel, if you study and follow Torah, you are considered an Israelite.

Beresheet

The first word of the Torah is Beresheet which means in the beginning. But, according to the Zohar, it does not say the beginning of what. It has been assumed to mean the beginning of Creation but this cannot be correct because there was Creation before the Torah was given to the Hebrews. Beresheet appears 4 other times in the Bible, each time referencing a King or Kingdom. Kabbalah says that Beresheet references the beginning of Time. The word for Kingdom in Hebrew is Malchut, the lowest Sephira so this means that there is a connection. Malchut is the root of time and the ultimate goal is to make God King of Creation. God is already King of Creation but the goal is for Humanity to recognize Him in this way.

Kabbalah says that there is an essential need to have a King to prevent reality from degenerating. The Zohar says that the rectification of a nation is dependent upon having a King as without a King, civilization will eventually degenerate and fall. When I was in the *Montauk Project*, we were consistently indoctrinated with the idea that Humanity needs controllers. Otherwise, we were told, society falls into chaos and everyone fights against each other. A strong leader or King who is benevolent is important to rule as a director rather than a dictator. Of course, thousands of years ago all rulers were Kings, so this is why this word is chosen.

Kabbalah says that the King should unite the people around a central focus directed by the King. It also says that before the Messiah comes, the face of the generation will be like the face of a dog. A dog always looks to its master as the leader for direction. Right now, the population is like dogs who look to their masters for direction. Every now and then they are thrown a metaphorical bone which makes them like their masters. It goes on to say that the leaders will do what makes the people like them, not what is most correct and beneficial for the populace. For example, in this time people state governments increased unemployment which encouraged people to stay home and do nothing. The people may like them for this but ultimately it hurts the people, it does not help them. A lack of true leadership combined with a lust for control compromises a leader's ability to act for the good of the nation and instead, endangers it.

Kabbalah says that the world was created for the nation of Israel. According to the Torah if Israel does not produce a King there can be no rectification/tikkun for the nation and therefore no rectification/tikkun of the world. So, Israel has to have this King that will lead them and then the whole world gets pulled along up with it and that is supposed to be when the Messiah comes. Ancient teachings say that it is God's Will to manifest His Kingship. There cannot be a King if there are no people and conversely, there cannot be a people if there is no King. The King is the head of the nation and it is his persona that brings about the rectification of the Kingdom. This means that the leader of a nation needs to represent the totality of the mind-pattern of the people. Whatever the leader does to improve him/her Self reflects upon what happens to the people. Rectification must come from the heart and happens with love, kindness, and positivity. Rectification cannot be accomplished with assertiveness, criticism or negativity.

The Zohar says that it is a Mitzvah, or good deed, to appoint a King, stating *appoint you shall appoint a king over you*. Yes, it uses the word appoint twice. The first time refers to God meaning that you will appoint God as your King. The second appoint refers to appointing a Human to be your leader on Earth. In other words, you need a spiritual leader as well as a Human leader. Interestingly it is common for most countries to have political leaders as well as spiritual leaders. The Pharaoh of Egypt considered himself the representative of God on Earth. The Pope considers himself the representative of Christ on Earth. This is exactly what the Zohar states, but today most leaders are not benevolent.

A Kingdom must be established by a courageous King to unite the nation and safeguard it from evil. Only after this happens can the people of the nation benefit from kindness. Kabbalah says that the Messiah will come with chadrach. In Hebrew chad means sharp; rach means soft. This means that the Messiah will be sharp with the nations of the world but soft toward Israel. He will be tough with nations that do not follow God's Word and soft toward those that do. Kabbalah says that this will be accomplished with pleasantness and Light that repulses the darkness. The Messiah will reach the height of unification between judgment and compassion.

Isaiah Chapter 60, verses 17-22

17 Instead of the copper I will bring gold, and Instead of the iron I will bring silver, and instead of the wood, copper, and instead of the stones, iron, and I will make your officers peace and your rulers righteousness.

18 Violence shall no longer be heard in your land, neither robbery nor destruction within your borders, and you shall call salvation your walls and your gates praise.

19 You shall no longer have the sun for light by day, and for brightness, the moon shall not give you light, but the Lord shall be to you for an everlasting light, and your God for your glory.

20 Your sun shall no longer set, neither shall your moon be gathered in, for the Lord shall be to you for an everlasting light, and the days of your mourning shall be completed.

21 And your people, all of them righteous, shall inherit the land forever, a scion of My planting, the work of My hands in which I will glory.

22 The smallest shall become a thousand and the least a mighty nation; I am the Lord, in its time I will hasten it.

Observing what is currently happening is extremely relevant because of what happened to President Trump in the US and Benjamin Netanyahu in Israel. Benjamin means the son of the right hand, which is God. Netanyahu means netan/to give; ya/God, hu/to them, or God gave him to you. Like Trump, Netanyahu says that he's going to come back.

Mar Cheshvan

The ***Book of Formation***, also called ***Book of Yetzirah***, says that each month of the Jewish year has a Hebrew letter that connects to a Zodiac sign, one of the 12 tribes of Israel and controls a limb of the body. Mar Cheshvan is the 8th month of the Jewish calendar and occurs mid-October to mid-November on the Western calendar. Mar means bitter, so this implies that Mar Cheshvan is a bitter month. Mar Cheshvan is also called the month of the bull because of the Hebrew word mabooll. Mabooll means flood. This is because Noah's flood began on the 17th of Mar Cheshvan and ended the following year on the 27th of Mar Cheshvan. The following day on the 28th Noah made a sacrifice to God to thank Him for ending the flood.

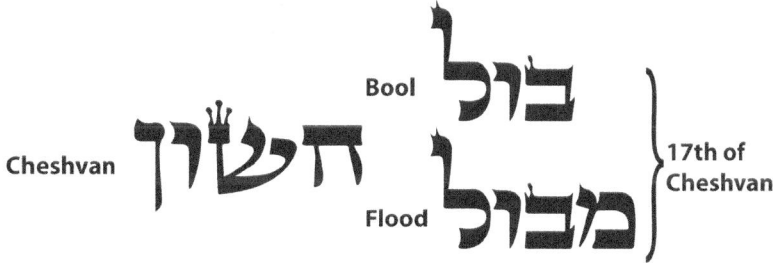

Mar Cheshvan is the only Jewish month that has no Holidays or special commandments. This is because Mar Cheshvan is reserved for the Messiah who will inaugurate the Third Temple during this month. The eternal revelation of the supernatural is signified by the number 8 implies that you can return to a rectified nature. The Zohar says that the harp of King David had 7 strings but the harp of the Messiah will have 8 strings. This signifies the completion of this world and moving into something more. The number of completion is 7; 8 represents Spirituality. The Soul of the Messiah is in a continuous state of consciousness to manifest rectification, representing a burning love for God and Israel.

The Hebrew letter Nun is related to the Messiah because the Bible says in Psalms Chapter 72:17 *May his name be forever; before the sun, his name will be magnified, and [people] will bless themselves with him; all nations will praise him.* In Hebrew, Nun means to reign, and as a noun, it means the Heir to the Throne.

Akrav/Scorpion

The Ancient sages said that the Akrav/Scorpion was the deadliest of poisonous creatures and is an archetypal figure related to the snake. Akrav means heel, like the heel of your foot. The Bible says the snake shall bite him at the heel. Metaphorically this means that the vulnerable part of you (heel) gets tempted by evil (snake) which then bites you. Messiah, in Hebrew is Mashiah which has the Gematria of 358. Snake, in Hebrew is Nachash which also has the Gematria of 358. This means that the Messiah must rectify and upgrade the energy of the snake.

The snake is crooked and bent like the letter Nun but during the month of Mar Chesvan it will straighten out like a Nun Sofit. When Nun is in the middle of the word it is curved but when it is at the end of the word it is a straight line. This means that in the end, the energy of the snake will be straightened out and ended. The Gematria of King David is 14, which when added to the Gematria of Messiah 358 becomes 372 which is the Gematria of the Scorpion. This means that a Scorpion equals Messiah + King David and the Messiah is descended from King David.

358 + 14 = 372 (Mashiach + David)

Akrav - Scorpio עקרב = 372

Heel עקר

Mashiach משיח = Snake נחש = 358

David = 14 דוד

Tribe of Manasseh

Manasseh is the firstborn son of Joseph, the father of all 12 tribes. Using Hebrew letters, Manasseh can be permutated to become Neshama which means soul. Menasha represents the revealing of the Divine Soul in Israel. In one place in the Bible, Moses/Moshe is called Manasseh. This is because adding the Hebrew letter Nun to Moshe turns it into Manasseh. The Zohar says that Moses did not attain the 50th Gate of Understanding, which is the understanding of God, Himself. But 50 is the Gematria of Nun and also Mar Cheshvan, so when Moses returns as the Mashiach/Messiah he will be the reincarnation of Moses. He will be a final redeemer who has achieved the 50th Gate as well as the secret of Manasseh. The Zohar says that when Moses passed from this world he received the 50th Gate. The Mishnah is a description of laws and the word is a derivation of both Manasseh and Mashiach. They're all connected which means that at the time of the Messiah the 50th Gate of Understanding will be revealed.

Menasheh מנשה Soul נשמה Moses משה
Mishnah משנה Neshama Moshe

Smell

Kabbalah says that smell is the most spiritual of all the senses and that smell is the only sense that the Soul enjoys but not the body. Smell is the only one of the 5 senses that was not blemished or polluted by the sin that took place in the Garden of Eden. The Hebrew word for smell is ruach. Ruach also means Spirit when the Yud is changed to a Vav as you can see in the following graphic.

In Isaiah 11:3 the Bible says *and he shall smell with the awe of God. He shall judge by smell rather than by sight or hearing. By his sense of smell his Holy Spirit the Messiah will know how to connect each Jewish soul to the divine root and thereby identify its tribe in Israel.* Because everyone is a genetic mix, rather than take this literally understand that this is about reading your frequency to know your origin.

The priest would grind grain into minute particles to include with the sacrifice. In Hebrew the word for intestines is dakeen; minute is da-ka, grain is dak and to grind are all related. This means that there's power to dissect into fine, refined parts. All the sacrifices in the Temple services were meant to produce a satisfying aroma to please the Divine sense of smell. This symbolized God's satisfaction with the service of his children, Israel, and in particular with Creation. The sages say that the phrase satisfying aroma means that God is satisfied and His Will has been fulfilled. Divine satisfaction with Humans and Creation was first expressed on the 28th of Cheshvan when Noah offered his sacrifice to God. As a result, the Torah explicitly expresses that God swore to Noah that He would never again destroy the world by flood.

The color associated with Mar Cheshvan is Violet which is the color of protection and filtration.

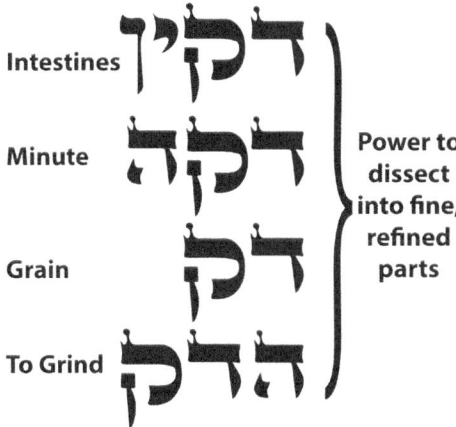

Witchcraft

The Zohar gives background information about witchcraft even though technically it is banned by the Torah, saying that you should not be a witch, warlock or sorcerer. Yet, there are cases where witchcraft was used for positive purposes such as healing and making amulets, all tolerated by Jewish tradition. Witches and witchcraft were viewed as a vice in which every woman will indulge. The Talmud does not approve of witchcraft, yet the Rabbis assumed that their own wives engaged in it. Mediterranean societies were more tolerant of witches than Northern European societies. In the Books of Exodus and Leviticus, as well as the Sanhedrin Court, witchcraft is considered a capital offense. Witches in the Bible are often shown in positions of power, employed by such personages as King Manasseh. Queen Jezebel was a witch and Hillary Clinton is the reincarnation of Jezebel. Wizards were employed by the Kings of Babylon and Egypt. The Jews of the Ottoman Empire were viewed with more acceptance as the Sultans used witches to do magic for them to extend their Empire.

The First Book of Enoch says that witchcraft was taught by the fallen Angels to their mortal wives. The Bible says that Lilith, the first woman, transformed into a demon or witch using the Tetragrammaton. Most people do not realize that you can use a *Name of God* to do such a thing. Jews were generally regarded to be exceptional magicians. Even some Rabbis used incantations and potions during healing rituals. However, in Rabbinical literature witchcraft is associated mostly with women even though it says that both men and women can practice it. Witches in Biblical literature were thought to be generally engaged in malevolent activities such as interfering with fertility and childbirth, cursing rivals, jealousy, envy, personal profit, giving the evil eye, and even killing people. In Sefer Hassidim, witches share attributes with werewolves and vampires, shapeshift, fly, and bloodlust, and can become the undead.

Homework

1. Visualize the word Akrav which in Hebrew means Scorpion
2. Put the letter Nun and/or Nun Sofit at your Pineal Gland to see what comes up for you.

Homework Review

Comment: I saw the color Brown which then changed to Red. I was told that the Scorpion is avoided by all other creatures, especially when angered. The words stung, vicious bite, stay away and venom came into my mind. When I visualized Nun at my Pineal Gland I got an image of a candle in the dark.

Response: Nun is the first letter of the word Nair in Hebrew, which means candle. so it is interesting that you saw a candle when you visualized the letter Nun.

Comment: When I visualized Akrav I felt my Self inside of a home during Biblical times. I saw a Chasidic scholar in his 40s or 50s with round eyeglasses studying the Torah.

Response: Many people see images from other lifelines when using Hebrew letters as visualizations. This means that in those other lifelines you are also studying this information. You are here now to continue with your studies.

Comment: I saw a three-dimensional DNA Archetype spiraling around in a Black background. Then it changed to Violet and then Clear.

Response: Violet is the color for the month of Cheshvan and Scorpion frequency.

Comment: I heard a force that was very fierce, strong, and protected. I also smelled roses.

Response: Sometimes each Sephira is referred to as a petal of a rose.

Comment: I heard and saw magic using the letters Nun and Hey for the purpose of creating either a miracle or tragedy using frequency. Intention is important.

Response: Creation is about duality and twin frequencies. This is how the God-Mind created all of Existence.

Comment: The Hebrew letters bring up memories from my childhood when I was in elementary school.

Response: Do the *Green Spiral Staircase* visualization to see what you need to look at that is associated with what you are studying at the current moment.

Comment: In my meditation, I am walking through a thick lush jungle of vegetation. I stopped and saw a flash of a man's thigh and buttocks. Then I heard the words naked you came, naked you will return.

Response: This means that everything will be revealed and exposed in your lifetime.

Comment: I was given a statement that said the real poison is refusing to give the gift of releasing, the bread of Shame, and balancing with absolute trust with Source.

Response: This means to have no guilt, no regret, and to be still, know, trust and have certainty. Be still with your thoughts, know that everything will be okay, trust in the Higher Power, and have a certainty that all will come out in the best possible way.

Comment: I visualized Nun at my Pineal Gland which created a change frequency and could be an antidote or poison. I saw vague fragments of trauma that I experienced in the hospital when I was 5 years old.

Response: This has twin meanings. Put the images at your Pineal Gland and then do the *Green Spiral Staircase* to determine the connection.

Comment: I had a feeling of traveling to another planet far away with dark skies. The Scorpions were about 6 feet tall. They felt a bit like people wearing, large Scorpion shells. And they were at a beach sitting upright on their tail as if the tail is like a built-in stool to sit on. When they finished their meeting, they go back into the water.

Response: Very interesting. Fossils have been found of Scorpion creatures that were 6 feet tall.

Noahides

God used the Hebrew Bet to create the planet Saturn which is in the month of Cheshvan. According to the Zohar, this connects to the story of Noah which is about the human consciousness. Noah in Hebrew is Noach, which means comfortable. Noach did not care who died during the Great Flood, which was a result of the collective negative mind-pattern of Humanity.

The dimensions of the Ark given in the Bible were not of a ship that wouldn't sink. Rather, the Ark had to do with mind-patterns and energy fields. The Zohar says the Ark was a security shield, not a ship. When Noah built the Ark, he was learning how to create a magnetic energy field of protection around Humanity and the Earth. The Bible says that the Great Flood resulted from 40 days and 40 nights of rain, but the Zohar says the Great Flood occurred when hot underground geysers erupted with steaming water that melted flesh.

Noah was commanded to protect 7 clean and 2 unclean animals. This refers to positive and negative energies because 7 is the number of completion and 2 is bipolar/unbalanced. Animals that are unclean are bipolar/unbalanced which is why they are not Kosher. The Torah says never ingest an unbalanced animal. The Zohar states that everything that exists is beneficial and of the Light force of God. This means that even unclean animals have a Holiness to them and represent an aspect of God Mind.

The Hebrew word for destruction is Mabul and has a Gematria of 78. This relates to the Great Flood. The Gematria of YHVH is 26. When multiplied by 3, the number of perfection and creation also becomes 78. This means that if destruction is 78 and 3x YHVH is 78, then within Creation is also the formula for destruction. They are twins.

Noahide is a word used to describe any nonJew who is a descendant of Noah. Of course, everyone allegedly is a descendant of Noah because he and his family were the ones left after the flood. Genesis 9:9 *says God speaks to Noah and his children as they exit the ark and God says, behold I establish my Covenant with you and with your seed after you.*

Because Islam is strictly monotheistic, Muslims have always been considered to be Noahides. Throughout history, Muslim nations welcomed the Jews to live there. During the Spanish Inquisition in Spain, Jews went to North Africa and the Middle East where they lived peacefully amongst the Muslims. In the Middle Ages, Jews acknowledged that the Christian doctrine of the Trinity was not the same as idolatry and so then Christians were also recognized as Noahides.

The Sanhedrin is the Ancient Hebrew Court that still exists in Israel. Jewish Courts enforce the Noahide Laws if a Christian or Muslim is brought into a Jewish Court. Some interpretations of the Noahide Laws say that it is unacceptable for nonJews living under a Jewish Authority to not accept Noahide Laws. Jewish Law says that you cannot make a Noahide convert or accept the Torah. Moses, however, commanded all people to accept Noahide Laws. None of the legal codes mentions an obligation to impose the Noahide laws or to punish nonJews for violations of the Noahide laws. In contrast, when Jews sin or commit a crime, other Jews are obligated to try and prevent that sin through intervention and education. Jews are to impose the law on other Jews but not on nonJews.

The Jews perceive that non-Jews are bound by a set of laws even if they're not bound by the full range of the Torah laws. That means that the Noahide laws stand as a testament, to the Jewish belief, in the need for the rule of law to protect all people. God gave the Jews 613 Mitzvot to follow, but He only gave the Noahides 7 Laws. Mitzvot is often translated to the word commandment, but it means connection. So Jews were given 613 connections to God to follow. The Zohar says that takes many lifetimes to fulfill all these Mitzvot in one lifeline, rather this is done over many incarnations. The Zohar also says that each Noahide must follow all 7 Laws during his/her lifeline.

Seven Laws of Noahides

1. Establish Laws Noahides are obligated to create a system of law according to the 7 Noahide Laws. Courts are to be established in every town and basically, nonJews are supposed to have the same laws as Jews.

2. Don't Curse God.

3. Don't Practice Idolatry. Do not bow down to any statue. Only pray to God.

4. Don't Engage in Illicit Sexual Activity. This includes 6 specific forbidden sexual relationships: with one's mother; one's father's wife; with another man's wife; with your sister from the same mother; in a male homosexual union; with an animal.

5. Don't Participate in Bloodshed. No murder, no violence.

6. Don't Rob. This includes kidnapping, cheating, and usery, which means high-Interest rates.

7. Don't Eat the Flesh of a Living Animal. The Rabbis say this comes from Genesis 9:4 where it says *flesh with its life, which is*

blood you shall not eat. This means you are not allowed to eat the blood of any creature which is part of the Kosher rules. When Jews eat meat they first soak it in salt water to draw out all the blood and then rinse it several times.

The first 6 Laws were given to Adam. The 7th Law was added after the Great Flood when Noah was given permission to eat meat. Because these 7 Laws were associated with Adam, it was implied that these laws were established as part of the Creation of the natural world.

There is a big debate about whether turkeys are Kosher or not. The *Book of Deuteronomy* gives the laws of Kosher animals. It says that when the Israelites were about to enter the land of Israel, they were permitted to eat meat more freely than they could in the desert. The Bible then lists certain types of animals that were specifically Kosher such as land mammals but they must chew their cud and have split hooves. It also lists animals like pigs and camels that you might mistakenly believe to be Kosher but they are not due to other characteristics not as easily noticed. To be a Kosher fish, it must have fins which is why shellfish are not Kosher.

Deuteronomy Chapter 14:11 says *You may eat any clean bird*, but it does not provide any way to identify a clean bird. Instead, it lists 20 types that are not kosher plus it says bats are rodents and are not Kosher. For a bird to be Kosher it must have an extra toe, a crop, and a gizzard and it cannot be predatory. Turkeys were not introduced to Europe until the 1500s because they came from North America. When they were brought to Europe from the New World there was much debate about whether or not it was Kosher. Eventually, the majority of European Jews accepted them as Kosher and now Israelis eat more turkey per capita than any other country in the world.

Weapons

Jewish law prohibits hunting for sport on the grounds of animal cruelty and risk to the hunter. Hunting for food is permitted however land animals must be ritually slaughtered to render them Kosher. There is a Talmud directive that says if someone comes to kill you, then you must kill them first. Not defending your Self is a sin. The Mishnah has a passage from a Talmudic sage known as Rava that permits a homeowner to kill an intruder in self-defense if the trespasser arrives at night. The rabbinical perspective says that you must avoid unnecessary danger. Gun ownership is therefore considered risky and dangerous and should be avoided if possible. But, denial of the right to self-defense is violating God's law. Isaiah prophesied that there will be a time when nations will beat their swords into plowshares. An ideal society in Judaism exists without any weapons.

Very few American Jews own firearms. According to a 2005 American Jewish committee study Jews had the lowest rate of gun ownership of all religious groups. At that time only 13% of Jewish households owned firearms compared to 41% of nonJews. Some people say that if Jews had possessed guns in Nazi Germany the Holocaust may not have occurred. However, during World War II there were many Jews who actively resisted the Nazis and then later went to fight for Israel. In Israel, guns are highly visible on soldiers who carry large automatic weapons in public. While most Israelis serve in the army and are trained to operate firearms, private gun ownership rates in Israel are low. Israel has extensive restrictions on guns and unlike the United States, Israel has no right to bear arms. Only certain groups of citizens are eligible for gun ownership and 80% of Israeli gun license requests are refused.

B'nai Israel

There are 3 Jewish communities in India. One is called Baghdadis which came from Bagdad. One is called Cochin which came from a northern part of India. They live in Bombai in the Kolaba district of Maharashtra State where most of the 3rd community, B'nai Israel, work as carpenters, farmers, and sesame seed oil pressers as well as in the shipyards. They were known for inventing new kinds of tools which made them highly regarded.

The B'nai Israel, meaning Children of Israel, follows religious observances based on Ancient Biblical Judaism. They do not have Torah Scrolls, prayer books, or synagogues so they follow Rabbinic Judaism or Jewish law. Their leaders, called Kazis, travel from village to village to tend to the needs of the people. The B'nai Israel say that they are descendants of 7 couples from a country to the north who were the sole survivors of a shipwreck off the Konkan coast near what is now Mumbai. Some people say that the B'nai Israel originated in Persia or Yemen but the B'nai Israelis say that their ancestors lived in the Holy Land of Israel during the time of Elijah in the 8th Century BC.

In 1813, Reverend John Wilson of the Church of Scotland came to Bombai where he worked with the Indians. Here, he identified the B'nai Israel as remnants of Israel and called them native Israelites. They didn't speak or understand Hebrew, so he introduced them to this language. In 1832, he wrote and published **The Rudiments of Hebrew Grammar** in Marathi, the language of Bombai. Many of his pupils learned English from him and became proficient in Hebrew. Some even became Hebrew professors at the University level where they also translated classical Hebrew texts into the Marathi language. Many Christian groups tried to convert the B'nai Israel to Christianity with zero success.

I believe that the B'nai Israel are the descendants of the Children of the East. Remember, after the death of Sarah, Abraham married Keturah and had 6 sons with her. Then he sent these sons to the East. Or, they could be the descendants of Jmmanuel and his sons who all went to India. Finally, they could be descendants of Saint Thomas, the twin of Christ, who went to India in 60AD and began the Chaldean Church. It is also highly likely that they are descendants from all 3 of these groups.

Interestingly, Israel's largest embassy in the world is located in India, and Israel and India have an extremely close relationship. Now, many of the B'nai Israel live in the Indian cities of Pune, Ahmedabad, and Delhi. Some are in Pakistan in the city of Karachi. After 1948, many emigrated to Israel. Today more than 60,000 B'nai Israel live in Israel. Others now live in the United Kingdom, United States, Canada and Australia.

Mezuzahs

Mezuzahs are small cases with two portions of Deuteronomy 6:4-9 and 11:13-21 written on a parchment scroll in their original Hebrew as per Biblical commandment plus Sha-dai, one of God's names.. The Mezuzah is attached to your doorframe to help protect your home. Rabbinical Law says that you are supposed to slant the top facing in and the bottom facing out.

Rashi, an 11th century French Rabbi said that mezuzaht should be completely vertical. His grandson, Rabbeinu Tum, wrote that the mezuzah should be horizontal because the 10 Commandments in the Torah scrolls are kept horizontally in the Ark in the Temple. Rabbi Jacob ben Asher, 150 years later, said that the best thing to do is to split the difference and put the mezuzah at a slant. Then 300 years after that another Rabbi known as Ramah codified the slanted mezuzah among the Ashkenazi Jews of Western and Central Europe. The Sephardic Mediterranean Jews and the Mizrachi Middle Eastern Jews still place the mezuah vertically.

Christopher Columbus

The Spanish name of Christopher Columbus, who was known as the Admiral of the Ocean Sea, was Cristobal Colon. Colon was a Jewish surname in Spain. His father was a weaver, one of the few trades that were open to Jews in Genoa, Italy where Columbus lived. His mother Susanna was the daughter of Kobol Fontanarossa, also a

Jewish surname. Letters from ancient archives hint at Jewish origins, such as this example:

I am not the first Admiral of my family. Let them give me whatever name they please, but when all is done, David that most prudent King was first a shepherd and afterward, chosen, king of Jerusalem and I am a servant of that same Lord who raised him to such a dignity.

In his ship's log, he made frequent references to the Hebrew Bible, Jerusalem, Moses, David, Abraham, Isaac and Sarah. He calculates the age of the world according to the Jewish calendar as well as writes that it was 1413 years since the destruction of the Second Temple. In his Last Will & Testament, Columbus bequeaths 10% of his estate to the poor girls for their dowry to be given to them anonymously. This is typical of Jewish charity.

In Lisbon, Columbus consulted professional Jewish astronomers and navigators of the Royal Court, such as Joseph Vecinho, a pupil of Rabbi Abraham Zacuto. Rabbi Zacuto was a renowned professor of astronomy at the University of Salamanca. Vecinho gave Columbus Castilian translations of calculations for travel. Columbus was unable to obtain funding in Portugal so he went to Spain. At the Spanish Court in Andalusia he met a small group of Royal officials, including Louis De Santangel, a converted Jew. De Santangel pledged a sizeable amount of his own money which helped convince the Queen and King of Spain to do the same.

On April 29, 1492, the date Columbus received authorization to equip his fleet was also the day the Edict of Expulsion took effect in many of the larger Spanish cities. On this day, the Jews were forced to leave Spain unless they converted to Catholicism. The Queen and King used the forfeited Spanish property of these Jews to help fund Columbus. Several conversos, or Jews who had converted to Christianity to escape the Spanish Inquisition, joined the crew including Alfonso de la Calle, a Bursar who eventually settled on the Caribbean Island of Hispaniola, and Rodrigo Sanchez of Segovia, a surgeon. Some people were baptized just in time to join the journey. There were also multilingual Orientals who signed on as translators thinking they were going to India. Many of these Jews who had to claim to be Christian to join Columbus settled in the Caribbean Islands.

In 1493 when Columbus wanted to return to the Caribbean, the Queen and King of Spain used the remaining forfeited Jewish wealth to finance his second trip. Anyone who wanted to settle in a Spanish Colony of the New World in America had to be of pure Spanish heritage. This was called Limpieza de Sangre which means purity of the blood. For the right price, the new Christians/conversos could buy permits of exemption which allowed the ship's captain to take them to secret locations in the Gulf of Mexico in what is now Mexico and Honduras where they started Jewish colonies. There were as many as 2,000 conversos who settled in Mexico City, Guatemala City, Guadalajara, Puebla, and even migrated as far north as New Mexico and Florida. Jamaica and Hispaniola, Dominican Republic

Jews wanted to go to the Americas and the Caribbean because they knew that the native people had Jewish ancestors. They settled in what is now Jamaica and Hispaniola and the Dominican Republic. Peru, in Hebrew, means be fruitful. Iberia, in Spain and Portugal, means land of the Hebrews. The original name of Ireland was also Iberia because the Jews went from Spain to Ireland. There are even 50 million people in Pakistan who claim to be descendants of Hebrew tribes. Even though they practice Islam they claim to be Hebrews and asked the Sanhedrin in Jerusalem to recognize them.

The name of Brazil comes from the Hebrew word Barzel which means iron. King Solomon sent his Navy there to get iron to build the Holy Temple. King Solomon's Navy went all over the world, including the Americas. According to geneticists, the population of Brazil has 60% Hebrew DNA.

Homework

Use the word Noahide as a focal point at your Pineal Gland in Brown block letters on a Royal Blue background to see what connection you have to Noahides.

Homework Review

Comment: I was shown that these laws help to avoid things that would ultimately bring misery and create a happier world for everyone.

Response: There is a very good quote from Hillel that says, *what is hateful to you do not do your fellow. This is the whole Torah the rest is the explanation. Go and learn.*

Comment: I gave my thanks and I left knowing that I'm welcome.

Response: Interestingly when everyone started looking at the word Noahide everyone started seeing movies, like with Charlton Heston; not too much programming within all of you.

Comment: The word Israel came up. I feel touched inside, a strong emotional connection. Stewart made me aware that my family had a farm at the origin of the river Danube, which sounds like the Tribe of Dan.

Response: The Tribe of Dan colonized most of Western Europe from Ireland all the way through Germany. The Tribe of Dan was known as a seafaring tribe. When they arrived in Ireland, they were called the Danaan and became the origin of the Irish people. This means that if you have Irish genetics or your family is from Central Europe in the Danube or Danzig area, you are from the Tribe of Dan.

Comment: I was walking in the desert with determination to an Egyptian city with pyramids. I was working to break the people out of Egypt and felt this was a metaphor.

Response: There is a lot of desert imagery in the visualizations. God freed His people from Egypt as a metaphor to free the minds of people. The entire Torah is a metaphor, so you are correct.

Comment: I saw a white bearded man who I knew to be Noah either before or after the Great Flood. It seems very peaceful and feels as if it had just rained. Then I saw a man whose face was contorted. He had long red hair and a red beard standing in the shallow part of the water. I saw an image of the painting of Quetzalcoat, the bird-like man from the Mexican Aztecs. Perhaps they might be a connection between Lucifer and Quetzalcoatl, in reference, to the bright and shining star of the morning.

Response: There is also a lot of bearded man imagery in the visualizations. Yes, Quetzalcoatl is a Feathered Serpent so there is a big connection to Lucifer.

Comment: I saw Jezebel and thought that we should find the Light of her story because people only look at the dark side of Jezebel.

Response: Everybody always looks at the dark side of Jezebel. Hillary Clinton is the reincarnation of Jezebel. The Light of Jezebel's story showed how she used her strength to balance with masculine energy. The result was a *Tree of Knowledge* rather than the *Tree of Life*. Her story emphasizes the importance of the Shekinah to balance the masculine energy. This is the *Tree of God*. Jezebel showed us what not to do.

Comment: I heard a military horn, which I interpret as the Shofar. The exercise was stressful for me.

Response: Usually when the work is difficult or stressful this means that there is something that you need to look at. Most likely this is because this works brings up very deep and old stuff with which you now need to deal.

Comment: I saw Shin and Mem. Mem has the Gematria of 40, which is a reference to the 40 days and nights of the flood, plus the 40 years in the desert, plus the 40 days of Christ in the desert. Mem is very, very important letter. The words became woodlike in texture, like a tree trunk. The words tree, wisdom, and nature wisdom came up. This group of Souls called Hebrews or Jews are experiencing restrictions and punishments for some unknown reason to me.

Response: The reason is that they didn't obey God's laws. You know the story of the Golden Calf, for example. This is the reason why the Temple was destroyed and the Jews dispersed.

Comment: I'm wondering how reincarnation fits in if you are Jewish in one life and a shaman in another life.

Response: It is all about the Tikkun; the correction. Each person's story is unique but it always has to do with the correction of your mind-pattern and experiences.

Cosmic Code

The 22 books of the Zohar are written in Aramaic which most people do not understand. The Zohar says that simply scanning the words from right to left opens up other dimensions. Even when read in Aramaic they often do not make sense because the Zohar is written in code. This means that many layers must be considered to understand it including the Gematria and symbolism. For example, the Zohar hints that Adam and Eve were giants, meaning that they physically might have been giants or perhaps spiritual and mental giants. The Zohar says that simply scanning

The Zohar says that the Torah is a Cosmic Code as well as an instrument of spiritual technology detailing the formulas of how God Created everything. The Zohar states to not take the stories of the Bible literally and that the revelations of the Torah are for all people. The Old Testament is comprised of the *5 books of Moses* which the Zohar says refer to as the Sephirot. The Sephirot are levels of Creation, regardless of what planet you are on or what universe you are in. The *5 books of Moses* are about Keter, Chokhmah, Binah and the Zeir Anpin, the middle 6 Sephirot as well as the bottom Sephira of Malchut, the synthesis of the 9 above it. Humankind is personified by Malchut which represents the desire to receive. Binah, the 3rd Sephira represents the desire to share. Keter was the 1st Sephria to be Created and is the seed that represents the potential of everything. Keter remains concealed so that you cannot connect with it directly but only with what emerges from it.

Yira is a Hebrew word often translated as fear, but a more accurate translation is awe of God. Yira has the same root as ruach which means to see. Seeing in awe equals Creation. You are in awe of what is manifest. Recognizing your awe of God is the beginning of your ability to have knowledge of all Creation. Humanity controls the Earth and the entire universe even if you do not understand this in the moment.

The first word of the Torah starts with Bet, the second letter of the Hebrew AlefBet. Bet is the first letter of the Hebrew word Brachah which means blessing. Bet is also the first letter of the Sephira of Binah which means Understanding. Bet has the Gematria of 2 and represents Chokhmah, which means Wisdom and was the 2nd Sephira to be created. Just this first letter of the first word has many layers of meaning. The Zohar says it takes 70 years to understand all the means of the first line of the Torah so this is why people continue to incarnate.

The very first word in the Torah begins with the word Bereisheet. Here is the transliteration of the original Hebrew and the translation:

b'-ray-SHEET ba-RA e-lo-HEEM AYT ha-sha-MA-yim v'-AYT ha-A-retz

In the beginning of God's creation of the heavens and the earth. (Beresheet 1:1)

The Torah says that God created Existence in 6 days. The Torah talks about Day One; it does not say first day. Day One is a code for infinite dimensions. There was no physical measurement beyond time, space and motion because these did not exist. Some interpretations say that one day equals 1,000 of our days and 1 hour is 1,000 of our years.

Beresheet, the very first word of the Torah, is two words. Bara means create and sheet is the number 6. Barasheet means creating 6. This refers to creating the 6 middle Sephirot called the Zier Anpin. These could not have been created unless the top 3 already existed. In my Hyperspace work, I tell you that Creation is the result of 3, which numerically symbolizes perfection. This is God-Mind, Christ Consciousness, and the Angelic Frequency which correlates to Keter, Chokhmah and Binah. The Fall from Grace refers to the Creation of the lower 7 Sephirot. When you study Hyperspace/Oversoul work you are studying Zohar. The concepts may be worded differently but underneath they are the same.

The Hebrew word et, spelled Aleph, Tav from right to left, provides emphasis to the word immediately following it. The word et has no translation, it only alerts you to focus on what comes next. Aleph and Tav are the first and last letters of the Hebrew AlephBet which the Greeks translated into the Alpha and Omega, meaning the first and the last. Aleph in Greek is Alpha and Tav in Greek is Omega. Greeks are Hebrew descendants of the Tribe of Dan.

The word et is the smallest Hebrew word but has the most powerful significance. With this word, God connects Binah/sharing with Malchut/receiving which implies free choice of all that is created.

Medat Hadean

During the Age of Aquarius, the Zohar says that there will be immediate judgment so you will immediately experience the effects of your actions. This is called Medat Hadean. Medat means experience or time period; Hadean means judgment. The Zohar says this is called the Strings of the Universe referring thousands of years ago to what is now called String Theory. Previously, Humanity was in a period called Medat Heragamien which is the effect of Mercy. This means there was a time lag of Mercy to give you the opportunity to mitigate your actions to change the end result. Now, there are no more delayed retributions and you experience the consequences of your actions immediately.

Eternal Light

Ain Sof/Without End/Eternal Light never undergoes changes; it is always the same. The Zohar says that binding by striking is the secret of Ani Sof. This means that when you strike something you connect with it. The Zohar describes the Creation of the Sephirot as when each one was created, it struck the next one to create sparks. Sparks come from resistance. When 2 rocks are hit together, the sparks create a circuit or completion of the energy connection. Questioning creates resistance and the resistance creates conflict. A question creates a spark/light/ revelation and this is why conflict is necessary. Conflict creates a metaphorical spark that helps explain the 2 sides of 1 issue.

This is an analogy between the Zeir Anpin and Malchut, the lowest form of Creation. This further explains the clash between Heaven and Earth because they complement each other. Heaven shares and Earth receives. The Torah calls this Yom Achat which means one day or unity of intelligence because it is both sides of the same thing. This is the secret of the Tzim Tzum. First, there was a restriction, then expansion, next striking resulting in sparks. Opposites must communicate to attain unity. This further explains why Creation is about twinning; there are always 2 sides to every single thing in Existence. Eve coming from Adam is the metaphorical story of 2 sides of the same thing. Saying that she came from his rib is a mistranslation. The correct translation is a part or section. Eve coming from Adam simply means that physical reality came out of the nonphysical.

Zohar explains that something must first exist in a potential state before expanding. This means that everything in Creation was present from the beginning as a potential. Intervention is required to activate potential. This further explains why Rosh Hashanah is considered the Head of the Year, or the New Year, even though it is the 7th Hebrew month. The 1st Hebrew month was the potential of all that would come after. But it was the 7th month, the month of completion, that the intervention happened to create Existence from the potential.

The story of God creating Heaven and Earth is an analogy of the separation of the upper and lower waters which in turn symbolizes the separation of the left and right columns of the Sephirot. That separation began with the Sephirah of Chesed which means Love and Kindness. Love and Kindness are the internal energy of Chesed. Chesed is symbolized by water which is why all life comes from water. You're born in amniotic fluid; your body is mostly water; the Earth is mostly water. All of this is from Chesed. Water has the power of unity and this is why it is 80% of the body and 70% of the Earth. Water is the root of all healing, so this is why when you drink an infusion tea it is mixed with water. Steam-distilled water is water in its most pure form. The left side, or physical aspect of Creation, came from the split in Chesed. Females make things flourish and are equal to the Sephira of Malchut. Malchut is the totality, or culmination, of all the energies of Creation. This is the level where humanity exists.

The Sephria of Chesed always manifests as water. This means that the problem is the solution. For example, wherever you find poison ivy the antidote of the jewel plant is always close by. In the same way, the water could be a flood or it can make things grow. The Hebrew word Kad means water jug or picture and appears 9 times in the Bible. Kad has a Gematria of 24. 24 x9 = 219 which is the Gematria as the *72 Names of God* which is 72 x3 letters each = 216.

The Heart Chakra area of Tiferet was created for balance and peace between the left and right sides of the Sephirot. On the *Tree of Life*, Tiferet is the 1st middle Sephira of Physical Creation. Keter was the 1st Sephira of Nonphysical Creation.

The Hebrew word Nachem is spelled Khaf, Chet, Mem Sofit right to left and means to comfort. This has the same Gematria as Tzach spelled Tazddi, Chet right to left and means to cleanse. This means that Light can clean your space or cleanse your energy which goes back to the Sephira of Chesed and water. Further, this is related to the Mikvah, the ritual bath which contains 40 units of se'ah, which is a measurement of water from ancient times. The Torah says that 1 se'ah equals 144 average-sized eggs. 144 is 12x12 and is said to remove chaos and contamination from a person. 12 is also the number of months in a year, zodiac signs and tribes.

Mavdil means a separation that brings about a connection or joining of forces. This means that there must be a separation before there can be unity. The word for Heaven is Shamayim. Shamayim is the contraction of 2 words; eish means fire and mayim means water. When the 2 come together, they neutralize each other. Gehinnom, the Hebrew word for purgatory, was created because of anger and fire from the left side of the Sephirot. The Hebrew word for hell is Sheol. This is where Christianity got its idea of purgatory and hell. The Zohar says that you create your own hell.

Satan is an effect of human negativity and negative consciousness. That's why in the Torah in the Hebrew Bible it's not called Satan, instead, it is called The Satan. The Satan is not a Being, it is a position that is created with the compilation of negative thoughts of Humanity. The Satan did not and could not exist until the manifestation of negativity which created the need for choice to exist. Negativity/evil exists for contrast so that you can see both sides of the same coin/experience. You cannot learn from neutrality in the same way. The separation of opposing energies gives you a choice. This means that you are responsible for all your issues. Rosh Hashanah and Yom Kippur are opportunities for you to take responsibility for your sins and correct past errors.

The Zohar says that the end never justifies the means. In other words, even if your intention is good but your actions are manipulative to get what you think is a better outcome, you have acted incorrectly, in a sinful manner. If you seek revenge, this is the equivalent of blaming someone else who is not taking responsibility. You must even think very carefully before giving advice because this can interfere with their Tikkun. Accepting responsibility is the key to all success.

The Zohar says that humankind was created with total control of every situation in life. You can repeat Chazach, Chazach, Chazach 3 times in succession which means strength, strength, strength. This has the same Gematria as *Name Frequency #5 Healing* from the *72 Names of God*. Just saying Chazach one time is the Name of God for victory over addictions.

The Zohar also says that the ego is The Satan's mind-pattern which makes you think you are in control when you may not be or vice versa. Doubt and confusion come from The Satan who is called The Dark Lord. The Satan is given permission to give you problems so you can learn to strengthen your connections to the life force and remove all the negativity. Wherever there is confusion and mystery, there is also Light. You must strive to be righteous, remove envy and jealousy as well as treat your worst enemy with dignity. In the New Testament, Christ said that Satan is the prince of the world. Thousands of years before this, the Zohar said that The Satan rules the world. Christ was a Kabbalist and studied the Zohar. Christianity is Zohar.

When Moses led the Children of Israel out of Egypt and they arrived at the Red Sea with the army of the Pharaoh behind them, they cried out to God to help them. God replied that they had the ability to help themselves because they created the situation. God does not interfere so that you can learn to correct your thoughts and mind-patterns. God wants you to do the work. People always ask for Divine Intervention. The Israelites told Moses to pray to God for them. God said, *why are you asking me? You can do it, so do it*. The first person jumped in up to his nose in the water and then the sea parted. Remember that you, too are going to be pushed to your limit until you say, *okay, I can change this, I can do something*. What you are experiencing in the world right now is pushing you up to your nose. This is forcing you to say, *okay I'm changing and correcting this now.* God is showing you that you can do this. When you have a child who wants your help, you help him and then tell him to do it. Sometimes the child gets hurt, cries, and whines but eventually he learns to do it on his own.

The Zohar says you must be totally committed to anything to ensure success. Doubt creates blockages and destroys. Use *Name Frequency #46 Absolute Certainty* from the *72 Names of God* to help more through doubt and confusion.

Crucial Coded Words of Creation

There are 4 crucial coded words of Creation. Tohu is often translated as chaos, but the correct translation is restriction or cause and effect. Cause and effect is regarded as Mercy. Chaos is simply a lack of understanding of what is not yet known or understood. True Reality is an energy consciousness that the 5 senses cannot perceive. This means that True Reality is a mind-pattern. Vohu is often translated as a void, but the correct translation is curtain, time or compassion. This means that time is a Mercy that allows you to remove the curtains/coverings of your issues so that you can work them out with compassion before the results are finalized. Choshech means darkness because you cannot see the Light of Ain Sof when you are in the illusion of time and space. Ruach has been translated as wind or spirit which means a correction or making decisions. The expression *winds of change* are because change redirects just as wind redirects. A windy day means you need to start making changes. A tornado or hurricane means that you are not making necessary changes so it is being done for you.

4 Crucial Coded Words of Creation

Tohu = restriction (cause and effect) – mercy

Vohu = curtain (time) – compassion

Choshech = darkness (illusion of time/space)

Ruach = correction (wind) -making decisions

The Zohar says that positive energy always precedes the negative. Human negativity is what creates chaos. Circuitry needs, opposing poles, or opposing energies, which of course are male and female. The Bible says male and female created, He them, referring to share and receive in the metaphorical story of Adam and Eve. There are 2 stories of Creation in the Bible.

Genesis 1 refers to Nonphysical Potential and Creation

Genesis 1 talks about evening and morning. After God does this the first time, God said this was Yom Achad which means 1 Day, not Day 1. 1 Day means it was complete and a unified whole, a seed that contained All.

Thought energy or intelligence is a code for sharing. The Zohar calls this male energy Zakhar. Physically this represents sperm or transmission. The code for female receiving energy is Nukva. Physically this represents the ovum that receives the sperm. This is another layer of male/female sexual relationships. Humans, and even humanoids from other planets, have the greatest capacity to receive from Ain Sof than any other species.

Cain and Abel

In Hebrew, Cain is (Kayin) and Abel is (Havel). The Bible says that Cain bit Abel's neck causing him to bleed to death. This is why the story goes on to say that the blood of Abel was on the ground and in the soil. This was the first murder in Humanity. However, the Bible uses the word Neshika with a Khaf. Neshika means Kiss. Neshikha means bite. These are the same letters except there is a dot/dagesh in the letter Khaf. This dagesh changes the word from bite to kiss. The Bible says that Cain committed Neshikha. The dot in the Language of Hyperspace means intelligence or awareness.

The Zohar says: Cain/Kayin bit the neck of Abel/Hevel

This means that because Cain had no awareness of death or murder, a kiss and bite meant the same thing. Had Cain kissed Abel on the neck, death would have been unknown in Creation. Before Cain, there was no concept of death or murder. There was only Eternal Life. This shows what a difference one small dot/dagesh can make.

End of Days

Over 1000 years ago, the Zohar gave the color codes of Green, White, and Red to avert destruction and annihilation using the Sephirot. The Zohar did not distinguish the shades but you know from your Hyperspace/Oversoul work to use Medium Green, White and Pale Red. At your pineal gland visualize the left column of the Sephirot in Pale Red, the right column in White, and the central column in Medium Green. Use this visualization to avert the destruction and annihilation of your goals so that you successfully bring them to fruition.

The Zohar says that the colors of the rainbow as well as the rainbow are assembled to save the world. The White Light of Ain Sof passes through the prism of physical reality which breaks it up into the colors of the rainbow. These colors are represented in the Chakra Bands which help to save your energy and correctly create your reality. There is a reason why the controllers of the LGBTQ+ community have chosen the inverted rainbow as its symbol.

A healing technique came to me came one day while I was working with the Hebrew letter Hey in White. On the Oversoul level, I was given permission to do energetic healing work on Florida Governor Ron DeSantis's wife who has breast cancer. I was visualizing the White

Hey in that area of her body when suddenly I was sitting in front of her with Governor DeSantis to my right. I was shown to take my right hand and hold it in her right hand as I filled my Self with the Light of Ain Sof so that I became very strong, powerful White Light energy that I transmitted through my hand into her hand. Then I was told that she was healed of breast cancer. Shortly thereafter it was announced in the press that she is now cancer-free.

I have a young friend in Romania who recently had a kidney transplant. Unfortunately, he was told that his creatinine levels were very high, indicating his body was rejecting the kidney. So, I did this healing work with him. The next day he called me from the hospital to say that his creatinine levels dropped, his kidney is working and the hospital is sending him home. I had another older friend who was in the hospital as a result of a stroke, with feeding tubes and not doing well. After I did this healing work with him the hospital took out the feeding tube and sent him to a rehabilitation facility. Then, I was told that my almost 91-year-old father's pacemaker was falling apart so he would need immediate surgery or his heart would stop. I did this healing work with him, he survived the surgery and is now home, going strong.

Now I have changed the visualization by crossing my hands so that an Infinity Archetype is formed between me as I hold both of their hands, left hand to the left hand, right hand to right hand. Always fill your Self up first with the White Light energy of Ain Sof, then cross your hands to create the Infinity Archetype as you hold the hands of the person with whom you are working. Then allow that energy to flow through you into them. There is no need for filtering or protection because this is the White Light energy of Ain Sof/God and God doesn't need any filtering or protection. The Zohar says that even organs and limbs will be able to regenerate during the Messianic times.

Erev Rav

The Erev Rav are creating situations globally to destroy Humanity as you know it. In Hebrew, Erev means evening or the night before. Erev Shabbat means the night before Shabbat. Erev Rosh Hashanah means the night before Rosh Hashanah. In Hebrew, Rav means teacher. These Hebrew words together mean teachers of the night/darkness/dark energies According to the Zohar there can be no redemption of Humanity until the Erev Rav are completely destroyed because they are the evil ones who return every generation to create problems. The Zohar states that only one-fifth/20% of those that left Egypt were Israelites; the rest were Erev Rav who had converted to Judaism and came from other nations. God is now giving the Erev Rav the opportunity to convert to the Light before they are destroyed. This is part of the *End of Days*.

The Erev Rav/Deep State used Looking Glass technology to look at the future. Looking Glass technology requires human input but the output must be correctly interpreted. Various options were analyzed to determine the outcome but regardless of input the outcome was always the same. The Erev Rav/Deep State was not going to win. This is why they are throwing poison to create the most disruption possible before they ultimately lose. Of course, everyone creates his/her own enemies. The Erev Rav can only exist because of the mind-patterns of each person. Without the negative, hostile mind-patterns of the people, the Erev Rav could not exist as a reflection back.

The Zohar says that the Erev Rav are the incarnations of those who existed from the 7 Pre-Adamic Civilizations as well as descendants of Cain and they live within the Earth. The Zohar, thousands of years ago, specifically says that there were 5 species, not groups and that these were shapeshifters. Erev Rav has been mistranslated over the centuries. One definition of Erev Rav is mixed multitudes because when the Hebrews left Egypt the Erev Rav went with them. The Erev

Rav were Egyptians that converted to Judaism and included Sumerians and Ethiopians as well as people from other nations.

It was the people of these mixed multitudes who created the Golden Calf when Moses went up on Mount Sinai to receive the 10 Commandments. The Erev Rav told the Hebrews that this Golden Calf was their real God. The Zohar says that the Golden Calf spoke, sang, moved, and was actually a computer. Translated from Hebrew, the Zohar says this was an Android made by the Erev Rave to replace Moses and wanted the Golden Calf to be the only physical God in reality that the Hebrews worshiped. This is why when Moses came down from the mountain after 40 days that he threw and broke the Tablets and had the Golden Calf destroyed. The Zohar states that there's no such thing as an inanimate object. Everything has consciousness, even rock and every grain of sand. Nothing is inanimate.

Of course, the representation of the Golden Calf/Bull still exists in front of Wall Street in downtown Manhattan in New York City. This symbolizes that the US economic system is based on the Golden Calf of the Erev Rav. Until this economic system is destroyed, the Messiah cannot come. So now, the destruction of the economy instituted by the Erev Rav is being destroyed and will continue to fall. The issue is will its replacement be better, worse, or just different.

The Amalek is the very first species referred to by the Zohar and even in the Torah. When the Hebrews left Egypt, crossed the Red Sea, and arrived on the other side the first Beings to attack the Children of Israel was a civilization known as the Amalek. The Amalek was extremely evil. According to Hebrew tradition, you are to destroy the Amalek wherever they are found. The descendants of the Amalek are the leaders of the Deep State; the politicians, CEOs, and world leaders.

The Zohar calls the next species the Nephilim. In the Hebrew language, the Nephilim means those who have descended from above. The Book of Enoch refers to them as giants. The Nephilim and their descendants are sexual predators who create and promote pornography, pedophilia, and rape culture. The Zohar gives the impression that the Nephilim are not humans and are not from this planet; in other words, the Zohar implies that the Nephilim are aliens. Anyone who has a predilection for viewing pornography or participating in sexual aberrations is supporting the sexual slavery of both males and females. The actors in these videos have been victims of sexual slavery since childhood, often taken from their parents or even created elsewhere to fulfill the desires of the Nephilim.

The third species is called the Giborim by the Zohar. This species is referred to in the Bible as the Men of Renown. They rebel very strongly against God, projecting a false spirituality. They do not want you to believe in God in the correct way. Examples of the Giborim include religious leaders like the Pope, Islamic Imams, and fire-and-brimstone Christian preachers.

The Rafaim is the fourth species referred to in the Zohar. The Rafaim are evil spirits called by the Zohar traitors to Humanity and Nations. The Rafaim will report you to the authorities and go against you. The participants in Black Lives Matter and Antifa are examples of the Rafaim.

The fifth species in the Zohar is called the Anakim. In Hebrew, Anakim means giants, not necessarily physical giants, but giants in status. Examples of the Anakim include the extremely wealthy, sports figures, entertainers, and any charismatic figure that people will blindly follow. The Anakim mock religion and want you to be an atheist and their beliefs are related to communism. They claim to be something that they are not, so they are frauds. In Hebrew, another layer of meaning of the word Anakim is necklace. This is symbolic of the false information that they metaphorically wear around their necks. You cannot trust them.

Erev Zair

The Erev Zair are not part of the Erev Rav but are a group of Torah-observing Jews that distort the truth. These religious leaders embed themselves in the Chasidim, Satmar, and other Jewish groups that purport to be strict observants of the Torah. In the 15th and 16th centuries in Europe, there was a Jewish group called the Sabbatians who distorted the truth of the Zohar and Torah. The Sabbatians promoted such things as child pornography, spouse-swapping, murder, and creating Golems. The Zohar also speaks about the group called the Hamas. The Hamas is an Islamic fundamentalist political organization that controls Gaza and parts of the West Bank. In Hebrew, Hamas means thieves and robbers.

Tzaddikim

Thankfully, the Zohar States that in every generation there are 36 people called Tzaddikim who hold the Holiness of God together so that the world can continue. These 36 people exist at all times in every generation to keep the Earth from being destroyed. These are Souls from the previous worlds that are incarnating now. In Hebrew, 18 is the number of long life and derives from the Hebrew word Chai. Chai is spelled with the Hebrew letters Chet and Yud. Yud has the Gematria of 10; Chet has the Gematria of 8, so Chai has the Gematria of 18. 36 equals 2 times 18, meaning double long life plus another layer of meaning refers to twinning, which is very important in Creation.

Moshiach

The Moshiach/Messiah is coming. There will be 2 of them; the political one and the spiritual one. The political one will be killed and then the spiritual one will lead Humanity to the finality of the Great Challenge. Everything will happen very quickly. One day you will wake up and there will be a new government, new financial system, and new Internet which you will have to accept. The new system will be designed with more egalitarian circumstances for everyone. The process for everyone to settle in and harmonize may take 10 to 20 years or perhaps even longer. This is not a time of fear but a time of excitement for change. Working on your mind-pattern now gives you a head start because it is your mind-pattern that brings you exactly what you need when you need it. This does not mean that you will have what you want, but it does mean that your needs will be met. Hold in your mind-patterns that your family and loved ones are getting exactly what they need as well in the most correct and beneficial way. Everyone is his/her own Savior. Be a living example so others can mirror this back. Each person saves the world, one person at a time until this mind-pattern reaches a crescendo which in turn allows a physical Moshiach/Messiah to manifest. The Messiah will bring changes to all physical laws including government and science. Everything will change because the Messiah means that the entire energy of Existence will shift.

The Earth is changing and all of Humanity and civilization is coming to a major turning point. The life that you knew before 2020 and Covid is not ever coming back. What is coming could be beneficial if Humanity makes the correct choices. This information will prepare you to help your Self and help others who will listen. I was told by very high intelligence sources that there will be casualties as well as people who will refuse to adjust. There are alien civilizations who want to pass on knowledge to humans on Earth so humans can progress. News will be given to the public designed to scare them. For example, China launched a Hypersonic missile that can go around the world very quickly and then return to land. Next, China may launch another Hypersonic missile telling the world that onboard is nuclear weaponry. This missile will not come back to Earth but will remain perpetually in Earth's orbit. China will say it can activate its nuclear weapons anywhere, anytime, and cannot be stopped. China does not have this capacity but the news will scare people into thinking this may happen.

There will be difficulties but ultimately you will adapt. There will be an abrupt change into a different type of society and structure that will accommodate what Humanity needs for survival. This means that there will be the formation of Super States, a change in the global financial system and what people need, not necessarily what they like. Michigan's SECAM/ Space-Enabled Communications and Advanced Mobility Center will become the central headquarters of the global Space Program. Michigan's location provides the capability of a polar launch which is easier than an equatorial launch.

Be prepared for a complete crash of the economic system. Shortages and hyperinflation will continue because this is designed to destroy the current economy so a new economy can be implemented. Purchase now with longterm planning in mind. Travel within the next 2 years before the 2024 elections because there will be a time when you are not able to travel freely. Eventually, you will be able to travel more freely within your own super state but expect global borders similar to World War 2 or perhaps even stricter. Do not be afraid but be prepared so that you have what you need during this time of upheaval. Without these changes, the only other choice would be the complete destruction of the Earth and that is not going to happen. What you are learning now will help you better adjust to the forthcoming time period which will be known as the Great Challenge. You are here to be a participant because you were born knowing that this was all going to happen. You are an important player or you would not be here.

There is no more choice. This is the *End Times*. As difficult as the next few years may be, ultimately it will be better, or otherwise what would be the point? Life will get more challenging before it gets easier. Like cleaning your house is a lot of work but when you are done you are glad you did it. The forthcoming cleansing of the world won't be fun or easy but when it's done it will be wonderful. You have the tools to do this and when you use them you will be Soul-satisfied. You must keep your focus on where you are and where you are going/growing.

Remember that your Soul was born to experience this period in history. You can't put your head in the sand and wake up when it's over. You may worry about your family and friends but you can see that people are still being born because they want to come here during this time period. Even though it is going to be rough, this is what you signed up for and so did everyone else who is here. Know that everyone is safe and going through what each needs to go through, just like you. They chose to be here. When you feel fear for Self or loved ones, give it all up to your Oversoul and God-Mind knowing that they have chosen this opportunity to learn in their own way.

Thoughts Create Reality

The sin of Adam HaRishon in the Garden of Eden removed the power to which Humanity was originally entitled. The Zohar says that Abraham reestablished the majority of this power via the Bris/circumcision which in Hebrew is called Milah. Milah means covenant in Hebrew. The foreskin is called the Klipot, representing the covering of evil over good, the embodiment of The Satan, and the negative energy that surrounds the person. Circumcision removes evil. In the Bible, oxen is a code for circumcision because oxen remove burdens which in turn removes The Satan. The foreskin/Klipot is a covering that blocks creative abilities. When this covering is removed, the burden of Satan is removed. Circumcision is not a symbol of religion, rather it is a tool to remove evil. The Klipot is removed on the 8th day after the birth of the baby boy because 8 is 7 + 1. The 7 symbolizes the 7 lower Sephirot and 7 Days of Creation and the +1 symbolizes going beyond the physical. The surgery is done in the morning when the Sephira of Chesed is the strongest. Kabbalah says that females are born circumcised which is why only males are circumcised.

There is another Bris/circumcision ceremony called Pinyon Haben for the firstborn male of a first pregnancy where there were no previous pregnancy events like miscarriages and the baby was born vaginally, not by Cesarean. This is the redemption of the firstborn male that removes evil energy and death, alluding to the 10th plague of Egypt which was the slaying of the firstborn. This ceremony is symbolic of purifying the Sephirot by removing the Satanic seed. Anyone who attends this ceremony also benefits. However, because of the lifestyle of the way most people live, this ceremony is not common.

Kabbalah says that sperm equals the energy of intelligence that transmits to the Soul during sexual intercourse. This means that the sperm is a template of the mind-pattern of intelligence. Kabbalah says therefore a first born of a woman may not be the real first born if the man is thinking of another woman at the time she is impregnated. Kabbalah gives the example of Joseph and his son Reuben. The story is that when he was creating Reuben he was thinking of somebody else and so Reuben was not her first son. Remember, no time, no space. Even during intimate moments, if you're not focused properly, the energy can manifest in unexpected ways.

Kabbalah teaches us to access the potential of Adam by connecting to the actuality of no time/no space. If you go back to the moment of Adam Kadmon, that energy represents the potential of everything that exists. When you have a potential and then it's released, that energy creates the pathways and functions of Creation. In Ancient Hebrew times, a seed was considered more important than the tree it would become. The tree is final regardless if it is a big or little tree, or perhaps it may die or be killed. The seed is always the potential; it is up to you what happens to the seed. This is the same in all of Creation. Regardless of the potential, it is up to you what you do with any metaphorical seed.

The Zohar says that you must maintain positive thinking, even when it is challenging. Every word you speak, every action, and every thought projects out an energy that not only affects you but is projected into the Totality of Creation. When you feel depressed, negative, curse or do bad things, you bring down all of Humanity as well as all of Creation. You must constantly monitor Self in everything you think, say and do.

Everything in the Bible is symbolic. This is why you must look at the various layers of meaning, including the Gematria of words. Rabbis in Ancient times interpreted the Biblical too literally, perhaps based on their mind-pattern filters. If you have 5 Rabbis and ask them the same question, you may get 15 different answers. Kabbalah says that all answers are correct and it is up to you to determine which is most applicable. This implies that you, too, have valid interpretations of the information.

You use energies beyond the physical all of the time. The physical is simply the last stage of manifestation of thought. What you desire, is what you get. Be careful what you wish for because you just might get it. How many times have you wanted something and gotten it only to realize that what you got is not what you thought it would be. This could be something as simple as ordering a drink at a restaurant that does not meet your expectations or as complicated as a marriage that is not what you thought it was going to be. This is what it is like with all aspects of life. You don't always receive what you think you are going to get. When this happens then you need to look at why your mind-pattern created the result that you received. You cannot blame anyone or anything else. As with every part of your life, you must take responsibility.

The Zohar says that the highest state of consciousness is born from the most unholy unions. The Zohar uses as an example Lot's daughter who made her father drunk and then slept with him so she could have a child. who she named Moab, which means from my father. Moab became an Amorite. From Moab came his descendant King David and eventually from him, Christ. This sexual trickery happened after the destruction of the city of Sodom and Gomorrah.

God said that He would save the city if 100 righteous men could be found amongst its thousands of inhabitants. Then he requested that 50 righteous men be found. Finally, God destroyed the city when not even 10 righteous people could be found. Lot's wife was turned into a pillar of salt because she looked back at the destruction after being told to not do so. Of course, this was a result of radioactive bombardment that turned her to ash. Because Lot's daughter was not married and did not have children, she thought her only choice was to become pregnant by her father. So from this Unholy Union came the Christ. The Zohar says that this is an example of how the most painful negative energy can be transformed into the seed of the most wonderful energy. In the same way, all the unholiness in the world can eventually lead to something good. This is a time period of restriction which leads to the Light at the end of the restriction. Even the energy centers of the Earth allow you to access the Light force from the Ain Sof.

When Abraham received his nephew Lot from Sodom he only had 318 people in his entourage. In Hebrew, the phrase God is help has the Gematria of 318. Abraham had a servant named Eliezer. The Gematria for Eliezer is 318. One interpretation of the Zohar is that Abraham did not have 318 people but rather he had this 1 servant with this Gematria.

3 Column System

Kabbalah says that the first 3 Sefirot are joined as one. This forms a Triangle Archetype which is the first one you learn in Hyperspace/Oversoul work. The 3 sides of this Triangle Archetype are formed by Keter, Chokhmah and Binah. Technically, this is all that should have existed until God continued Creation with the lower 7 Sephirot which are arranged in a 3 column system. Everything in the universe is structured with this 3 column system of the Sephirot.

In the beginning, God created Existence from Keter/nonphysical all the way down to Malhut where the physical world exists. Malhut is the final stage of Creation. In the same way, you have a right, left and central column. This is the pattern of Creation. The 3 Holy Fathers in Judaism, Abraham, Isaac, and Jacob represent the Sephirot within Creation. Abraham represents the Sephira of Chesed/sharing. Isaac represents the Sephira of Gevurah/receiving. Jacob represents the Sephira of Tiferet/restriction and that restriction creates antimatter which is the Light of Mercy.

Kabbalah says that when the Bible mentions a half shekel that this is a code for sharing and receiving God in Its strongest form, which is antimatter. A shekel is a coin with a whole value but Creation is made of matter and antimatter. This indicates that antimatter is the other half of a whole coin. The Zohar says that Aaron, the brother of Moses, was a conduit for the Sephira of Chesed which represented antimatter. Chesed translates as mercy and sharing.

There are 3 stories that the Zohar says are all connected. First is the story of Abraham's circumcision which teaches that you can remove evil. The second is how Sarah became pregnant teaches that anyone can be rejuvenated. The third is the Binding of Isaac which teaches that when you let go of something you can get it back. All 3 stories teach that humans are created to control their environment.

The Bible says that Sarah lived to be 20 years and 7 years and 100 years. It does not say that she lived 127 years. Her age represents the 3 upper Sephirot of Keter = 100, Chokhmah + Binah = 20 plus 7 for the number of lower Sephirot. This also shows you that the secret of Chochmah and Binah is to never separate from each other. They're always together and between them is Da'at which is not a Sephira but is necessary to maintain the balance between Chokhmah and Binah. The 3 column system represents healing, rescue from catastrophes, and physical regeneration, which is what happened to Sarah.

Each Sephira contains another 10 Sephirot. 10 Sephirot x 10 within each means you have 100 Sephirot. These are related to the letters in the Torah which come in 3 sizes large, regular and small. The small letter Khaf controls nature, reverses the aging process, and makes physical reality smaller until it's reduced to nothing. Use the small letter Khaf to work on these issues. Reducing Khaf reduces illusion and emotion. If you have mental, emotional, or physical issues, visualize the small letter Khaf until it is reduced to nothing so that the same thing happens you're your issues.

= Small Khaf Controls Nature - Reduces Aging

The Gematria of Khaf is 20 which according to the Zohar means it has 10 Sefirot of Direct Light and 10 Sephirot of Reflected Light. This means energy is sent from 2 forces. For example, a flashlight directs light out and that light reflects back. Shining out is one force; reflecting back is the second force. When reflected light strikes the light shining forth there is friction causing Creation.

There are 3 important words beginning with Khaf. Kavod means your honor and standing in life. Kiseh is your position or title in life. Ke'as is your anger issues. You should not be connected to any of these. You must rise above all 3.

Some Hebrew words in the Torah have 3 dots over them. The Zohar says that these represent the 3 Angels that came to Abraham and Sarah while they were sitting in their tent in the heat of Summer as written about in the Book of Genesis. From the door of the tent, Abraham saw

3 figures approaching from the desert. He ran to welcome them and washed their feet with water. When the 3 Angels told Abraham and Sarah that she would get pregnant, Sarah laughed. Then she told them that she was 90-years-old. God asked her why she was laughing. Sarah replied that she was laughing, but God repeated that she was. This is why Sarah named her son Yitzhak/Isaac because his name means the one who laughs.

76 Energy Centers

The Zohar says that there are 76 energy centers on the Earth which are listed in ***Revelations of Time & Space, History and God***. The Zohar adds YHVH as an additional 4, with a total of 76. The Zohar does not list where these are, but I believe them to be in Mt. Sinai, Mt. Moria, Mt. Zion, Sea of Galilee 7 + 6 = 13, the number of Totality of Energies in Creation. This means that the *72 Names of God* + 4 (YHVH) = 76 = 7 + 6 = 13.

Kiriat Arba, City of 4

Those who are buried here correlate to YHVH. This is the Spiritual entrance to the Garden of Eden, the *Tree of Life*, and represents the twinning energies of God. Creation is always about the number 2: matter/antimatter; plus/minus; positive/negative; male/female.

Yud = Adam and Eve

Hey = Abraham and Sarah

Vav = Isaac and Rebekah

Hey = Jacob and Leah

Kiriat Arba is located in an area called The Plains of Mamre. In Hebrew, Mamre is spelled Mem, Mem, Resh, Aleph, right to left. Mamre has two Mems, another twinning. Mem represents a vortex. When Sarah died Abraham needed a place to bury her. He chose the Cave of Machpelah which was owned by a man named Efrom. Efron means afar or dust, so this is a reference to physical death that takes you afar. The double Mems reference a vortex through which you can travel elsewhere. The Planes of Mamre and the Cave of Machpelah represent the resurrection of the dead. Abraham bought the cave for 400 Shekels. 400 = 4x100. 100 = 10 x 10 Sephirot, or 10 Sephirot within each 10 Sephirot. 4 represents the 4 letters of YHVH. The Zohar says that there are 400 Gates of Impurity in the physical world, implying levels of understanding and layers of intensity.

You can visualize Mem moving into Mem Sofit, both in White, to create a vortex. Then, mentally go through the middle of them to see what comes up for you. The Zohar often says to use a black background but from a Hyperspace perspective, Royal Blue is best. Try it both ways to see how you feel about what you get. The Torah is written in Black on White. The Zohar says to also look at the space between the letters in the Torah which represents the nonphysical while the letters represent the physical. The Zohar says there are 600,000 letters in the Torah including the white space.

Protection

I recently spoke to my friend and colleague who is a NASA physicist with a Q-level security clearance and has an attorney in Spain who is part of the oldest law firm in Europe. This scientist has worked on projects for NASA for over 40 years and came to the United States from France under a special program, which may no longer exist, for extremely intelligent people or what is called an extraordinary person.

He told me that the Earth is moving into a very energetic area of space that only happens every 26 million years. He says that in this area there is an energy pulse that is moving toward the Earth at a rapid pace. When it hits the Earth it will cause much destruction. The energy comes from Eta Carinae, between the Orion and Sagittarius arms of the Milky Way 7,500 light-years from Earth. He says *I thoroughly investigated this theory, which appeared to be true after I visited with serious astrophysicists, particularly at the observatory in Hawaii, where I stayed for several days. Eta Carinae is the most energetic site that we are visiting every 26 million years. It is a long cycle. It could be very slowly harmful. And what we are seeing is just the beginning.*

He will be creating a huge complex in the Pyrenees, on the border of Spain and France close to the country of Andorra, on the Spanish side, which he says will be a safe place from geological upheavals. His goal is to create a Helium 3 project as an energy source to revitalize the Earth after this event happens. The energy is moving so quickly that computers on this planet are only able to determine the exact point of impact within 2 days before it hits. This is why they are not telling anyone because the number of people impacted will not be able to move out of the impact area within only 2 days. The physicist says that this will happen in 2023 while the space director says that it will happen in 2024. There will not be total destruction but there must be a plan on how to take care of the survivors of the impact area. The physicist wants to create a shield that will mitigate the impact on the Earth as well as deflect the energy back into space where it can be stored and then used for decades thereafter.

He says that he's been tracking this since 1994 when he first discovered it. He has observed that the storms on Earth have been getting more severe. For example, he mentioned that he measured a lightning bolt that was 40 miles long. He said that the energy coming in already from the edges is forcing the sun to a grand minimum so there is an ice age coming. The energy coming in is an incredible force of an electromagnetic nature that acts as a concussion force moving at a speed that is incomprehensible. Right now, they don't have the capability to figure out exactly where it's going to hit because the speed is faster than what the computers on Earth can calculate

Perhaps the controllers of the Earth know this and they are not the evil people that you envision. Perhaps they are doing what is necessary to protect the survivors of such catastrophic events. Perhaps evil is not what you think it is. Perhaps the beta tests they are conducting have much more far-reaching consequences than you can imagine and serve a benevolent purpose. Perhaps the controllers are working with alien forces to protect the people from what is coming from space. There are groups that already have the technology to mitigate the impact of this gravitational wave. Even if the controllers are only doing it for their own benefit, with the correct mind-pattern you will still draw the benevolence that you need. The controllers may not want to lose their assets, which include you or their territory. Those who are damaged by this event may ultimately benefit because they will be forced to work for the good of Humanity for survival purposes. In the short run, life may be extremely challenging but in the long run, Humanity may be better. This will be an opportunity for the best qualities of Humanity to come forward.

Remember the people of Joplin Missouri whose children were saved by Butterfly People during a horrendous tornado. So many children said that they had been picked up and carried to safety by Butterfly People or Angels that the town created a mural as a memorial to these testimonies. All kinds of things happen beyond what you are taught in linear thinking so having an Absolute Knowing that you are safe, protected, and have exactly what you need opens the pathway for this to happen in unexpected ways. Do your work know that all is in accordance with God's Plan. There is even a book written that says by 2050 Michigan will be the safest place on Earth to live:

> According to geopolitics and globalization expert Dr. Parag Khanna and his colleague Greg Lindsay, nowhere in the world looks more promising to be in 2050 than the state of Michigan. That's an academic assessment and not a personal one, Khanna stressed. He lives in Singapore and doesn't have any ties to Michigan. "I think I've been to the state twice," he said, "So I do this as a geographer and a political scientist."Khanna's new book, **Move: The Forces Uprooting Us**, sheds light on what it means for the Great Lakes region to become what he calls a "climate oasis," and about the complex forces shaping the future of global migration.
>
> https://www.michiganradio.org/show/stateside/2021-11-29/the-best-place-to-live-in-2050-michigan-says-globalization-expert

Now you know why I'm in Michigan, the space program will be located here, and why it is highly possible that eventually the capital of the new American Superstate will be located here. Of course, there will be other safe places such as where the NASA physicist is relocating in the Pyrenees in the North of Spain. He said when the energy wave impacts wherever there is a weak tectonic region or fault line the Earth will move significantly. If there's a volcano, that will also erupt. Right now scientists are working to mitigate geographical changes. They know where the tunnels and lava are as they do not want to lose their people/assets. Even if their benevolence is economically motivated you still have what you need. Perhaps growing meat in laboratories is a way to feed people when the Earth goes through its changes. You may be eating vegan meat and be happy about that. Perhaps the controllers are not evil; perhaps they are economically motivated which ultimately is to your benefit. Work on your mind-pattern so that whatever the situation you continue to pull to your Self and your loved ones all that is most correct and beneficial. Create a mind-pattern that says your loved ones thrive and move forward with you.

Think about what is going on in the world right now. Think of all the lazy people who won't work and contribute to society. Think of the bad, mean people who commit crimes every day and who allow themselves to be controlled and motivated by evil. The planet will survive. How it survives and what happens to its people is another thing. Stay focused on your inner level work that elevates and mitigates. As you know you are never given a problem without a solution. This means that the solution already exists and it just needs to be brought forward into the conscious minds. Hold the mind-pattern that the solution to this situation is already resolved in the way that is most correct and beneficial for everyone and everything.

Prayer of Protection

The Shema Israel Prayer is the most important Hebrew prayer to know and say. This prayer is said every single day in every Temple service. Even the first line of the prayer protects the person praying. You also are supposed to say this before you go to go to sleep at night and when you wake in the morning before even getting out of bed to create an energy field of protection around your Self. You can read the English version or Hebrew transliteration if you do not know Hebrew.

The Gematria of this prayer is equal to the totality of the structure of your body. As you say the prayer every part of your body is energized and protected. This prayer is about God being One with all of Creation. Even just saying the first line Shema Yisroel, Adonoi Eloheinu, Adonoi Echad means Listen Israel, God is our Lord and God is One. This prayer connects you to the highest level of your Self.

Transliteration of The Shema

Cover your eyes with your right hand and say:

Sh'ma *Yis-ra-eil, A-do-nai E-lo-hei-nu, A-do-nai E-chad.*

Whisper: *Ba-ruch sheim k'vod mal-chu-to l'o-lam va-ed.*
V'a-hav-ta *eit A-do-nai E-lo-he-cha,*
B'chawl l'va-v'cha,
u-v'chawl naf-sh'cha,
u-v'chawl m'o-de-cha.
V'ha-yu ha-d'va-rim ha-ei-leh,
A-sher a-no-chi m'tsa-v'cha ha-yom, al l'va-ve-cha.
V'shi-nan-tam l'-va-ne-cha, v'di-bar-ta bam
b'shiv-t'cha b'vei-te-cha,

uv-lech-t'cha va-de-rech,

u-v'shawch-b'cha uv-ku-me-cha.

Uk-shar-tam l'ot al ya-de-cha,

v'ha-yu l'to-ta-fot bein ei-ne-cha.

Uch-tav-tam, al m'zu-zot bei-te-cha, u-vish-a-re-cha.

V'ha-ya, im sha-mo-a tish-m'u el mits-vo-tai

a-sher a-no-chi m'tsa-veh et-chem ha-yom

l'a-ha-va et A-do-nai E-lo-hei-chem

ul-awv-do b'chawl l'vav-chem, u-v'chawl naf-sh'chem,

V'na-ta-ti m'tar ar-ts'chem b'i-to, yo-reh u-mal-kosh,

v'a-saf-ta d'ga-ne-cha,

v'ti-ro-sh'cha v'yits-ha-re-cha.

V'na-ta-ti ei-sev b'sa-d'cha liv-hem-te-cha,

v'a-chal-ta v'sa-va-'ta.

Hi-sha-m'ru la-chem pen yif-te l'vav-chem, v'sar-tem,

va-a-vad-tem E-lo-him a-chei-rim, v'hish-ta-cha-vi-tem la-hem.

V'cha-rah af A-do-nai ba-chem, v'a-tsar et ha-sha-ma-yim,

v'lo yi-h'yeh ma-tar, v'ha-a-da-ma lo ti-tein et y'vu-la,

va-a-vad-tem m'hei-ra mei-al ha-a-rets ha-to-va

a-sher A-do-nai no-tein la-chem.

V'sam-tem et d'varai ei-leh, al l'vav-chem v'al naf-sh'chem,

uk-shar-tem o-tam l'ot al yed-chem,

v'ha-yu l'to-ta-fot bein ei-nei-chem.

V'li-mad-tem o-tam et b'nei-chem, l'da-beir bam

b'shiv-t'cha b'vei-te-cha, uv-lech-t'cha va-de-rech

u-v'shawch-b'cha uv-ku-me-cha.

Uch-tav-tam, al m'zu-zot bei-te-cha, u-vish-a-re-cha.

L'ma-an yir-bu y'mei-chem, vi-mei v'nei-chem, al ha-a-da-ma

a-sher nish-ba A-do-nai la-a-vo-tei-chem, la-teit la-hem

ki-mei ha-sha-ma-yim al ha-a-rets.

Va-yo-meir *A-do-nai el Mo-she lei-mor:*

Da-beir el b'nei Yis-ra-eil, v'a-mar-ta a-lei-hem

v'a-su la-hem tsi-tsit, al kan-fei vig-dei-hem l'do-ro-tam,

v'na-t'nu al tsi-tsit ha-ka-naf p'til t'chei-let.

V'ha-ya la-chem l'tsi-tsit, ur-i-tem o-to

uz-char-tem et kawl mits-vot A-do-nai, va-a-si-tem o-tam,

v'lo ta-tu-ru a-cha-rei l'vav-chem,

v'a-cha-rei ei-nei-chem

a-sher a-tem zo-nim a-cha-rei-hem,

L'ma-an tiz-k'ru, va-a-si-tem et kawl mits-vo-tai

vi-h'yi-tem k'do-shim lei-lo-hei-chem.

A-ni A-do-nai E-lo-hei-chem,

a-sher ho-tsei-ti et-chem mei-e-rets Mits-ra-yim

li-h'yot la-chem lei-lo-him;

A-ni A-do-nai E-lo-hei-chem... Emet

https://www.chabad.org/library/article_cdo/aid/282822/jewish/Transliteration.htm

If you would like to learn how to read Hebrew, this book is a really great course that teaches you to do so in 6 weeks. **Learn to Read Hebrew in 6 Weeks** by Miiko Shaffier.

When Amen is said at the end of a prayer or even a positive statement, this word elevates and unifies everything in the world. Amen means it is so/so be it. Ya'minu, which is in the Bible, is a derivative of Amen and means they will believe.

Amen connects the nonphysical aspects of God with the physical level, thus unifying and elevating. You're bringing down the highest level of God to the physical level. The Gematria for Amen is 91. The Gematria for YHVH is 26. The Gematria of Adonai, which means God on Earth/God-Mind energy within physical reality, is 65. 26 + 65 = 91, the Gematria of Amen. The Hebrew letter Vav, which is in YHVH, brings the nonphysical into the physical. Putting the Vav down the central column of the Sephirot connects Ketter to Malchut. Simultaneously saying Amen helps to manifest the nonphysical into physical reality. More proof that the Torah came from beyond this world.

Increasing Power

Kabbalah says that spelling out a Hebrew letter materializes and expands its power. For example, Yud is spelled Yud, Vav, Dalet right to left. This is how Existence was created. Yud represents the Sephria of Chokhmah in the Tetragrammaton.

Kabbalah uses Gematria and permutation/rearrangement of the letters to formulate different energies and find layers of meanings. There are 6 possible permutations of Yud. On the chart above, you see the spelling of Yud as Yud, Vav, Dalet. Yud has the Gematria of 10, Vav has the Gematria of 6 and Dalet has a Gematria of 4 so the

Gematria of Yud when spelled out is 10 + 6 + 4 = 20. There are 6 permutations with the Gematria of 20 so this part of the formula is 6 x 20 = 120. There are also 6 lines of 3 letters each so 6 x 3 = 18. There are 6 permutations in total adding 120 + 18 + 6 = 144, a number that is Biblically significant.

Yud has 6 possible combinations when spelled out:

Yud, Vav, Dalet
Yud, Dalet, Vav
Vav, Dalet, Yud
Vav, Yud, Dalet
Dalet, Yud, Vav
Dalet, Vav, Yud

6 combinations x Gematria of	20 =	120
18 letters	3 x 6 =	18
6 combinations		6
Total		144

There are 10 Sephirot within each of the 10 Sephirot.
10 x 10 = 100 Levels Sephirot.
There are 10 Levels of Creation x 100 Levels of Sephirot = 1000.
The symbol of the Messiah is 1000 because it takes 1000 Levels of Experience to get to the Messianic Level.
The 144 from the preceding chart x the symbol of the Messiah 1000 = 144,000 which according to the Bible is the number saved.

10 Sephirot x 10 Sefirot = 100 Levels
100 Levels x 10 Levels of Creation = 1000
1000 = Symbol of the Messiah
1000 x 144 = 144,000 Saved

If out of the 8 billion people on Earth, there are going to be a lot more than 144,000 saved. This number refers to 144,000 Oversouls or genetic lineages. The Zohar says that there are not only 10 levels of the Light force but also 10 levels of the Dark Lord/Dark Force and that there are contaminations from 400 Levels of the Dark Lord/The Satan on the Earth. These 400 Levels = 10 Sephirot x 40. The number 40 is mentioned almost 150 times in the *5 Books of Moses*. The Zohar says that evil allows you to have choices. Without the existence of evil, you would only do one thing. The definition of sin is the severance of the relationship between human and Light Force of the Creator. This means that cutting off your relationship with the Light Force leads you into sin and doing evil things.

Zohar says to not follow evil influences but if someone comes to kill you, you have an obligation to kill him/her first. It says, do not follow evil influences. However, if someone comes to kill you rise up, early to kill him first. The Zohar goes on to say that The Satan has an open field with males until 13 years old and females until 12 years old. In Judaism, 13 is the age a male is Bar Mitzvahed and 12 is the age that females are Bat Mitzvahed. According to the Bible, they become adults at these ages and were allowed to marry in Ancient times. In other words, The Satan can attach to a child who is not fully physically mature so that it can mold and influence him/her.

Kabbalah calls repentance a teshuva technology. Remember that the root of teshuva is teshuv which means to return. Teshuva corrects the root of your issue returning you to your positive side so that you can consciously return to God.

Teshuva existed before Creation and is a time travel technology that allows you to go back in time and become the person you were before the sin. To do this you can use *Frequency #1 Time Travel* of the *72 Names of God*. You can also go up into Keter which is outside of time and space. Kabbalah says that by going back in time and becoming the other person you create another timeline and a parallel universe. It says that every situation is an illusion and you cannot blame anyone for anything.

The Zohar says to reach a goal requires difficulties and that all sin can be repented and forgiven. Repentance and forgiveness are the same as a correction of mind-pattern. The Zohar states that you must deal with the Bible, not just study it. When it says deal with the Bible it means you have to apply what you know. Many people only study but they do not apply what they learn. Religious people from all walks of life often study from morning through night but they do not apply what they learn. You must apply as much as you can to mitigate negativity. However, thought is still more important than action. God is always with you. The Hebrew word Emanuel means that God is with you.

Blueprint of Creation

The Zohar also says that the Soul is part of Creation and that the Torah is the Blueprint of Creation. The Bible was never meant for religious services; it was meant to be studied to learn the layers of the Blueprint of Creation so that you could learn about your Self. Kabbalah says that atoms are indestructible thought energy and intelligence that can be directed with your mind. Humankind is necessary because there is no other way that the Creator can express Itself. The Hebrew letters control the movement of the atoms. In the Sephriot, Chessed represents Protons; Gevurah represents Electrons and Tiferet represents Neutrons. Combining these create the Chariots or Merkavah.

According to the Zohar, 4 sides of the world gathered together to create the body. I interpret this to mean the 4 protein bases of your DNA. The Blueprint of your Body is your DNA which of course is comprised of 4 protein bases. Then it says that the 4 spirits of Chessed, Gevurah, Tiferet, and Malchut or the 4 spirits of Chokhmah, Binah, Tiferet, and Malchut unify to = YHVH = DNA/4 Protein Bases.

Physical pain cleanses and removes problems. When you have pain, focus on that area. Identify the mind-pattern that creates the pain to remove your mind-pattern of negativity.

In Hebrew, Toldot means generations. This means you, your children, grandchildren, great-grandchildren, and so forth. The Zohar says Toldot is about the resurrection of the dead to bring back those from exile. In other words, you resurrect the dead through your progeny; the same Souls come back from exile and are physically reborn/resurrected again.

Eliminating Chaos

This information that I am passing along to you from the NASA physicist is important because this helps you better understand this time period that we are in called the *End of Days*. He explains that there will not be a galactic explosion but rather there will be a huge emission of gamma rays part of which is coming from Zeta Orionis which is very active in the Orion Belt and adds intensity to the energy coming into this solar system. His laboratory which he needs to help create the shielding for the Earth will be built in the Pyrenees on the Eastern side between Andorra and Barcelona. Beneath this area is a huge block of granite that has been formed he says, as part of the Mycenaean plate and Empirical plate as a result of huge temperatures in the asthenosphere layer. The asthenosphere is a layer under the Earth's crust and upper mantle comprised of thick malleable rock that allows for the movement of tectonic plates. The granite that is in these locations will not break up and whatever is on top will remain intact. According to him, there will not be any movement of the tectonic plate in the Pyrenees or the Alps which is why he located his laboratory there. He says that most paleontologists and climatologists are unfamiliar with or refuse to put this information out.

He further explains that this is why the French built their ITERN Fusion Reactor in this particular part of the Alps. These 2 sites are unique in the world. He says that time is of the essence as radio communication will become difficult. The Space Director has confirmed the information of this physicist. A few days ago the Russians blew up what they said was an inoperable satellite in orbit around the Earth. A couple of weeks before this the Chinese sent a Hypersonic rocket around the Earth. The Space Director told me that this would happen and that what you are seeing now is just the beginning. He said that the satellite the Russians blew up in high orbit in a specific place was not inoperable but it had technology that they did not want the Chinese or the Americans to get. If the Russians had blown it up in low orbit the debris would have fallen through the atmosphere and burned up. But because they blew it up in high orbit the 1500 plus pieces of debris are strategically located about Cape Canaveral so launches from this place on the North American Continent are almost impossible. This shuts down the US space program.

The Space Director confirmed that they have a technology that creates an electromagnetic net that can be thrown over the debris and scoop it up, but first the satellites must get up there. He said that the American space demonstration will be coming soon and these types of demonstrations of power will increase in number and intensity. He said that space has become a region of technological warfare between the superpowers and is called the New Frontier. He says all future wars will be fought from space including geological and weather warfare some of which have already been seen. He does not deny the existence of alien technology but does believe that the revelation of the alien presence on Earth will take place in 10 years or less. I was told that all the wars and events that are happening now are being controlled from behind the desk of the 4th Reich people who control the US and most of the world. This explains why China and Russia are doing things against the Nazi US.

Codes

The phrase *coming out of Egypt* is found 50 times in the Bible. Number 5 represents healing energy and 10 represents the Sephirot and the Levels of Creation. 5 x 10 = 50 which gives the phrase *coming out of Egypt* the significance of healing Creation. This means that there is an opportunity to eliminate chaos which is simply a pattern not yet recognized or understood.

Kabbalah says that the elimination of chaos is the reason a man leaves his parents to be with his wife. This is because there must be balanced male and female energies. The Zohar says that one reason for the existence of females is to help males with their Tikku and that the male consciousness is not raised until marriage. This is one of the reasons that the Kabbalah says males cannot study it until they are married and at least 40 years old. This is interesting because one of the most famous kabbalists known as the Arizal died at the age of 38 and was never married. The first 6 months of the Hebrew year are male energy and the last 6 months are female energies. Meditating on the 2 Hebrew letters that represent each month gives you the ability to control The Satan.

In Hebrew the word for I AM or I, is Ani. Anochi is a similar word in the Torah with quite a different meaning. Anochi also means I AM but this is what God says about Himself and His high spiritual level that is connected to the lower level of Himself. In other words, Anochi is the male and female presence connected together of the I AM. Anochi is the Name of God before He connected with the Shekhinah, the female energy of God. The Zohar says that the true meaning of Jacob's Ladder Dream on Mt. Moriah is symbolic of ascending up the gates from Sheckhinah to Yesod and so on. Remember that Jacob dreamed of Angels going up and down a ladder and then started wrestling with one all through the night. Finally, the Angel stopped, telling him that he was no longer Jacob but was to be called Israel. Of course, Yesod and Malchut are gates or levels of understanding through which you are to ascend to elevate your level of consciousness. Elohim is the word used to represent God in the lower levels of the Sephirot connecting to the level of Malchut. The Zohar refers to dreams as Nevuah which means prophecy. All your dreams are connected to prophecy and a powerful system of information that represents a status report of your mind pattern. This means that what you do with the information you receive in your dreams determines the outcome. The status report gives you the opportunity to correct your mind-pattern if necessary or tells you to keep doing what you are already doing.

Jacob had four wives and 12 male children, each one eventually becoming head of one of the 12 Tribes of Israel and 1 female child. Jacob met one of his wives at a well who was drawing up water. This is symbolic of pulling up the power of Malchut, which is represented by water. Water represents life and the well represents the Source of life. Together, this represents drawing life from the Source. The Zohar says you can change the sex of a fetus in utero and gives the example of Leah, Jacob's first wife. Leah changed the fetus growing inside of her from a male to a female, calling her Dina. A female is always XX chromosomes and a male is always XY. As the fetus is developing, the mother can change the Y to an X to create a female child or an X to a Y to create a male child.

Jacob's Uncle Laban tricked him into marrying his youngest daughter Rachel, even though Jacob had wanted to marry Leah. Then, he had to work as a sheep herder for another 7 years to earn his marriage to Leah. In Hebrew, Laban means White. The colors of Laban's flock of sheep were described as Akudim/streaked, Nekudim/speckled and Uvradim/spotted which the Zohar says are Codes of Creation. The Zohar says these codes describe the first moment of Creation, contain all the secrets of the universe and can manipulate the universe for benefit as well as organizes chaos. Streaks represent energy streams from Ain Sof. As they coalesce they start to look like speckles. Finally, the speckles concentrate into spots. When you want to create something, you send out energy streams from your mind which coalesce and form whatever it is you want. You can use this as a visualization.

All Bible stories are symbolic. If you do not look beneath the surface you will be stuck with surface conditions. Too many people on Earth never look beyond the surface level in their lives which is why they cannot correct their issues. Your inner level work allows you to understand these secrets. The language of Kabbalah is mathematics which provides Gematria and a formula for understanding the layers of underlying meanings.

The Zohar says that the Angel Sandalfon receives all the prayers of Israel and brings them to God. Sandalfon contains the word sandal/shoe. Sandalfon is the Angel that controls or monitors the physical reality of the Earth and then takes the energy of your prayers, hopes, and visualization up to the nonphysical. You are supposed to accept all that God has created for you and complete this energy circuit by sharing it. Prayers increase this energy that you are given. According to Judaism, you cannot pray in a Temple unless you have 10 men present to create a Minyon. The reason male energy is needed is that males project while female energy receives it. A Minyon creates an energetic vessel that propels the prayer into the nonphysical. This does not mean that you can't pray on your own, but 10 is the most supreme energy. The New Testament says that when 2 or more gather to pray the prayer has more power.

There are 3 important names of God:

Yehowahe = Always will be. Yud in front of a verb means the verb is to be constant.

Ehyeh = Is now. Aleph in front means it is now and that Name is connected to the Sephira of Keter.

Adonai = My Lord and has to do with the physical reality Name of God.

When the Hebrew words Adonai and Yehowahe are written next to each other, the end of Adonai is the beginning of Yehowahe as you can see in the preceding chart. On the last line of this chart are Yud, Yud with 2 dots under each one. Whenever you see this in a prayer Adonai is said but the next word is not. The top dot means God; the bottom dot means Creation/Humankind. The God dot is always above the Humanity dot. This brings the nonphysical into the physical. The nonphysical cannot be pronounced so this is why you only say Adonai. A dot called a dagesh that appears on Hebrew letters represents the Light of God.

These Names together have the Gematria of 112. This equals the word Ybok which means wrestle. The root of Yabok is Avak which means dust or ashes. This refers to the words of the Torah that says you were created from dust and to dust you will return. Judaism does not allow cremation because ashes cannot be resurrected nor can bodies be embalmed. The only time embalming is ever allowed is if someone passes away in a faraway place and the body must make a long journey back for burial. However, when a body is left in the ground it eventually returns to dust and ashes.

The central column of the Sefirot is symbolic of the restriction of the Tzim Tzum. The 6 Sephirot between the head and legs represent the

Star of David. When connected this is called the Magen David. The Sephira of Tiferet is in the Heart Chakra Band. Bread is the symbol for faith and the heart. The City of Šchem, which is now called Nablus, is a Palestinian City on the West Bank. The Zohar says this city is a symbol of the Sephira of Yesod.

Ana B'koach Prayer

Ana B'koach represents all of Creation coded into the prayer. There are 6 words and 7 lines so 42 words, 6 x 7. When you take the first letter of each word on each line, they create another code. The first letters of each word in the first line are Aleph, Bet, Gimmel, Yud, Tav and Tzadik. This code removes all blockages and negativity from the physical world as well as the *Tree of Knowledge*. The first letter of each word in the second line spells the Hebrew words of Kra Satan which means to tear away Satan, or literally to remove evil from your life. The first line is a time travel line that takes you back to the very beginning of creation before all the corruption began. Then the second line removes evil. So this prayer is a gigantic formula to create perfection, peace, and harmony in your life and the world. You can apply this to the word Democrat. In Hebrew, Demo means his blood and crat means cutting away or tearing away his blood. When you apply this to what it represents in the United States, you could say that it represents tearing you away from the blood of the Messiah. The third line has the letters Yud, Khaf, Shin which allows you to go back to the embryonic state before the issues in your life began. Khaf in Hebrew means monkey and supplies the corrupt sequences in human bodies. This stands for the word Ketz which means end or finite and removes The Satan. These are more reasons why you should say this prayer at least twice per day.

There is also a Rejuvenation Code embedded in this prayer of Yud, Khaf, Shin. Visualize these letters in White anywhere in your body or even through your entire body to rejuvenate.

 - Yud, Khaf, Shin

Secret Names of God are embedded in the Ana B'Koach that invoke supernatural powers. In the following chart, the second column from the left has six Hebrew letters which are the first letters of each of the words in the sentence before it. A combination of these is what Moses used to part the Red Sea and to kill an Egyptian soldier. It is said that using various combinations can render you invisible or allow you to fly through the air. Just looking at these combinations or meditating upon them can have powerful effects on you. Kabbalah says they should only be verbalized by someone who knows what he/she is doing or there can be dire consequences.

Purpose	Letters							#
Removal of time, space and motion. Removing the negative influence of physical matter from our lives. Unconditional Love	אבג יתץ	צְרוּרָה tzerurah	תַּתִּיר tatir	יְמִינְךָ yeminecha	גְּדֻלַּת g'dulat	בְּכֹחַ b'koach	אָנָּא ana	חסד Chesed	1
Restricting the reactive system. Closing the gates from Satan. Forgetting all limited thoughts	קרע שטן	נוֹרָא nora	טַהֲרֵנוּ taharenu	שַׂגְּבֵנוּ sagvenu	עַמְּךָ amecha	רִנַּת rinat	קַבֵּל kabel	גבורה Gevurah	2
Opening the channel of sustenance. Retrieving the Light from the Klipot. Removing hatred for no reason	נגד - יכש	שָׁמְרֵם shamrem	כְּבָבַת k'vavat	יִחוּדְךָ yichudecha	דּוֹרְשֵׁי dorshei	גִּבּוֹר gibor	נָא na	תפארת Tiferet	3
The power to persevere	בטר צתג	גָּמְלֵם gamlem	תָּמִיד tamid	צִדְקָתְךָ tzidkatecha	רַחֲמֵי rachamei	טַהֲרֵם taharem	בָּרְכֵם berchem	נצח Netzach	4
Clairvoyance – to be able to see the connection between cause and effect. To see the Big Picture	חקב טנע	עֲדָתְךָ adatecha	נַהֲלֵל nahel	גְּמוּל tuvche	בְּרֹב b'rov	קָדוֹשׁ kadosh	חָסִין chasin	הוד Hod	5
Spreading spirituality throughout the world, enlightening others particularly through Kabbalah	יגל פזק	קְדֻשָּׁתְךָ kdushatecha	זוֹכְרֵי zochrei	פְּנֵה p'neh	לְעַמְּךָ l'am'ach	גֵּאֶה ge'eh	יָחִיד yachid	יסוד Yesod	6
The power to manifest things in the right way. Renewal and restoration	שקו צית	תַּעֲלוּמוֹת ta'alumot	יוֹדֵעַ yodeh	צַעֲקָתֵנוּ tza'akatenu	קַבֵּל kabel	וּשְׁמַע ush'ma	שַׁוְעָתֵנוּ sha'vatenu	מלכות Malchut	7
		יָעַד ya'ad	לְעוֹלָם le'olam	מַלְכוּתוֹ malchuto	כְּבוֹד kevod	שֵׁם shem	בָּרוּךְ baruch	(silently)	

The second column from the left has Hebrew letters transliterated into the Western Alphabet in the next chart with the purpose of each line.

1. ABGYTTz   Interdimensional condition
2. KRA STN   Tear away Satan
3. NGD YKSh   Against Yachsh/Demons

4.	BTR TsTG	Better a poor horse than no horse at all
5.	KhKB TNA	Timelessness
6.	YGL PZK	Equalizing spiritual energy
7.	ShKV TxYT	Shake a lighter/Reset

You can see how many codes are hidden within codes. When the time is correct and you are ready, the code reveals itself to you. The Zohar reminds you that the process is the goal. For example, if you are baking a cake, the cake is not really the goal. The goal is the process of gathering the correct ingredients, mixing them correctly, baking them correctly, and ultimately what you learn during the process. Once you obtain the result of the cake, your learning stops. When the Bible talks about destiny, it means playing out your role in Creation. In every incarnation, you have a name because your name is a statement of your purpose in life. Your name is not an accident; you chose it for a specific reason. This is why you should never change your birth name. Changing your birth name means removing your ability to complete your purpose for existing in this incarnation.

Jewish Humor

A religious Jewish man got married and said to his wife, *remember, I'm the head of this household.* His new wife replies, *okay, you can be the head but remember that I am the neck; whichever way the neck goes is where the head goes.*

Choose Elevation

One of the reasons that destruction is coming to the Earth is because of the mind-pattern of Humanity that unfortunately is choosing degradation over elevation. People are choosing to debase subhuman demonic activities which are becoming accepted as normal by too many people just like in the times of Sodom and Gemorrah. The Space Director says that the White House is actually in the control of the Pentagon, but there are older people who don't agree with the new agenda who will be purged. This means that those who do not agree are out. He says that the older military people still believe in war on the ground but new technology means that war will come from space. Any war that comes will be shortlived because of new technology.

He says that China will extend its territory to include the Philippines and Vietnam and most likely will include Malaysia. There will be aluminum shortages and China does not have its own source of aluminum so there will be shortages of anything that requires aluminum parts including automobiles, airplanes, and home appliances. Prices for these items will continue to increase so anything you intend to buy you should do it as soon as possible. Even if China lost half its population it would still have a huge population base. Afghanistan was given to China which now occupies the eastern part of Central Asia. The United States relied on Afghanistan for their lithium and batteries needed for the space program. However, according to the Space Director, the Congo is an additional source of lithium and he has a negotiation team in the Congo working on this.

The Internet will eventually go down for approximately 3 days and when it comes up it will be completely different. However, the entire changeover of the Internet may take 3 years, approximately 2024 to 2027. There will not be diversity of opinions or freedom of discussion. Whatever you have on the Internet that you want to save, you need to print it out and put it away. You may not be able to get books so build your library now. There will be virtually no trade between the Superstates so especially if you want something from another continent you need to acquire it now. There was talk of putting a former Soviet woman in charge of the Federal Reserve who wanted to remove all private bank accounts, making them a part of the Federal Reserve. This means that you would have less control over your money than you do now, but he said that this person would go away, which she did.

He told me that the 4th Reich is in control of the United States even though they hate Communists and are being controlled by China. He said the solution is a little more complicated saying that there is a hybrid political issue. This means that Fascism will be combined with both Communism and Capitalism. He said the elite of China is the most successful capitalists in the world but they label themselves as Communists to distract people from the truth. China's middle class is the largest in the world, including the entire population of the United States and Europe put together.

The US will become a dictatorship but of course, it already is. The US was fake and all of the freedoms, benefits, and dreams were fake. Now, people are experiencing the reality of what it always was. The Space Director says that he is very positive and welcomes the changes, believing that eventually, people will accept the changes and all will be successful. He says this time period will be known as the Great Challenge. People will be more concerned about their survival than anything else. The situation will be dire for most people, but this is the reason why you are working on your mind-pattern. Your mind-pattern that you create helps to mitigate all these outer effects. In this way, you will have what you need, how you need it when you need and you cannot dictate how this comes to you. These times are big tests for everyone, so prepare as best you can and know that you will be tested.

You may wonder how God can allow this to happen but even the Space Director says that this is what people have created with the collective mind-pattern of Humanity. While most people think of themselves as good people, there is still Darkness lurking within. Each person must eliminate evil within Self. Evil is such things as saying, *I'm ugly, I'm fat, I'm not good enough*. This is the periphery of evil. You need to know these things so you can change your mind-pattern and become a positive virus within the system to help uplift and elevate Humanity. Your positive attitude and mindset will be needed when the time comes, wherever you are in the world. You were born onto this planet in this time period knowing what was coming. This is not a surprise because somewhere inside you knew this was going to happen and you're still here. People of all ages are passing away now because they know what is coming and they do not want to experience it. There is more Soul growth when you're under stress than when you are not pushed.

Whether you like the plan or not, everything that happens is ultimately God's choice. You will always be in communication with each other via the Oversoul level because once the Superstates come into place you most likely will not be able to communicate or do business across Superstate borders. You may want to stop these experiences but remember that everyone is here for a reason. You may be able to mitigate some of it but you cannot take away the lessons of others or the lessons for which you came. Otherwise, everyone will have to do it again and it can always be worse. You have to tools to deal with all of the forthcoming world changes. For example, you can use the *72 Names of God* to release fear and depression as well as for protection and security amongst other things. You can use all these experiences to accelerate your Spiritual work and Soul growth. We are working on a collective level already, helping each other and connecting like a big energetic net around the globe. As a team of Light Force, we are unstoppable.

These changes have always been on the schedule. This is not a punishment or a surprise. This has been known for many, many years but it is still your mind-pattern that creates these experiences. Yes, you can be taken to another universe or reality. Everything can happen. Remember the Butterfly People of Joplin who took those children up out of the tornado and held them. But know that running away and escaping doesn't solve anything, because you're going to bring your mind pattern with you, wherever you go. So, you might as well stay here and do what you came here to do. God is not seeking the destruction of Humanity, rather people are being given a big choice. People need to make the decisions to do the correct thing and stop allowing evil to bend and twist their minds. Anchor into your Oversoul and God-Mind so that you are not affected by all the nonsense that is out there. No matter what comes at you, connect to Source so that you know the truth.

Here is a visualization to help protect the Earth and mitigate the effects of the gamma ray that is heading in this direction:

Create the image of Adam Kadmon in White, the primordial human, in front of the Earth. The Torah says Adam Kadmon stretched from Earth to Heaven, meaning that his energy connected from physical reality to nonphysical reality. Visualize Adam Kadmon holding open a White Torah Scroll facing the incoming gamma rays to deflect them and protect the Earth. Or, you could even just visualize the 10 Sephirot because Adam Kadmon represents these, and Adam Kadmon was the first Son of God, the Christ. You have to remember that the outcome always must be what's most correct and beneficial. If you change things without permission you can make the outcome worse for everyone.

Trust God

The Zohar says do not place your trust in humans, but only God. The left side of the Sephirot is considered female/negative. One layer of meaning is Miketz which means no memory. Shichecha means forgetfulness. Cosheh means darkness

Ketz means end. These are all illusions. In other words, no memory is only an illusion in physical reality.

The right column of the Sephirot is considered male/positive. One layer of meaning is Zachartani which means to remember me. The root of Zachartani is Zachar which means to remember. Zachiya means remembering the Light Force/Remembering God.

The central column connects memory. Focusing on the central column of your Sephirot balances and enhances memory. When the central column is injected into any idea, there is never failure according to the Zohar. For example, if you want a new job, visualize this at Keter and then pull it all the way down the central column through Tiferet and Yesod until it lands in Malchut. Of course, it is your intensity that determines when it will happen. Yesod represents the Hebrew letter Vav, which connects the nonphysical to the physical which explains why it is in the YHVH. When you put an image of what you want to create put the Vav right through the middle of your Sephirot. Then bring the image down from the Vav from Keter into Malchut to densify and energize the mind-pattern. Yesod also represents the male sex organ.

Conversely, Malchut must become one with Yesod to raise physical reality to the nonphysical and remove chaos. Physical reality only exists because of the failure of each piece of Adam Kadmon. Physical reality was created to administer the lessons and Tikkun to correct negative mind- patterns. This forces you to raise up the physical into the nonphysical. You can also use the *72 Names of God* to help make this happen.

Bringing up the central column and balancing each side of the Sephirot also helps eliminate depression called Atzvut. The root of Atzvut is Etzev which means nerve. According to the Zohar this means that there is an imbalance in your nervous system when you press down the Light Force within. Also, balance your T-Bar archetype to help balance your brain.

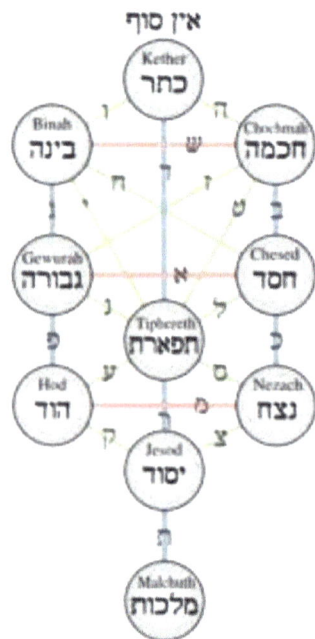

When visualizing the Shield of David, the upper triangle represents potential Creation. The lower triangle represents actual manifestation. Together, they mean As Above, So Below. This is why you must be extremely cautious of what you think, even in a fantasy, because this embeds in the energy of the nonphysical and somewhere it is going to manifest. This is why you must pass all your feelings up to your Oversoul so that it stays in the nonphysical and does not manifest in some physical reality.

Egypt

The Hebrew word for Egypt is Mitzrayim which means chaos, the place of Satan, and a place for Tikkun. This is why the Hebrews had to spend so many centuries in Egypt. The time spent in Egypt was their Tikkun. Remember the story of Joseph being sold into slavery in Egypt? There he was placed in the adviser's house of the Pharaoh where the adviser's wife falsely accused him of raping her. He was then thrown in prison until the Pharaoh had a dream of 7 fat cows and 7 thin cows. One of the prison guards told the Pharoah that Joseph could interpret dreams, so Joseph was brought before the Pharoah. Joseph said the dream meant that Egypt would have 7 fat years and then 7 lean years. The Egyptian people needed to prepare by saving food from the fat years so they could survive the lean years. This elevated Joseph's status in the eyes of the Pharoah who then placed Joseph as second-in-command of all of Egypt. While in this position, Joseph commanded that all Egyptian males be circumcised and follow the Hebrew religion. This is another reason why when the Jews left Egypt the Erev Rav went with them. The Erev Rav were the Hebrew converts as well as people from other nations who believed in the magical things the Hebrews could do. The Sages say that Joseph was premature in giving these commands to the Egyptians because they were not spiritually elevated enough to follow them. Therefore, all the Jews were punished for this. In addition, the striped coat of Joseph known as the Coat of Many Colors is Kol in Hebrew. Kol is spelled Khaf, Vav, Lamed, right to left which means voice.

The word Egypt in the Bible is a code that means the totality of negativity and chaos. The Sages say that Egypt is a place of high-level consciousness that became corrupt. Now, history is repeating uncompleted Tikkun from that time period in the *End of Days*. Another layer of meaning for Mitzrayim is constraint or limitation. The current world situation is similar to the constraint and limitations of the Hebrews in Egypt. These constraints and limitations are in place to give people the opportunity to be purged of the evil inclination. Kabbalah says that the labor of the children of Israel and Egypt is hard work. You must learn to not over intellectualize because then you tend to only look at one side and not the other. You must always look at both sides of the coin to find Truth and merge both sides into one coin. You may become tired of the process but this is what purges the evil inclination out of each person so that he/she can find Truth within his/her own opposites.

When God took the Hebrews out of Egypt this symbolically represents that God removed the evil and chaos from the people with a higher Light force. Kabbalah says that Israel is one of 7 energy centers of the Light force on Earth. Using *Name Frequency #1 Time Travel* from the *72 Names of God* you can time travel to all events in simultaneous existences to remove your sins. Every action creates an equal and opposite reaction. This is what is often referred to as Karma in Eastern religions. You remember that after Sarah died, Abraham married an African woman named Keturah with whom he had 6 sons. When they reached adulthood he sent them to the East, bringing their religion with them. The idea of Karma originated from these men who became known as the Children of the East.

Removing Exile

Some people only think of exile in reference to the Holy Land. But exile means that you have exiled your Self from the way that life is supposed to be. In addition, you are in exile from the true nature of your Soul-personality. Kabbalah teaches that making a connection to the 12 Tribes removes your inner exile and helps you identify who you are. Connecting to the names of the 12 Tribes daily brings down blessings. Of course, understanding the 12 Tribes can be a little confusing. The Tribe of Levi was removed because this tribe became the priests and the priests dispersed amongst the other tribes. This left 11 Tribes. The Tribe of Yosef/Joseph is divided into the 2 Tribes of Manasseh and Ephraim which were not part of the original 12 Tribes, but if you add these 2 Tribes in there are 13 Tribes. If the Tribe of Levi is counted even though they are dispersed this would make 14 Tribes.

Most of the people on Earth, including you, are the same Souls that went with Jacob to Egypt as well as from the time of the flood of Noah and the Tower of Babel. You are here now as a reincarnation of these Souls so that you can correct the errors of those time periods. The Zohar says that anyone with an affinity for the Light Force of God is an Israelite, regardless of your nationality. The *Names of God* are channels of light that you can use to help emerge from your personal exile.

Egypt, Mitzrayim, is also a metaphor for your own imprisonment, especially during these times of lockdowns with people having to stay home. Your home has become your prison and for some, it has become a living tomb. Pharaoh is a metaphor for The Satan within you. In Hebrew, the Phar in Pharaoh refers to evil and speech, so Pharaoh means evil speech. The Gematria of Joseph is equal to the Sephirot of Yesod which is also equal to the 6th line of the Ana B'koach Prayer. This means that the energy of Joseph makes chaos disappear.

Priya is the Hebrew word that means tearing a membrane, referring to the foreskin or Klipot. Klipot means covering of evil over physical life. Priya can be separated into 2 words, Parah and Yah. Parah means breaking or removing. Yah is an abbreviated version of Yahweh. Parah-Yah means you're removing a membrane or covering that will reveal God. The Satan cannot exist unless humanity supports it. The Satan has no power except what is given to it. Remember that the Satan is a frequency or a position that can be filled with negative energy. In Hebrew, there are 2 words for sin. One is Avon and the other is Pesha. The root is Avar which means to pass over a transgression.

Shabbat, the Sabbath

According to Jews, Shabbat is unique among world religions. Shabbat begins on Friday at sundown and ends on Saturday at sundown. On Shabbat, you are supposed to cease all your work so that you can focus on the Holiness of the day. There are 39 categories of work from which Jews must abstain on the Sabbath including lighting a fire, writing, and spending money. Instead, they must spend time with their community praying, meditating, singing, eating large meals, and even resting or sleeping. There are 7 reasons to observe Shabbat.

1. To connect with others such as participating in Shabbat meals and read the Torah preferably with others.

2. To experience personal renewal and inspire you to make the world a better place. People who observe Shabbat frequently report that it makes them better people, gives them more creative time for thinking, and a feeling of being refreshed before going into another week.

3. To connect to the natural world. God created the world in 6 days, saw what He had made, and rested on the 7th day. The Ancient Rabbis, called Sages, said that it made no sense for an all powerful God to need to rest. Rather, this means that He stopped the Creative process and gave His Creations to

Humanity. God does not need to rest. He's giving you a gift to be creative. He said that He Created and now it is your turn.

4. To make you stop feeling like a slave to your work. Shabbat creates the opportunity to remove your Self from your daily routine and remind your Self that you are in control.

5. To stop searching for life's purpose. Shabbat gives you the opportunity to step back from all your achievements and goals to be and exist; to not do anything.

6. To be challenged to calm your mind as you step away from the outside world. It takes effort to learn prayers and pray with Kavanah, meaning intention. You must focus your prayers on specific purposes of what you are doing in life. Shabbat is not simply a Holiday that happens to you; it is a Holiday that you make happen which sometimes can be difficult. You must create Shabbat for your Self. Your version may not coincide with the version of others.

7. To do what God says is to observe Shabbat.

The Zohar says that God did not rest on the 7th because why would God need to rest? This means that God passed on the power of Creation to his creations. The root of Shabbat is rita, which means to strike. This means that Shabbat is not about resting from work but instead to think about striking or understanding the sparks of Existence. The Shabbat is a day to balance the positives and negatives.

It is customary to light 2 Shabbat candles within 18 minutes before sundown on Friday. Shabbat starts Friday at sundown and concludes Saturday at sundown. In Jerusalem, the candles can be lit 40 minutes in advance of sundown. The earliest allowable time to light the Shabbat candles is 75 minutes before sundown. The Gematria for Chai, meaning long life is 18 so lighting the candles 18 minutes before sundown adds this energy to Shabbat. If the candles are not lit by sundown, they cannot be lit at all. Lighting Shabbat candles seems to have originated as an extension of the practice of lighting a flame before Shabbat because once Shabbat officially starts at sundown you cannot light any flame. In Ancient times before electricity, they lit Shabbat candles before sundown so they would have light in the house before they went to bed. Once lit, Shabbat candles cannot be moved or extinguished. The Torah does not say anything about lighting candles to welcome Shabbat. This is only a Rabbinical interpretation.

Lighting the Shabbat candles is generally the obligation of the woman of the household. If an adult woman is not present, a man is allowed to assume this obligation. Shabbat candles are traditionally White. A minimum of 2 candles per household are lit. Some say that the 2 candles represent the 2 times the commandment of keeping the Shabbat is mentioned in the Torah; once in Exodus *remember the Sabbath* and once in Deuteronomy *keep the Sabbath*. Others say that the 2 candles represent Creation and Revelation as well as Genesis 1 and Genesis 2. Some families light a candle for every person in the household.

The candles are lit from right to left and then the burning match is placed in the tray that holds the candles until it extinguishes itself. The female then waves her hands from top to bottom near the candle to bring the nonphysical into the physical. Some say this represents the Hebrew letter Vav; others say this represents the Sephirot of Keter, Chokhmah and Binah. Then she covers her eyes while she recites the following blessing:

Hebrew: *Baruch Atah Adonai, Eloheinu Melech haolam, asher kid'shanu b'mitzvotav v'zivanu l'hadlik ner shel Shabbat.*

English: *Blessed are You, Lord our God, Rules of the universe who has sanctified us with commandments and commanded us to light Shabbat candles.*

The blessing for the Shabbat candles is modeled on the blessing for lighting the Chanukah candles. Then Hamatzi, a blessing over the bread is said. Traditionally, blessings are said before you do something such as eat or drink. But on Shabbat, the candles are lit before the blessing. Lighting the Shabbat candles also represents bringing the Flame of God Mind into your home. The Talmud says that lighting the Shabbat candles is a Mitzvah or a commandment, but it doesn't mention the Shabbat candle-lighting blessing that is now customary.

Soul Growth

Last week, I had big anger issues. I was sitting in the office and heard the dogs barking at the side gate. A delivery man with a huge U-Haul truck had backed into my snow-covered driveway and was unloading gigantic boxes almost on the neighbor's property. I asked him why he was unloading there instead of on the front porch. He said it was his first time here. I told him he should have gone to the front porch and ring the bell. I didn't have a coat, the temperature was (-10)C, and had to carry all these huge boxes across the driveway, through the garage and into the house. As he was leaving I couldn't help my Self. I screamed at him across the street as he sped away. Then I tried to report him on the FedEx website but there was no place to speak to a live person. Then a survey popped up so I took the survey, gave them my name and phone number, and of course never heard from anyone.

On top of that, Janet had closed out her dad's brother's bank account in Las Vegas with the help of a banker there. She even got an email from the banker saying the account was closed. Then 8 days after the account was closed she received an overdraft notice from the bank. She contacted the bank and was told that the account was reopened because the Las Vegas Water Authority had sent an automatic payment. The bank then reopened the account, paid the bill and sent an overdraft notice. She was told that the bank had only soft-closed the account. Long story short, to get this resolved she finally had to contact the Better Business Bureau who contacted upper management at the bank to get the account closed, never to be reopened again. Then the attorney that Janet is using in Las Vegas to close out her uncle's estate, told Janet that she was asking too many questions and using up her valuable time. Janet had to tell the attorney that the attorney was wasting Janet's time and to do the job for which she was hired.

This is why the world is in the shape that it is in. This is only a tiny piece of our corner of the world. The world needs a slap to stop doing such ridiculous things. People need to stop bullying and intimidating others and take responsibility for their actions instead of trying to blame others for their inadequacies and lack of integrity. We had a delivery that was just thrown on the porch and when I opened the box it was full of broken glass. People don't seem to have a sense of morality or a sense of pride; it seems as though no one cares about anything. They are more interested in how big they can make their lips with Botox and other injectables. According to the news, Saudi Arabia had a beauty contest for camels, because that's really important. The prize was 49 million pounds. So 40 camels got disqualified because their owners gave them Botox face injections and facelifts. After all, that's what's necessary while people are dying and starving. This is what is being prioritized in this world. The priorities of people are messed up and they have no pride in their work. In my case, regardless of what I am paid I always do my best. This sets the precedence for the best to come back to you. This information is teaching you to reinject pride and Self-responsibility back into the world to make it a better place. The world needs you right now more than ever.

Recently there were 60 earthquakes within 24 hours off the coast of Oregon on the Cascadia fault line. This is continuing. This means anyone living on the Pacific Coast needs to move. There will also be volcanic eruptions in Washington State and Oregon, even in the Northern and Eastern parts of California, because those volcanoes are filling with magma at this moment. There was also a big earthquake in Kansas, where supposedly there are no fault lines. I was also recently told that Russia will take Ukraine and merge with Belarus. As I have told you, there is the new Soviet Union that is going to take back all the countries that once were a part of it. There are even Russian troops in Armenia that did not get there by military planes but rather on Aeroflot commercial airlines under the guise of civilian passengers. Yet, they wore military uniforms and carried weapons.

I was also told that Japan, which is not allowed to have a military since WW2, is now building up a large military force to confront China. China is about to merge with Laos and Mongolia before they assimilate Taiwan. The news has shown the Chinese lunar rover on the dark side of the moon amid claims that a mystery hut was found here. Of course, as I have already told you this is the Nazi 4th Reich moon base that has been there for many years, and now it is on public news. There will be a conflict with China somewhere between 2024 and 2027. I am working with NASA to help get a project going in the Pyrenees near the country of Andorra between France and Spain to save the Earth from gamma ray bombardment. I have been told that the military is taking over the United States. You can use the Star of David as a symbol of protection around your Self and your home. Turning it counterclockwise in a circle also helps block storms as well as other potential natural or human made disasters.

Kabbalah says that the more uncomfortable the physical body, the greater the spiritual growth. This means that the physical issues in your body are opportunities to understand the mind-patterns that created the issues. The **Alternative Medical Apocrypha** and **Heights of Health** both discuss physical issues and the mind-patterns that create them. Kabbalah also says that you cannot interfere in the Tikkun of others. You can offer in person or on the Oversoul level through your prayers but it is up to the other person to accept or reject. I think about the millions of people from British Columbia to California who will be affected by earthquakes and other natural disasters. I have told people this will happen and if they choose to stay this is their Tikkun. There is no such thing as being lucky or unlucky. You create your own reality. No one punishes you, everything comes from within you.

I recently had a 3 hour conversation/interview with author Linda Moulton Howe. Her father was the head of aeronautics in the state of Colorado. She confirmed that in 1999, a military person told her about the gamma ray burst that my NASA physicist friend told me about. Linda said that the military told her that if the gamma ray burst hits the Pacific Ocean that there will be 1,000 foot waves that will wash over California meaning that California will no longer exist. You have from the end of 2023 until 2024 to relocate. You should move away from the coasts, but especially the Pacific Coast from British Columbia all the way down to Mexico. Another source told me that both China and Russia will soon be doing more than one hypersonic test to show their superiority over the United States and Europe. You are fortunate to know that this is all planned so you do not need to be afraid. Get in your center and understand your place in Creation and why you chose to be here in this time period. New wars will be fought from space and this includes weaponizing weather. This current wave of tornado attacks in the Midwest was an attack. Tornadoes do not happen in December. One day it is 60F and the next day the temperature drops with blinding cold and snow. This is not natural.

Darkness means losing spiritual awareness but this is just an illusion because you cannot ever lose spirituality. The Light is always there even if you don't recognize it. The Zohar says that a plague is a code for fear of the unknown as well as fear of darkness. This means that if you are affected by any plague you fear of what you do not know. If you are afraid of the dark, afraid to sleep or sleep-walk, you are inviting evil to come in. Read the chapter in ***Decoding Your Life*** about fear. When you are vulnerable you attract the Angel of Death to eliminate you. The Zohar says the cause of death cannot be seen through physical means because there really is no death. Death is only an illusion. The Zohar also says to take control of the forces that compel you, meaning that you can change your mind-pattern. Freedom from fear and uncertainty means taking control over evil and not allowing yourself to be vulnerable. You cannot capture or remove darkness by force. You must only create and shine Light. For example, if you have an infestation of vermin in your house and you turn the light on, the vermin runs away. Shine Light on what you want to remove within and change the outer. Illuminate perceived chaos to effect permanent outer change. The cosmos is in a state of constant flowing Light. The Zohar says that from midnight to dawn is the most powerful and energetic time of the day. This is why those who study Kabbalah and Zohar get up just before midnight to start their prayers and spiritual work.

Talmud

The Talmud is a collection of writings that covers the full gamut of Jewish law and tradition, compiled and edited between the third and sixth centuries. Talmud is Hebrew for "learning," appropriate for a text that people devote their lives to studying and mastering. The main text of the Talmud is the Mishnah, a collection of terse teachings written in Hebrew, redacted by Rabbi Yehudah the Prince, in the years following the destruction of the Second Temple in Jerusalem.

Over the next several hundred years, the rabbis continued to teach and expound. Many of those teachings were collected into two great bodies, the Jerusalem Talmud, containing the teachings of the rabbis in the Land of Israel, and the Babylonian Talmud, featuring the teachings of the rabbis of Babylon. These two works are written in the Aramaic dialects used in Israel and Babylonia respectively.

https://www.chabad.org/library/article_cdo/aid/3347866/jewish/What-Is-the-Talmud-Definition-and-Comprehensive-Guide.htm

The Torah is the *5 Books of Moses*. Talmud means study and Mishnah means repeating. By studying the Talmud you learn the law. The Talmud has 6 sections: agriculture, sacred times, women and personal status, damages, Holy things, and Purity Laws. The Talmud and the Mishnah within it is like a casebook of law. The last section of the Talmud is the Gemara, which means learning. The Gemara began in Israel and was expanded upon in Iraq, called Babylonia during the time of exile. The Gemara addresses the logic of the Mishnah and Talmud. The Talmudic Yerushalmi was produced in Israel which includes the Mishnah and Gemara. This one is sometimes referred to as the Palestinian Talmud as well as the Talmud Eretz Israel/Talmud Land of Israel. This one is considered to be less authoritative than the Talmud Bavli. The Talmud Bavli was produced in Iraq/Babylonia which is the Mishnah and Gemara from Iraq/Babylonia. Bavli means Babylon in Hebrew.

Both Talmuds have the two layers of the Mishnah and Gemara. The Mishnah of both is almost identical. However, the Gemaras differ significantly in content and style. The Jerusalem Gemara is written in Aramaic, which is different than the Babylonian Aramaic. In those days, Aramaic was the language of the entire Earth even though the dialects varied. The Babylonian Talmud consists of quotes from Babylonian Rabbis while the Jerusalem Talmud quotes from the Ancient Hebrew Rabbis of Israel. The Jerusalem Talmud was used more by nonJews while the Babylonian Talmud was used more by the Rabbis and Jews. The language and content of the Jerusalem Talmud were influenced by the Greeks who at one time occupied the Middle East and controlled the Holy Land. Many Ancient Hebrews spoke

Greek, including the Apostles who spoke more Greek than Latin. Today, more Rabbis use the Babylonian Talmud with Jewish laws codified in Baghdad from the 8th to the 10th century. Interestingly, laws, regulations, and interpretations are in use today that originated in Iraq rather than Israel.

Protective Angels

> Rabbi Chaim Lowe (brother of the famed Maharal of Prague) explains that Talmud study is a form of spiritual protection. This is alluded to by the word gemara, which is an acronym for the four hosts of angels, each one headed by the archangels, who sing Gd's praise and surround the person to save him from harm:

Gabriel גבריאל

Michael מיכאל

Raphael רפאל

Uriel אוריאל

> https://www.chabad.org/library/article_cdo/aid/4617587/jewish/Why-Was-the-Talmud-Called-Gemara.htm

Many scholars have tried to say the Talmud is a source of historical inquiry, but it is an extremely controversial book due to its various interpretations.

The School of Shammai was known to be very strict and the School of Hillel was known to be more lenient. A Hillel Rabbi even said that anyone who followed the School of Shammai deserved to be put to death. In fact, the Rabbis even produced a series of curses that they could hurl at each other during their disagreements which they say are for the sake of Heaven. They called each other such things as vinegar, son of wine, demented ostrich or they sometimes said that the other should be sentenced to execution, cursed each others' ancestry, wished the other to be stung by scorpions, wished his words to be like vinegar on the others' teeth and like smoke in the others' eyes, wished that a horn would poke out the others' eyes or they even predicted the death of one another. All of these means that you need to consider what is written and then meditate upon it to see what answers and interpretations come up for you. Because everything has many layers of meaning it is quite possible that your studies will produce legitimate answers. Use *Name Frequency #46 Absolute Certainty* to remove doubt and confusion from your mind.

Midrash

The Midrash is writings that fill in the gaps of the Biblical text, compiled between 200AD and 1000AD. In the Bible, when you want to inquire into any subject including God's Word, the root Hebrew letters are Dalet, Resh, Shin. The word Midrash comes from these Hebrew letters. The Midrash is interpretive and seeks the answers to religious questions, both practical and theological, and has 2 categories. Midrash Halaka is about Law and Religious Practice. The text of the Torah is often very ambiguous when it comes to Law. The Midrash is the Rabbinical interpretation of Hebrew Law. Midrash Aggadah interprets Bible stories. Aggadah means telling. Anything that is not Law falls into this category. In the Midrash are such writings as the *Song of Psalms, Book of Ruth, Lamentations and Ecclesiastes*. These are usually read during the Holidays. Others are just commentaries or sermons that lead to Torah readings. All are subject to interpretation that needs to be applied to each time period. The Zohar says the Torah is timeless so each generation has its own interpretations of the same information. This is why there are so many interpretations.

History of the Yiddish language

Yiddish is about 1000 years old and is a form of German. Literally, Yiddish means Jewish and is spoken by Ashkenazi Jews from Central and Eastern Europe. Yiddish is derived from medieval German and integrates German, Hebrew, Aramaic, Slavic and Roman languages. It's impossible to determine exactly where Yiddish emerged, it is believed to have been formulated around the 10th Century or the 900s when Jews from France and Italy migrated to the German Rhine Valley. There, they combined their languages mixed with German to create Yiddish. As a result of the Crusades and the black plague, Yiddish spread across Central and Eastern Europe where Slavic languages intermingled with it. In the Ashkenazi societies, Hebrew was the language of the Bible and prayer, Aramaic was the language of learning and Yiddish was the language of everyday life. This is referred to as the trilingualism of the three languages. Yiddish, Hebrew, and Aramaic all use the same Hebrew AlephBet.

The first printed Yiddish sentence was done by scribes in 1272. In the 18th century, German-speaking Jews were quickly assimilated into Germany and Western Europe. At the same time, Yiddish started to flourish in Eastern Europe and reached millions of speakers. The growth of the Hasidic movement increased the popularity of the Yiddish language and the late 19th century brought in printed Yiddish literature. In 1908, the first International Conference on the Yiddish language was held and called to be the national language of the Jewish people. In 1925, the Yiddish Scientific Institute was founded in Vilnius Lithuania. In the early days of the Soviet Union, the communist government supported Yiddish schools, theaters, research, and literature as long as it did not mention government or religion.

During the Purge of 1937, many Yiddish writers and leaders were arrested and executed because Joseph Stalin said that Yiddish was anti-Soviet. Interestingly, in pre-state Israel from 1918 to 1948 Yiddish was banned in favor of Hebrew which was declared the national language. At the beginning of WW2, there were approximately 13 million Yiddish-speaking people in the world. However, the Holocaust destroyed most of that population. In the last half-century, Yiddish has been studied as an academic discipline and Yiddish literature recognized as a great contribution to the world. In the 1970s Yiddish and Eastern European Cultural Revival began. Isaac Bashevis Singer won the Nobel Prize for literature in 1978 for his Yiddish work. In addition, a style of music known as Klezmer became popular in Central and Eastern Europe as well as parts of North America.

Many people think Oy Vey, a common expression of hardship and depression with a bit of sarcastic humor, used by the Jewish people is Yiddish. However, the word Oy is a classical Hebrew word from thousands of years ago meaning woe is me. Then, Aramaic-speaking people started using the same expression but in Aramaic the word is Vey. Eventually, both the Hebrew and Aramaic words were joined to form the expression Oy Vey which means woe is me, woe is me. Webster's Dictionary traces the word Vey to the Middle High German word Vey which also means woe. There are many words in German that came from Aramaic or Hebrew. In Scottish, Oy can mean grandchild and is sometimes said as hoy or ahoy, such as used in maritime terminology. The Scottish, Irish, English, and Welsh people all originate from the Hebrews which is why Hebrew words infiltrate their languages.

Deeper Levels

You know that the first word of the Torah is Beresheet and begins with the Hebrew letter Bet. The Zohar says that another reason why Bet was chosen to start Creation is that it is made up of three of the Hebrew letter Vav. Bet is comprised of a Vav on the side, top and bottom. These 3 Vavs represent the 3 columns of the Sephirot. The Zohar calls this a super force because everything in creation exists in 3s. You already know that everything in Creation is about twinning. In addition, there are 3 sets of twins. The 6-pointed star is 3 x 2.

The Zohar says that Creation started with the letter Hey. While Bet is the 2nd letter of the Hebrew AlephBet, Hey is the 2nd letter in the *4-Letter Name of God YHVH*. This means that Hey represents the powerful physical force of the God-Mind. Bet initiated the Creation energies/formulas and Hey enhanced the physical manifestations. This is another layer of Genesis 1/nonphysical Creation and Genesis 2/ physical Creation. **Miracles in Motion** has an entire chapter about the *72 Names of God* and how they were formulated based upon 3 consecutive verses of Exodus 14:19-21. Each of the *72 Names of God* is comprised of 3 Hebrew letters. In each of these *72 Names of God*, the left letter represents the left side of the Sephirot, the right letter represents the right side of the Sephirot and the middle letter represents the middle of the Sephirot. The Zohar says that Bet is the seed of the universe and meditating upon it makes you a Holy One. To most effectively do this, mentally build it by visualizing first the Vav on the left side, then placing a Vav on the top and another Vav on the bottom. This visualization activates the mind over matter, initiating/activating change in whatever circumstances you desire.

> Exodus 14:13-14 says The Lord will fight for you, and you have only to be silent.

Name Frequency #58 Letting Go of the *72 Names of God* will help you do this by quieting you and your environment. The Hebrew letters are Yud, Yud, and Lamed, right to left. The Zohar says that restriction is the foundation of the *72 Names of God*, which is a technology and means not to be reactive. This means that when you want to react you must first be still and calm to allow what you need to do to flow into your conscious mind.

There is a section in the Torah that is different from all the other sections. It has a strange count of letters and spaces which is not the normal way of writing. This indicates that it is a formula or frequency. The Zohar says that there is one word in this section that is the secret for all future generations. In Hebrew, this section is called Az Yeshir which means he/it will sing meaning that there will be a frequency activated. But it has been incorrectly translated as *Song of the Sea*.

In this section, there is a sentence that addresses the war with Amalek, which the Torah says is the most evil nation that needs to be eliminated and wiped from memory. Amalek has the same Gematria as the Hebrew word Sufok which means doubt. Therefore this section symbolically refers to the evil of Amalek/doubt that needs to be eliminated within each person because Doubt is your worst enemy. Doubt eliminates opportunities by infusing negative energy into what you want. Doubt negates your positive inner level work. Doubt is your Amalek, your evil enemy that needs to be removed because all battles are within. You may see war and fighting but this is a projection into the physical world of what is happening within you. Reciting the Az Yashir in Hebrew will help you defeat your inner Amalek. As you know, the Hebrew language contains the Light Force of God that eliminates darkness.

The Zohar says to choose to keep people around you that have fear/awe of God. It says that there are 2 levels of fear and 2 levels of love, and that fear and love are opposites. According to the Zohar low levels of fear and love are from the animal Soul or animal mind. Examples of lower levels of love include such things as a love of specific foods and a love of travel. Examples of higher levels of love are recognizing the potential within others and seeing that there is a Spark of God even within the most evil or horrible people. The Zohar says that the people who do the most evil have the most potential to reach the highest levels of love. This also means that whatever negativity is within the darkest part of you contains the potential opposite of an even stronger Light Force that can bring out even more good. People who are only nice and wonderful often stay the same without growing higher.

Examples of low levels of fear are fear of bad weather, getting killed, and not having enough food to eat. Higher levels of fear are mistranslated from the Bible. Higher levels of fear do not mean hiding close and being afraid of God. Rather, the correct translations mean to be in awe of God. Examples of higher levels of fear/awe include standing in front of a gigantic mountain range and recognizing its enormous magnitude and beauty while you are physically only a speck in front of it. This higher level of fear/awe reminds you of the magnitude of God.

5 Levels of the Soul

There are 5 levels of the Soul. The lowest level is Nefesh with the highest level of Yechida. A female child is connected to Malchut, which is the physical reality that was in at the moment. A male child connected to Zeir Anpin, which is the middle six Sephirot from Yesod to the neck.

Nefesh (lowest)

Ruach

Neshema

Chaya

Yechida (highest)

The Zohar says that reincarnation allows for punishment and reward, specifically addressing punishments for specific actions by males. For example, if two men are fighting and a pregnant woman gets injured, then the husband of that woman can demand anything from those men and they must pay it. It also states that if a master hits and injures his slave but the slave recovers, there is no compensation due to the slave. Because the Bible is not to be taken literally, the Zohar says that Israelites dealing with slaves is symbolic of the rules of reincarnation. You are a slave to the baggage of other lifetimes. When you sin, you become a slave to the person that you have wronged. If you commit murder you must die in a subsequent lifetime. If you steal, you must return and be a slave or servant to that person. The Bible does not believe in prisons because prisons do not solve problems. Prisons do not provide correction nor does the victim receive anything as a result. Current prisons are to warehouse people, not to help them. The Zohar says that slavery is a code for addiction. If you are addicted to any person, place, thing, emotion, and/or action, you are a slave to that addiction. **Alternative Medical Apocrypha** has an excellent chapter called *Addictions*.

The Bible states that a Hebrew slave must work for his master for six years and The 7th year is known as the Shemitah Year. A master must provide his male slave with a wife from another nation. This changes the energy or genetics of the enslaved people as the wife and children of the slave belong to the master. Female children sold into slavery are treated differently than male children. The Zohar says that the perpetrator is not separate from the victim. They have the same mind-pattern which is why they attracted each other. As challenging as this may seem when you see hurt and injured people, these people all attracted each other as a result of their Tikkun/correction from other lifetimes. Your animal mind might emote and feel horrible for others but when you go up higher into Unconditional Love you recognize that these people must all go through these circumstances for their Soul Growth. Of course, if you see someone attacking another and you can stop it, this is your duty to do so. These days, violent crimes happen while others stand around videoing the event as entertainment. At one time the torture and murdering of others was a public spectacle that took place among throngs of people who did nothing. In some countries, this still happens. These are opportunities to correct what they did not do in other lifetimes. When you see something and don't try to stop it, you are also guilty. The Zohar says that a doctor who helps an injured person, even a felon can only ask for payment if the injured person is healed.

Healing

Aging should not exist because the body is always recreated anew in every moment. According to the Zohar, no person should ever age. It is the negative thoughts instigated by The Satan that cause the illusion and delusion of illness and death. There are 2 codes that can be used for healing as well as return you to your original format of Creation. The 1st code is Chet, Bet, Vav, from right to left. The 2nd code is Yud, Lamed, Yud from right to left. Simply visualize these at your pineal for them to be effective.

- Chet, Bet, Vav

- Yud, Lamed, Yud

These codes bring up many issues from your past because this is what initially created your issues. Be prepared for your emotions to get stirred up so they can rise to the surface, be dealt with, and therefore eliminated.

There is another code that removes the illusion of death. The Soul never dies, it is Eternal. Concentrating on the 3-letter code of Nun, Yud, Tav from right to left, is said to prevent the physical body from dying. You can add this to your other work, including *Name Frequency #54 Correct Death* from the *72 Names of God* so that you do not interfere in the life path of another. This code removes death.

 - Tav, Yud, Nun

Brain of God

The Ark of the Covenant represents the Brain of God and was comprised of 3 layers. The inner and outer layers were made of Gold while the middle layer was Acacia wood. This represented protection of finances, health, relationships and The Satan. The human brain also has three layers, one thin membrane, one thick membrane and the skull/bone. The Ark of the Covenant is the storage place for all the Revelation of Light revealed by the Torah. The physical dimensions were described in the Torah, including length, width and height. It is not possible put the Holy Scrolls and Tablets inside of it, but somehow they fit. This is because the Ark creates an interdimensional energy that goes beyond time and space.

In the same way, Holy Temple in Jerusalem created an interdimensional energy so that no matter how many people entered, there was always plenty of room. People who are abducted by aliens often say that the ship was very small but when they entered, the space was gigantic.

When the Bible talks about Archangel Michael, this is a code for moving your consciousness towards God. The Gematria of Archangel Michael equals 101. The high priest's clothing was designed to handle a Light Force and the energy of Archangel Michael. This references the priest's direct connection to the God-Mind. The priest wore a breastplate which the Bible describes as Urim and Thumim, meaning Light and Twins. Urim and Thumim allowed the priest to receive all the answers to all the questions. The breastplate was also a computer. The priest's clothing and its precious stones were an information system. The stones were arranged in an array that created specific vibrations/frequencies that became a communication device.

The High Priest of the Holy Temple was the only person with the Spiritual strength to go into the room that held the Ark. This only happened 1 time per year on Yom Kippur. To enter this room, he wore White linen, which served as a grounding cloth, before putting on Urim and Thumim. If the High Priest did anything wrong or misused the equipment something akin to a lightning bolt would be emitted from the Ark and strike him dead. If this happened, his body could not be retrieved by ordinary means. A hook had to be thrown into the room to pull his body out. If any person went in who could not spiritually wield the priestly garments, that person would die instantaneously. In 1967 students from the University of Minnesota built a replica of the Ark of the Covenant according to the directions in the Torah. When finished, it was so electrically charged it had to be destroyed before its power killed them.0

Tevet

Every Hebrew month of the year is associated with one of the 12 Tribes. The 13th month is associated with the Tribe of Levi, which is the tribe of priests dispersed among the other 12 Tribes. The Tribe of Dan is associated with the Hebrew month of Tevet which usually occurs during the month of December on the Western calendar. The Tribe of Dan was named after one of the 12 sons of Jacob and Leia.

Dan was born after Judah, who is described as the king. Christ came from the tribe of Judah. The Tribe of Dan is described as the least of the Tribes, but this Tribe took care of lost people, returning them to their families. The Tribe of Dan also helped people who were emotionally, mentally, and spiritually lost return to their true purpose and find their true identity and thus their true Self. The energy of the Tribe of Dan is to help people see through doubt and confusion in complex situations to make wise decisions.

Jacob's affection for the tribe of Dan is apparent in the blessing that he gave them before he died. He said *Dan will judge his nation like the one of the tribes of Israel. Dan shall be like a snake on the path, a horned snake on the road, which bites the horse's heels so that the rider falls backwards and I ask God for your salvation.* Genesis 49:1-27 is called the Blessing of Jacob, a prophetic poem that mentions each of Jacob's 12 sons, that Jacob says when he is about to die.

The Talmud tells the story of the burial of Jacob, who became known as Israel, by his sons in the cave of Machpelah. Esau, Jacob's evil twin brother, appeared to claim Machpelah as his burial place. Jacob's sons said that Jacob had purchased the burial plot from Esau years ago but the deed was in Egypt. Someone from the Tribe of Naphtali was dispatched to Egypt to bring the deed. Everyone else was forced to wait before Jacob could be buried. Chushim, the son of Dan, could not hear very well so he did not understand the negotiations. All he understood was that Esau was keeping his grandfather's remains from being buried, so he struck Esau in the head with his sword and killed him in one swoop.

Tribe of Dan has a special power to triumph. Chushim is an anagram for Moshiach because in Hebrew both words use the same letters. Jacob describes Dan as a snake on the path because the Gematria of Nechash/Snake equals the Gematria of Moshiach. This means that you can choose one or the other. This is why Moses used the same words for both Judah and Dan in Deuteronomy 33:2-27 is known as the Blessing of the Tribes of Israel by Moses. Moses said Dan is a lion cub and he also said Judah is a lion cub. Kabbalah says that the Chief of Staff of the Messiah will be from the Tribe of Dan and the Messiah will be from the Tribe of Judah.

Together they will be victorious. The following is the symbol of the Tribe of Dan.

It was the people of Danann who invaded Ireland and used this symbol because they were descendants of the Tribe of Dan. This means that if you have Irish genetics you are from the Tribe of Dan. The original name of Ireland was Hibernia meaning Land of the Hebrews.

Jewish Humor

In Heaven, there are 2 lines for husbands. One is for husbands who were completely controlled by their wives and the other is for husbands who were the man of the house. The line for husbands who were completely controlled by their wives stretched on for as far as you could see. There was only 1 man in the line for husbands who were the man of the house. A husband in the long line recognized this lone man and asked him why he was standing in that line. The lone man answered, *my wife told me to stand here.*

Healing Light

The Torah, Kabbalah, and Zohar all clearly explain that worship of God is strongly suggested but you are given free choice whether to do this or not. The Zohar says to worship God because you want to, not because you are commanded. If the worship of God was forced upon you, Kabbalah says this would be the same as idol worship. In Hebrew, Ohalo means Tabernacle. This is symbolic of your body that is filled with Light, not a physical building or location. Gold is the greatest manifestation of the Light Force which is why the elite and royalty wear Gold and keep Gold in their environments. In Hyperspace, Gold means God-Mind Wisdom.

Zohar Color Codes

Scarlet represents the Sephirah of Gevurah and acts like a generator. Scarlet is a dark, deep red similar to the color of dried blood red. So, for example, if you are outside in the cold, visualize Scarlet acting like a generator to increase your body temperature so you can stay warm. In Hyperspace work, visualizing bright Red in and around the body heats it up. However, in either case, this color can feed anger, so it is important to use the color without it using you.

The Zohar calls Purple all-inclusive and the best color. The Healer's Handbook has a color chart at the back of the book so you can see the difference between Purple and Violet. Purple is the color of royalty, deep space, and energetically the color of blood. Purple also represents deep prayer. The Zohar says that Blue makes things manifest but it does not give a specific shade of Blue. This means that Blue brings the nonphysical into the physical. In your Chakra system, Violet is the Crown Chakra, the Royal Blue Chakra Band is beneath that and the Ice Blue Chakra Band is beneath that. This shows how close that Blue is to the nonphysical.

The Zohar says that combining Blue and Purple is the color of YHVH, the Intelligence of All. Combining Blue and Purple with Scarlet unifies the 3 columns of the Zeir Anpin of the Lower Sephirot which includes Chesed, Gevurah, Tiferet, Netzach, Hod, and Yesod as well as Malchut. These represent the physical. The 3 Upper Sephirot of Keter, Binah, and Chochmah are not included because they represent the nonphysical.

Flame of God

In Hebrew, Nun, Resh spells Ner which means candle. Candle is a code for the Flame of God. This is another layer of why 2 candles are lit on Shabbat, to bring the Flame of God into the home as well as one candle for Nun and one for Resh. Nun is the first letter of Nefilah, which means falling. Reshis the first letter of Rash which means poor/poor person. Together, Nun and Resh represent the falling, or destruction, of poverty. Visualize a large Nun, Resh together to destroy poverty of all kinds in your life. These letters bring antimatter into your life to destroy chaos and negativity on all levels. Whenever you have a problem without being able to find a solution, visualize this formula to prevent negative energies from manifesting.

 - Resh, Nun

The Zohar says that there is no such thing as a sudden strike from the Dark Lord. There is always a warning of some kind. Even years ago on news shows, there would be scrolling news at the bottom of the screen which would be different from what the news presenter was saying. Sometimes, stories only appear once and are then never heard about again. This is how the Deep State tells you the plans because by telling what they are going to do, they are not hiding anything from anyone. Technically even under Spiritual Law, this absolves its responsibility. If you don't see it, understand it, or pay attention, then this is your issue. Just like now, you are being told that there is going to be death, disease, and destruction under the guise of science. You have the opportunity to prevent or neutralize the planned negativity. You can use the Nun, Resh to block the chaos.

The Zohar states then that when your heart is happy, everything around you joins in. This means that your happiness floods out to assimilate any negativity that is in your environment. Being depressed or sad is a sin against God. Being angry is identical to idolatry because it means that you are not accepting that God is the Creator of all of this and has a reason for whatever happens. It is important to recognize these forms of negative emotion within so you can begin to mitigate their intensity. The entire point of Kabbalah is to make your Light shine so brightly that evil cannot exist.

Darkness cannot coexist with Light. Consider 2 rooms next to each other, one dark and one light. When the door is opened between them, the Light goes into the dark, the dark does not go into the Light. Light is more powerful than dark. When you shine your Light, the dark must go away. Visualize your Self like a giant Light bulb plugged into Ain Sof through Binah, into Gevurah, and projecting this out, on, around, and into the physical world to remove the darkness. The Zohar says that the world needs Soldiers of Light, meaning that you need to be like a warrior under the energy of the God-Mind and Ain Sof to shine Light on evil and remove it. The Zohar states very clearly that the only way the Moshiach can come is with the end of the Erev Rav. There is a difference between the Illuminati and the Deep State. The Illuminati is the government of the Deep State. Destroying only the Deep State still leaves the Illuminati which is blended with the Erev Rav. To eliminate negativity and evil you must go to the Source. The Erev Rav only believes in mechanical physicality. They remove the spirituality of society.

Death

Before a person passes away, he/she writes an ethical will that records guidance for the descendants. In addition, there is a traditional deathbed confession, called the Viddui. Now, people are hired to recite the confession of the deceased in front of the mourners at the funeral. As soon as a first-degree relative, meaning parent, spouse, sibling, or child, hears of the death until burial, he/she says a blessing that the deceased should be judged with truth. It is also traditional to tear your garment as soon as death happens. Tearing the clothes has Biblical origins that symbolize that your heart is broken, so close relatives rip the clothes over their hearts. Sometimes instead of ripping garments, black ribbons are cut as if they are torn and pinned over the heart. A mourner's prayer called a kaddish is also said.

Judaism says that you must comfort the mourners and treat the deceased and their bodies with respect. The body is prepared with great care by a sacred burial society which includes rituals, purification, and dressing the body in a shroud. Many Jews hire a person to sit with the body from death until burial to ensure that the body is not desecrated or disturbed in any way. Of course, at one time another reason for sitting with the deceased was to make sure the person was dead and not just unconscious. Embalming is considered a sin and form of mutilation. The only time embalming is allowed is if the body must be shipped from a distance to prevent decomposition until it can be buried. Autopsies are forbidden except when the cause of death needs to be determined. Organ donations are permitted to save the life of another.

There's a powerful taboo against cremation because of the Jews who were burned in the crematoriums by the Nazis. Because there is no explicit Jewish law prohibiting cremation in Jewish legal sources, more modern Jews are opting for cremation. Some Rabbis interpret cremation as defiling dead bodies. Others say that Jews may have practiced cremation in Ancient times. According to Jewish mystical tradition, the soul does not immediately depart the body after death. Therefore, the process of decay in the Earth allows a gradual separation rather than the more immediate and painful one resulting from cremation. Because the body is considered to be the property of God and it's forbidden to defile it, some regard cremation as defiling the body. There is nothing in Jewish law that bars the ashes from being buried in a Jewish cemetery. Jewish law and custom require special cemeteries for Jews. Today, nonJews may be buried in Jewish cemeteries, such as a non-Jewish spouse.

The funeral must take place within 24 hours of the death. The casket must be made of wood that deteriorates very quickly in the ground, such as pine, so that there's nothing left. Nothing can be preserved. You must go from dust to dust. When the body is lowered into the ground at burial, it is considered an honor for the spouse or oldest son to throw a shovel of dirt onto the coffin; then the shovel is passed on to the next person to do the same.

Suicide is forbidden in Jewish law. It's presumed in Judaism that if anyone takes his/her own life, the person suffered from mental illness. According to Jewish law, anything that mutilates the body is illegal such as tattoos and body piercings of any kind.

Mourning

After the burial, there is a 7-day period called Shiva where mourners visit the family home and participate in prayer services. Family members sit on a wooden stool or box that is uncomfortable to punish themselves for any wrongdoings that they did to the deceased. This is followed by a 30-day period of mourning that includes special mourning prayers. Then, the family can return to a normal routine.

After 11 months a ceremony called an unveiling takes place in the cemetery where the gravestone of the deceased is revealed and sanctified. Every year on the anniversary of the death of the deceased, a Yahrzeit service is held and a 24-hour candle is lit in his/her honor.

Mi Sheberach

Mi Sheberach is a Jewish prayer for healing the sick or recovering from an illness or accident. This prayer invokes the Patriarchs Abraham, Isaac, and Jacob and the Matriarchs Sarah, Rebecca, Rachel, and Leah to have compassion for these people, to help to heal and a speedy recovery.

A "mi sheberach" is a public prayer or blessing for an individual or group, most often recited in synagogue when the Torah is being read. Because it is not an officially mandated prayer, there is a lot of room for creativity regarding whom to bless or how they can be blessed. Thus, there are mi sheberachs for just about any person in need of some divine goodness—most notably those requiring healing.

When we petition Gd to bring blessing or healing, it is customary to do so in merit of charity pledged. So if you request that a mi sheberach be said in your synagogue on someone's behalf, make sure to give some charity as well (of course not on Shabbat).

The prayer takes its name from its opening words, "mi sheberach," "[May He] who blesses." The standard opening line reads, "May He who blesses our fathers, Abraham, Isaac and Jacob bless . . ." and then continues with a personalized blessing.

Here is the Hebrew text and English translation of some of the most common mi sheberachs as they are found in the Chabad siddur:

To be said after someone receives an aliyah to the Torah on Shabbat or festivals:

מִי שֶׁבֵּרַךְ אֲבוֹתֵינוּ אַבְרָהָם יִצְחָק וְיַעֲקֹב, הוּא יְבָרֵךְ אֶת (name) בֶּן (father's name) בַּעֲבוּר שֶׁעָלָה לִכְבוֹד הַמָּקוֹם לִכְבוֹד הַתּוֹרָה וְלִכְבוֹד הַשַּׁבָּת (on festivals—וְלִכְבוֹד הָרֶגֶל), וּבִשְׂכַר זֶה הַקָּדוֹשׁ בָּרוּךְ הוּא יִשְׁמְרֵהוּ וְיַצִּילֵהוּ מִכָּל צָרָה וְצוּקָה וּמִכָּל נֶגַע וּמַחֲלָה, וְיִשְׁלַח בְּרָכָה וְהַצְלָחָה בְּכָל מַעֲשֵׂה יָדָיו (on festivals add—וְיִזְכֶּה לַעֲלוֹת לְרֶגֶל) עִם כָּל יִשְׂרָאֵל אֶחָיו. וְנֹאמַר אָמֵן:

May He who blessed our fathers, Abraham, Isaac, and Jacob bless (name) son of (father's name), because he has come up for the honor of Gd, for the honor of the Torah, and for the honor of the Shabbat (on festivals add: and for the honor of the festival). In this merit may the Holy One, blessed be He, protect and deliver him from all trouble and distress, and from all affliction and illness, and may He send blessing and success to all his endeavors (on festivals add: and may he be privileged to go up to the Beit Hamikdash for the festivals), together with all Israel his brethren; and let us say, Amen.

This mi sheberach is often modified to mention a donation given and to specific family members or friends to be included in the blessing.

Prayer for an ill male to be said on weekdays:

מִי שֶׁבֵּרַךְ אֲבוֹתֵינוּ אַבְרָהָם יִצְחָק וְיַעֲקֹב, מֹשֶׁה וְאַהֲרֹן דָּוִד וּשְׁלֹמֹה, הוּא יִרְפָּא אֶת (name) בֶּן (mother's name) בַּעֲבוּר שֶׁ(name) בֶּן (father's name) יִתֵּן בְּלִי נֶדֶר לִצְדָקָה בַּעֲבוּרוֹ, בִּשְׂכַר זֶה הַקָּדוֹשׁ בָּרוּךְ הוּא יִמָּלֵא רַחֲמִים עָלָיו לְהַחֲלִימוֹ וּלְרַפֹּאתוֹ וּלְהַחֲזִיקוֹ וּלְהַחֲיוֹתוֹ, וְיִשְׁלַח לוֹ מְהֵרָה רְפוּאָה שְׁלֵמָה מִן הַשָּׁמַיִם לִרְמַ"ח אֵבָרָיו וְשַׁסָּ"ה גִידָיו בְּתוֹךְ שְׁאָר חוֹלֵי יִשְׂרָאֵל, רְפוּאַת הַנֶּפֶשׁ וּרְפוּאַת הַגּוּף, וְנֹאמַר אָמֵן:

May He who blessed our fathers, Abraham, Isaac and Jacob, Moses and Aaron, David and Solomon, heal (sick person's Hebrew name and that of his mother), because (Hebrew name of the person who pledged charity for the sake of the sick person and that of his/her father) pledged charity, without a vow, for his sake. In this merit may the Holy One, blessed be He, be filled with mercy for him, to restore him to health and to cure him, to strengthen him and to invigorate him. And may He hasten to send him from heaven a complete recovery to his 248 bodily parts and 365 veins, among the other sick people of Israel, a healing of spirit and a healing of body; and let us say, Amen.

Prayer for an ill female to be said on weekdays:

מִי שֶׁבֵּרַךְ אֲבוֹתֵינוּ אַבְרָהָם יִצְחָק וְיַעֲקֹב, מֹשֶׁה וְאַהֲרֹן דָּוִד וּשְׁלֹמֹה, הוּא יִרְפָּא אֶת (name) בַּת (mother's name) בַּעֲבוּר שֶׁ (name) בֶּן (father's name) יִתֵּן בְּלִי נֶדֶר לִצְדָקָה בַּעֲבוּרָהּ, בִּשְׂכַר זֶה הַקָּדוֹשׁ בָּרוּךְ הוּא יִמָּלֵא רַחֲמִים עָלֶיהָ לְהַחֲלִימָהּ וּלְרַפֹּאתָהּ וּלְהַחֲזִיקָהּ וּלְהַחֲיוֹתָהּ, וְיִשְׁלַח לָהּ מְהֵרָה רְפוּאָה שְׁלֵמָה מִן הַשָּׁמַיִם בְּכָל אֵבָרֶיהָ וְגִידֶיהָ בְּתוֹךְ שְׁאָר חוֹלֵי יִשְׂרָאֵל, רְפוּאַת הַנֶּפֶשׁ וּרְפוּאַת הַגּוּף, וְנֹאמַר אָמֵן:

May He who blessed our fathers, Abraham, Isaac and Jacob, Moses and Aaron, David and Solomon, heal (sick person's Hebrew name and that of her mother), because (Hebrew name of the person who pledged charity for the sake of the sick person and that of his/her father) pledged charity, without a vow, for her sake. In this merit may the Holy One, blessed be He, be filled with mercy for her, to restore her to health and to cure her, to strengthen her and to invigorate her. And may He hasten to send her from heaven a complete recovery to all her bodily parts and veins, among the other sick people of Israel, a healing of spirit and a healing of body; and let us say, Amen.

Prayer for an ill person to be said on Shabbat or festivals:

For a man

מִי שֶׁבֵּרַךְ אֲבוֹתֵינוּ אַבְרָהָם יִצְחָק וְיַעֲקֹב, מֹשֶׁה וְאַהֲרֹן דָּוִד
וּשְׁלֹמֹה, הוּא יְבָרֵךְ אֶת (name) בֶּן (mother's name), בַּעֲבוּר
שֶׁ (name) בֶּן (father's name) יִתֵּן בְּלִי נֶדֶר לִצְדָקָה בַּעֲבוּרוֹ, שַׁבָּת
הִיא מִלִּזְעֹק וּרְפוּאָה קְרוֹבָה לָבוֹא, וְנֹאמַר אָמֵן:

For a woman

מִי שֶׁבֵּרַךְ אֲבוֹתֵינוּ אַבְרָהָם יִצְחָק וְיַעֲקֹב, מֹשֶׁה וְאַהֲרֹן דָּוִד
וּשְׁלֹמֹה, הוּא יְבָרֵךְ אֶת (name) בַּת (mother's name), בַּעֲבוּר
שֶׁ (name) בֶּן (father's name) יִתֵּן בְּלִי נֶדֶר לִצְדָקָה בַּעֲבוּרָהּ, שַׁבָּת
הִיא מִלִּזְעֹק וּרְפוּאָה קְרוֹבָה לָבוֹא, וְנֹאמַר אָמֵן:

May He who blessed our fathers, Abraham, Isaac and Jacob, Moses and Aaron, David and Solomon, bless the sick person (name) the son of (mother's name) because (donor's name) pledged charity, without a vow, for his/her sake. It is Shabbat when it is forbidden to plead; healing will come soon; and let us say, Amen.

Prayer for a woman who just gave birth to a baby girl (this also doubles as the baby naming):

מִי שֶׁבֵּרַךְ אֲבוֹתֵינוּ אַבְרָהָם יִצְחָק וְיַעֲקֹב, מֹשֶׁה וְאַהֲרֹן דָּוִד
וּשְׁלֹמֹה, הוּא יְבָרֵךְ אֶת הָאִשָּׁה הַיּוֹלֶדֶת (woman's name)
בַּת (mother's name) עִם בִּתָּהּ הַנּוֹלְדָה לָהּ בְּמַזָּל טוֹב, וְיִקָּרֵא
שְׁמָהּ בְּיִשְׂרָאֵל (announce child's name) בַּת (father's name), בַּעֲבוּר
שֶׁבַּעְלָהּ וְאָבִיהָ יִתֵּן בְּלִי נֶדֶר לִצְדָקָה בַּעֲדָן, וּבִשְׂכַר זֶה
יְגַדְּלוּהָ לַתּוֹרָה וְלַחֻפָּה וּלְמַעֲשִׂים טוֹבִים, וְנֹאמַר אָמֵן:

May He who blessed our fathers, Abraham, Isaac and Jacob, Moses and Aaron, David and Solomon, bless the woman who has given birth (Hebrew name and that of her mother) together with the daughter who was born to her in an auspicious time, her name shall be called in Israel (announce the Hebrew name of the newborn and that of her father), because her husband, the child's father, has pledged charity, without a vow, for their sakes. In this merit, may they raise her to Torah, to marriage and to good deeds; and let us say, Amen.

Prayer for a woman who just gave birth to a baby boy:

מִי שֶׁבֵּרַךְ אֲבוֹתֵינוּ אַבְרָהָם יִצְחָק וְיַעֲקֹב, מֹשֶׁה וְאַהֲרֹן דָּוִד
וּשְׁלֹמֹה, הוּא יְבָרֵךְ אֶת הָאִשָּׁה הַיּוֹלֶדֶת (woman's name)
בַּת (mother's name) עִם בְּנָהּ הַנּוֹלַד לָהּ בְּמַזָּל טוֹב, בַּעֲבוּר
שֶׁבַּעְלָהּ וְאָבִיו יִתֵּן בְּלִי נֶדֶר לִצְדָקָה בַּעֲדָם, וּבִשְׂכַר זֶה יִזְכּוּ
לְהַכְנִיסוֹ בִּבְרִיתוֹ שֶׁל אַבְרָהָם אָבִינוּ וִיגַדְּלוּהוּ לְתוֹרָה
וּלְחֻפָּה וּלְמַעֲשִׂים טוֹבִים, וְנֹאמַר אָמֵן:

May He who blessed our fathers, Abraham, Isaac and Jacob, Moses and Aaron, David and Solomon, bless the woman who has given birth (Hebrew name and that of her mother) together with the son born to her in an auspicious time, because her husband, the child's father, has pledged charity, without a vow, for their sakes. In this merit, may they be privileged to bring him into the Covenant of Abraham our father, and to raise him to Torah, to marriage and to good deeds; and let us say, Amen.

https://www.chabad.org/library/article_cdo/aid/2903187/jewish/Mi-Sheberach.htm

Addendums

King Solomon

Son of King David, builder of the temple, author of three biblical works and the wisest of men, Solomon looms large in Jewish tradition — and beyond.

BY MY JEWISH LEARNING

Solomon was the son of King David, the last sovereign of the ancient Kingdom of Israel, builder of the first Jerusalem Temple, and is traditionally viewed as the author of three biblical books: Ecclesiastes, Proverbs and Song of Songs. He was renowned for his wealth, wisdom, abundance of wives and concubines, and the peacefulness of his reign. Later in his life, he would succumb to the temptations of idol worship, for which he was punished by having his kingdom split into competing domains with his son ruling over the smaller one.

Virtually all of what is known about Solomon comes from biblical accounts and other ancient texts, and scholars are divided on how accurate they are. Little archaeological evidence has been found to corroborate the Bible's florid descriptions of Solomon's wealth and the lavish construction projects he undertook in Jerusalem, though that may be due in part to the difficulty of digging in a city at the epicenter of centuries of religious and political strife.

Whatever the historical facts, Solomon looms large in Jewish tradition — and beyond it. Two of his works are read in synagogue on fixed days in the calendar — Ecclesiastes on Sukkot and Song of Songs on Passover. The final chapter of Proverbs, the hymn known as Eishet Hayil, is customarily sung at the Shabbat evening meal. But Solomon — and his temple specifically — is also a central symbol of the Freemasons, who often name their lodges temples (or even King Solomon's Lodge). Legends of Solomon's ability to control demons, create gold out of other materials and perform other supernatural feats have been embraced by adherents of magic and occultism since medieval times.

The Life of Solomon

Solomon reigned over the kingdom of Israel about a millennium before the dawn of the Common Era. The most extensive account of his life is found in I Kings. There we learn that he was the daughter of Bathsheba, the woman David famously saw bathing on a roof and took for a wife after sending her husband away to die in battle. After assuming the throne upon David's death, Solomon began carrying out a purge, ordering the death of his older brother Adonijah, who had sought to usurp the throne, and Joab, the commander of his father's army.

The source of Solomon's wisdom is contained in a story related in the third chapter of I Kings, which describes God coming to Solomon in a dream and offering to grant him a wish. Rather than ask for riches or power, Solomon asks for wisdom. This response pleases God, who responds by granting him wisdom along with the riches and glory and long life that he didn't ask for. Solomon thus became the wisest of all men. "I grant you a wise and discerning mind; there has never been anyone like you before, nor will anyone like you arise again." (I Kings 3:12)

This incident is followed in I Kings by what is perhaps the most famous Solomon story of all, in which two women come before him both claiming to be the mother of a baby. Solomon calls for a sword and says the solution is to cut the baby in two and give one half to each woman. One of the women is amenable to this solution, but the other protests, saying she would rather give the child up than see it killed. Solomon thus determines that the latter woman is the child's mother. As the final verse of the chapter relates, the story burnished Solomon's credentials as the possessor of transcendent wisdom: "When all Israel heard the decision that the king had rendered, they stood in awe of the king; for they saw that he possessed divine wisdom to execute justice." (I Kings 3:28)

Solomon the Builder

Solomon's kingdom was vast, wealthy and prosperous. According to the biblical account, he possessed 1,400 chariots and 12,000 horses and presided over a significant trading enterprise. Solomon's reign was also a peaceful one.

With those blessings in hand, he determined to build a temple in Jerusalem in fulfillment of a promise God had made to David that his son would build a house for God. He secured cypress and cedar wood from Lebanon and hewn stone from the finest quarries, and the interiors were overlaid with gold and adorned with carved reliefs of cherubim and palm. Construction took seven years.

The Temple was by far the most important construction project Solomon undertook, establishing Jerusalem as the locus of Jewish prayer to this day. But it was not the only thing he built. He also built a lavish palace fashioned from hewn stone, choice woods, and bronze. I Kings describes the details of this palace at length, including the size and materials of all its various structures as well as the decorative elements. He also fortified cities elsewhere in his kingdom, in Hazor, Meggido and Gezer, and built garrison towns.

Solomon's Wives

Solomon's retinue of consorts was also legendary — 700 wives and 300 concubines, according to the biblical account. Among these was the daughter of the Egyptian pharaoh, whom Solomon set up in her own residence in Jerusalem. Only one of Solomon's wives was ever named — Naamah, the mother of Jeroboam, who would succeed Solomon in ruling over the split kingdom of Judah.

Among the more enigmatic stories of Solomon's dalliances is his encounter with the Queen of Sheba, a story told twice in the Bible (in the 11th chapter of I Kings and then again in the ninth chapter of I Chronicles) and elaborated upon in later Jewish sources. In the biblical narrative, Sheba hears of Solomon's legend and travels to Jerusalem to meet him with a large entourage. According to the text, Sheba is so impressed with Solomon's wisdom and palatial surroundings she is left breathless. She gifts Solomon gold, spices and precious stones before returning home. A later tradition suggests the two had a relationship that resulted in a child who would eventually give rise to Nebuchadnezzar, the Babylonian king who would destroy Solomon's temple in 586 BCE.

Solomon's many wives included women from nations that God had commanded the Israelites never to marry lest they lead their husbands to worship foreign Gods. And this is precisely what happened to Solomon, who began to worship foreign gods and even build shrines to them. As punishment, God decided to take the kingdom away from Solomon, but out of deference to his father, God does so only after Solomon's death, leaving only one tribe for his son to rule.

The Talmud offers conflicting takes on Solomon's piety. Some rabbis labor to rehabilitate him, which requires some heroic feats of exegesis, as the text in I Kings is rather explicit in multiple places that Solomon sinned, even going so far as to assert that he committed "evil" in God's eyes and was not loyal to God like his father King David.

Other talmudic sources are more frank about Solomon's wrongdoing. In an echo of the legend about Solomon siring the lineage that would ultimately lead to the destruction of the temple, the Talmud records a teaching that after Solomon married pharaoh's daughter, an angel implanted a reed into the sea and a sandbar grew around it that was the eventual site of Rome, which destroyed the Second Temple in 70 CE.

Solomon's Legacy

In Jewish life, Solomon's influence is felt primarily through the three canonical works that are traditionally ascribed to him: Song of Songs, Proverbs and Ecclesiastes. Scholars are generally dubious of the truth of this claim, but the rabbinic tradition is mostly unambiguous that these three are works of Solomon, not least because Solomon is mentioned as the author in the opening verse of all three (or in the case of Ecclesiastes, "son of David.").

There is a tradition that the three works are products of three stages of Solomon's life: the youthful eroticism of Song of Songs, the middle aged wisdom of Proverbs, and the life retrospective of Ecclesiastes. All three are also read at major observances of the Jewish calendar. Ecclesiastes is read publicly in synagogues on the Shabbat of the Sukkot festival, and Song of Songs is read on the Shabbat of Passover. Eishet Hayil, an ode to the "woman of valor" which is the final chapter of Proverbs, is traditionally sung by men to their wives just prior to the Friday night meal.

The legend of Solomon has also been embraced by the Freemasons, the fraternal organization said to trace its origins to the stonemason guilds of medieval Europe. For the spiritual heirs of these stone cutters, Solomon's temple, whose craftsmanship was thought to be unequalled in the ancient world, remains a powerful metaphor for personal development. "This structure depicts the capabilities of men when they work collaboratively, using the right tools to diligently develop themselves in order to be better for the world," one Masonic website says.

Solomon has also long had a presence among enthusiasts of magic and the occult. The origins of this likely trace to a strange story in the Talmud in which Solomon, seeking the secrets necessary to build the temple, has an encounter with Ashmedai, the prince of the demons, in which he tricks him into helping him with its construction. The story makes mention of a ring inscribed with God's name, which would come to be known as the Ring of Solomon, a symbol popular in medieval magic.

Solomon died after ruling for 40 years and was laid to rest in Jerusalem. He was the last ruler of the united Kingdom of Israel. After his death, he was succeeded by his son Rehoboam, who was rejected by the ten tribes in the north, splitting the kingdom between the Kingdom of Israel (led by Jeroboam) and the smaller Kingdom of Judah (led by Rehoboam). Solomon's reign is therefore remembered, in many respects, as a golden era in Israelite history.

Tale of Two Talmuds: Jerusalem and Babylonian

The two versions of the Talmud developed simultaneously in the two major Jewish communities of the rabbinic era.

BY RABBI JILL JACOBS

When people speak of "the Talmud ," they are usually referring to the Talmud Bavli (Babylonian Talmud), composed in Babylonia (modern-day Iraq). However, there is also another version of the Talmud, the *Talmud Yerushalmi* (Jerusalem Talmud), compiled in what is now northern Israel. The Yerushalmi, also called the Palestinian Talmud or the *Talmud Eretz Yisrael* (Talmud of the Land of Israel), is shorter than the Bavli, and has traditionally been considered the less authoritative of the two Talmuds.

Want to learn Talmud with us? Daf Yomi is a program of reading the entire Talmud one day at a time, and My Jewish Learning offers a free daily email that follows the worldwide cycle. To join thousands and thousands of Jews on this learning journey, sign up here!

Like the Talmud Bavli, the Talmud Yerushalmi consists of two layers — the Mishnah and the Gemara. For the most part, the Mishnah of the two Talmuds is identical, though there are some variations in the text and in the order of material. The Gemara of the Yerushalmi, though, differs significantly in both content and style from that of the Bavli. First, the Yerushalmi Gemara is primarily written in Palestinian Aramaic, which is quite different from the Babylonian dialect. The Yerushalmi contains more long narrative portions than the Bavli does and, unlike the Bavli, tends to repeat large chunks of material. The presence of these repeated passages has led many to conclude that the editing of the Yerushalmi was never completed. Others, however, have argued that these repetitions represent a deliberate stylistic choice, perhaps aimed at reminding readers of connections between one section and another.

Comparing the Two Texts

While the Bavli favors multi-part, complex arguments, Yerushalmi discussions rarely include lengthy debate. For instance, both the Bavli and the Yerushalmi discuss the following Mishnah:

"For all seven days [of Sukkot], one should turn one's Sukkah into one's permanent home, and one's house into one's temporary home. (Sukkah 2: 9).

The Bavli Gemara embarks on a long discussion of the validity of this statement in the Mishnah:

The rabbis taught, 'You shall dwell [in booths on the Holiday of Sukkot]' (Leviticus 23:42) means 'you shall live in booths.' From this, they said 'for all seven days, one should make the Sukkah [temporary booth or hut] one's permanent home, and one's house temporary home. How should one do this? One should bring one's nice dishes and couches into the Sukkah, and should eat, drink and sleep in the Sukkah.' Is this really so? Didn't Rava say that one should study Torah and Mishnah in the Sukkah, but should study Talmud outside of the Sukkah? (This statement appears to contradict the Mishnah's assertion that during Sukkot, one should do everything inside the Sukkah.) This is not a contradiction. [The Mishnah] refers to reviewing what one has already studied, while [Rava's statement] refers to learning new material [on which one might not be able to concentrate while in the Sukkah]" (Talmud Bavli Sukkah 28b-29a).

As proof of this resolution, the Bavli goes on to relate a story of two rabbis who leave their Sukkah in order to study new material. Finally, the Gemara suggests an alternate resolution of the apparent conflict– namely, that one learning Talmud is required to stay in a large Sukkah, but may leave a small Sukkah.

In contrast, the Yerushalmi offers very little discussion of the Mishnah:

"The Torah says, 'You shall dwell in booths.' 'Dwell' always means 'live,' as it says, 'you will inherit the land and dwell there' (Deuteronomy 17:14). This means that one should eat and sleep in the Sukkah and should bring one's dishes there" (Talmud Yerushalmi Sukkah 2:10).

After this brief definition of terms and law, the Yerushalmi moves on to a new discussion.

Parallels Between the Two Talmuds

As might be expected, the Bavli quotes mostly Babylonian rabbis, while the Yerushalmi more often quotes Palestinian rabbis. There is, however, much cross-over between the two Talmuds. Both Talmuds record instances of rabbis traveling from the land of Israel to Babylonia and vice versa. Many times, the rabbis of one Talmud will compare their own practice to that of the other religious center. Early midrashim and other texts composed in Palestine appear more frequently in the Yerushalmi, but are also present in the Bavli.

Both the Bavli and the Yerushalmi follow the Mishnah's division into orders, tractates, and chapters. Neither contains Gemara on all 73 tractates of the Mishnah. The Bavli includes Gemara on thirty-six and a half non-consecutive tractates. The Yerushalmi has Gemara on the first 39 tractates of the Mishnah. Some scholars believe that the differences in the Gemara reflect the different priorities and curricula of Babylonia and of the Land of Israel. Others think that parts of each Gemara have been lost.

Within the Yerushalmi, quoted sections of the Mishnah are labeled as "halakhot" (laws). Citations of the Yerushalmi text usually refer to the text by tractate, chapter, and halakhah. Thus, "Sukkah 2:10" (quoted above) means "Tractate Sukkah, Chapter 2, halakhah 10." Some editions of the Yerushalmi are printed in folio pages, each side of which has two columns. Thus, Yerushalmi citations also often include a reference to the page and column number (a, b, c, or d). In contrast, the Bavli is printed on folio pages, and is referred to by page number and side (a or b). These differences result from variations in early printings, and not from choices within the rabbinic communities of Babylonia and the land of Israel.

In most editions of the Yerushalmi, the Talmud text is surrounded by the commentary of the 18th-century rabbi, Moses ben Simeon Margoliot, known as the P'nai Moshe . The P'nai Moshe clarifies and comments on the text of the Yerushalmi, in much the same way that Rashi (Rabbi Shlomo ben Yitzchak, 11th century) explains and discusses the text of the Bavli.

Medieval sources credit Rabbi Yohanan, a third-century sage, with editing the Yerushalmi. However, the fact that the Yerushalmi quotes many fourth and fifth-century rabbis makes this suggestion impossible. From the identities of the rabbis quoted in the Yerushalmi, and from the historical events mentioned in the text, most contemporary scholars conclude that this Talmud was edited between the end of the fourth century and the beginning of the fifth century CE. The codification of the Bavli took place about a hundred years later.

Cultural Concerns

The discussions of the Bavli and the Yerushalmi reflect the differing concerns of the cultures from which the texts emerged. A comparison of the narrative elements of the two Talmuds suggests that the rabbis of the Yerushalmi had more interaction with non-rabbis–both Jews and non-Jews–than the rabbis of the Bavli did. The Yerushalmi, produced in a place under Hellenistic control, reflects Greek influences, both in its language and in its content.

Traditionally, the Bavli has been considered the more authoritative of the two Talmuds. This privileging of the Bavli reflects the fact that Babylonia was the dominant center of Jewish life from talmudic times through the beginning of the medieval period. The first codifiers of halakhah (Jewish law), based in Baghdad in the eighth through 10th centuries, used the Bavli as the basis of their legal writings. Reflecting the prevalent attitude toward the Yerushalmi, the Machzor Vitri, written in France in the 11th or 12th century, comments, "When the Talmud Yerushalmi disagrees with our Talmud, we disregard the Yerushalmi."

Today, there is renewed interest in studying the Talmud Yerushalmi. This interest reflects the current academic emphases on tracing the development of the Talmudic text, and on understanding the cultures that produced these texts. Many scholars attempt to learn about the history of the talmudic text by comparing parallel passages in the Bavli and the Yerushalmi. Comparisons between the two Talmuds also yield new information about the relative attitudes and interests of Babylonian and Palestinian rabbis.

The traditional approach to learning Talmud, which emphasized the legal elements of the text, tended to dismiss the Yerushalmi as incomplete and non-authoritative. Today, interest in the literary, cultural and historical aspects of traditional texts has prompted a rediscovery of this Talmud, and a willingness to reconsider its place in the Jewish canon.

Rabbi Jill Jacobs is the Rabbi-in-Residence for the Jewish FundS for Justice.

Dan: The Tevet Personality

The Dan tribe embodies special characteristics needed for this time of the year

The Dan Personality

The new month of Tevet represents the coldest month of the year, the month that is most associated with the winter. Every month of the year is associated (according to the Arizal and based on *Sefer Yetizrah*) with one of the Twelve Tribes (with the thirteenth month, the second Adar, that appears in intercalated years, being associated with the tribe of Levi). The Tribe of Dan is the one associated with the month of Tevet. Let us see how Dan warms and illuminates the cold winter.

Dan: Lost and Found

When the Children of Israel walked through the desert, the tribe of Judah walked at the front of the procession and the tribe of Dan brought up the rear. Participants in an army hike or a trek know that a strong person is needed for the rear. It has to be someone who knows how to encourage everyone to keep going and ensure that nobody is left behind or gets lost. The sages say that Dan's role at the rear was to find and return lost items. More importantly, it was Dan's role to take care of the people who got lost, to return them to their families and their place.

Translating the Dan tribe's role into the psychological and spiritual dimensions, reveals that their role is to help people find themselves. Sometimes, people lose their way, their self-confidence, their sense of purpose, their identity. The tribe of Dan knows how to help all those people, to get them back on their feet and show them the way. In a sense, they return to a person his or her most important possession: their self.

A Simple Jew

What is the source of this talent of the tribe of Dan? After Leah gave birth to four sons, Rachel asked Jacob to marry her maidservant, Bilhah. Bilhah gave birth to Dan. He did not boast the illustrious lineage of the sons of Leah and Rachel. He was the son of the maidservant, who, on the surface, married Jacob just to enable her mistress, Rachel, to 'compete' with her sister Leah.

Dan was born just after Judah was born to Leah. But it seems that there is a great distance between them: Judah marches at the forefront of the nation, while Dan is at the rear. Judah is the king and Dan is described as "the least of the tribes." But it is specifically for this reason that Dan merits something very straightforward. The people of Dan embody the character of the simple Jew, nothing more. Dan did not have illusions of grandeur. He did not have to fill a lofty role and therefore is not obliged to fulfill great expectations. As a result, he does not bear the complexes that sometimes characterize more important and wise people. Dan merits simple, robust mental health with which he can help his brothers find their way and their identity.

Dan knows how to make decisions when others may get confused by complex situations and arguments. The Talmud relates that when the sons of Jacob came to bury him in the Cave of Machpelah, Esau appeared and delayed the burial, claiming that the place in the Cave was reserved for him (since Jacob had already used up his allotted spot to bury Leah). The sons retorted that Jacob had bought Esau's plot from him years ago and that the deed was in Egypt. The quick-footed Naftali was dispatched to hasten back to Egypt to bring the deed, while everyone was forced to wait, while Jacob lay in shame. It truly was a painful and disgraceful situation.

Chushim, the son of Dan, was hard of hearing and could not hear the negotiations that had sent Naftali off to Egypt. All he understood was that Esau was keeping his grandfather's remains from being buried and that this was a shameful situation. So, he raised his sword and terminated the dispute with a blow to Esau's head.

I Hope, God, for Your Salvation

Jacob's affection for the tribe of Dan is also apparent in the blessing with which he blessed them before he died: "Dan will judge his nation, like the one of the tribes of Israel. Dan shall be [like] a snake on the path, a horned snake on the road, which bites the horse's heels, so that his rider falls backward. I hope, God, for Your salvation" (Genesis 49:16-18).

While giving Dan this blessing, Jacob saw Samson, the illustrious hero and judge from the tribe of Dan, smiting his enemies like a snake—all in his mind's eye. Jacob vicariously experienced Samson's last moments and his cry, "Remember me and strengthen me, just this time, *Elokim*, and I will take revenge of the Philistines for one of my two eyes" (Judges 16:28) and cried together with Samson, "I hope, God, for Your salvation" (Genesis ibid.)

The tribe of Dan has a special power to triumph. They 'finish the job' with one fell swoop. Samson bears a spark of the future, a messianic spark, passed on from Chushim, the son of Dan. In fact, the name Chushim is an anagram for Mashiach! Jacob also describes Dan as a "snake on the path." In *gematria*, "snake" also equals "Mashiach."

Before his death, Jacob attempts to see and reveal the time of the redemption to his sons. "Gather and I will tell you what will happen to you at the end of days." The end, however, was concealed from him. God's Essential Name, *Havayah*, is also not written in the Torah portions read during the month of Tevet about the descent of the small family of Israel to Egypt. But when Jacob blesses Dan, the light suddenly shines, a bright messianic light to illuminate the darkness of Egypt: "I hope, God (*Havayah*), for Your salvation." This is the one and only time that *Havayah* is mentioned in Tevet's Torah portions.

There is a special Aramaic expression in the Midrash (Vayikra rabba 24:3): "*Didan notzach* which means, "triumph is ours." This clearly alludes to Dan. The first word contains the name Dan, while the remaining 5 letters in the phrase, which equal 162 or 3 times 54, the value of "Dan". Thus the numerical value of the entire phrase, "*Didan notzach*" is equal to 4 times Dan. (In Chabad, the fifth day of Tevet is known as *Didan notzach*. This is the day that the Lubavitcher Rebbe won the so-called Book trial).

Mashiach of Chaos

Samson is a supernatural figure. He is considered one of Israel's judges and saviors. Everything about him is extraordinary, from his birth until his death. He always worked alone, literally like a snake. He has tremendous powers, but they are not always channeled to the right place. Samson's tremendous power is indeed messianic. It appears however in a wild form, unprocessed, irregular. Thus, it ultimately breaks.

In Kabbalistic terms, Samson is associated with the World of Chaos, which has 'many lights and few vessels." It is tremendous energy that makes an explosion for lack of a fitting vessel to contain it. The ultimate purpose is to achieve the World of Rectification, in which energies appear in an orderly and balanced fashion, with the inner light settling firmly into the fitting external vessel.

We do not, however, want to completely forgo the immense power of chaos. The path of Mashiach is described as, "the lights of chaos in rectified vessels." In other words, the tremendous power, like that of Samson, the "Mashiach of Chaos," within orderly vessels and parameters, which do not result in death and destruction, but rather, in creativity and life.

Proper Anger

The comparison of Dan to the snake expresses his attribute of anger. Anger is dangerous, and we must generally distance ourselves from it as if it were fire. It has the power of chaos and is not something to be played with. Dan's anger, however, is positive and fitting. He knows how to fight with Israel's sworn enemies, who do not understand any other language.

In Kabbalah, the sense of anger is the sense of the month of Tevet. The *gematria* (numerical value) of "Tevet" equals "chaos". We can conclude that the month of Tevet can be used to rectify the attribute of anger, which has the great power of chaos, and apply it in correct measure and in the proper situations.

Dan's real place in life is in the role of Judah's "right hand man." Despite the differences between the two, they have an interesting mode of cooperation. In the work of constructing the Tabernacle, the chief artisans were Betzalel from the tribe of Judah and Ohaliav from the tribe of Dan.

In Jacob's blessing, we see the same concept: "Dan will judge his nation, like the one among the tribes of Israel," referring to Judah, who is described as "the one," the most special, of the tribes. In his blessing to the tribes, Moses uses the same words for both Judah and Dan: "Dan is a lion cub," and "A lion cub is Judah." Finally, Kabbalah teaches that the Chief of Staff of Mashiach (who is from the tribe of Judah) will be from the tribe of Dan. Together, they are victorious—*Didan notzach*!

The History of Yiddish

Yiddish originated in Germany, but was eventually spoken by Jews all over Europe.

BY MORDECAI WALFISH

In its 1,000-plus-year history, the Yiddish language has been called many things, including the tender name *mameloshen* (mother tongue), the adversarial moniker zhargon (*jargon*) and the more matter-of-fact Judeo-German.

What is Yiddish?

Literally speaking, Yiddish means "Jewish." Linguistically, it refers to the language spoken by Ashkenazi Jews — Jews from Central and Eastern Europe, and their descendants. Though its basic vocabulary and grammar are derived from medieval West German, Yiddish integrates many languages including German, Hebrew, Aramaic and various Slavic and Romance languages.

The Origin of Yiddish

It is impossible to pin down exactly where or when Yiddish emerged, but the most widely-accepted theory is that the language came into formation in the 10th century, when Jews from France and Italy began to migrate to the German Rhine Valley. There, they combined the languages they brought with them, together with their new neighbors' Germanic, producing the earliest form of Yiddish. As Jews continued to migrate eastward –a result of the Crusades and the Black Plague–Yiddish spread across Central and Eastern Europe and began to include more elements from Slavic languages.

Early Yiddish

In Ashkenazi societies, Hebrew was the language of the Bible and prayer, Aramaic was the language of learning and Yiddish was the language of everyday life. Scholars refer to this as the internal trilingualism of Ashkenaz. Though they vary in sound and use, all three languages are written in the same alphabet.

The first record of a printed Yiddish sentence is a blessing found in the Worms Mahzor (*Vórmser mákhzer*) from 1272. Beginning in the 14th century Yiddish was commonly used for epic poems such as the *Shmuel-bukh*, which reworks the biblical story of the prophet Samuel into a European knightly romance.

Early Modern Yiddish

Yiddish publishing became widespread in the 1540s, nearly a century after the invention of the printing press. To ensure the broadest possible readership, books were published in a generic, accessible Yiddish, without the characteristics of any particular Yiddish dialect. In the 1590s, the Tsene-rene (also called *Tzenah Urenah*) was published for the first time (eventually, more than 200 editions were printed). The book, which retells the weekly Torah portions woven together with homiletic and moralistic material, became known as "the women's Bible," because it was read in particular by women on the Sabbath and Holidays.

By the 18th century, German-speaking Jews were quickly acculturating. In Western Europe, leaders of the Haskalah (the Jewish Enlightenment) campaigned heavily for the use of German over Yiddish, which they referred to as "barbaric jargon." At the same time, Yiddish was flourishing in Eastern Europe, where compact settlement helped the number of speakers reach the millions by the 19th century.

The rise of the Hasidic movement also did much to further Yiddish along — in both numbers of speakers and spiritual prestige. Two of the key early works of Hasidism were written in both Yiddish and Hebrew: *Shivkhey ha-Besht* (Praises of the Besht), which were stories about the Ba'al Shem Tov, and *Sipurey Mayses* (Telling of the Tales), a collection of stories from the Ba'al Shem Tov's great-grandson Nahman of Breslov.

Modern Yiddish

The late 19th century saw the birth of modern Yiddish literature. The "grandfather" of this new literary movement was Sholem Yankev Abramovitsh, known by his pen name Mendele Mokher Seforim (Mendele the Bookseller). I. L. Peretz, a Polish writer, poet, essayist, and dramatist became known as the "father" and humorist Sholem Aleichem, born in Ukraine, the "grandson." The realism, irreverence, satire and moralism found in the works of these three writers heavily influenced the development of Yiddish literature.

Yiddish in the 20th Century

In 1908, the first international conference on Yiddish language (the Czernowitz conference) declared Yiddish to be "a national language of the Jewish people." The purpose of the conference was to discuss all the issues facing the language at that time, including the need to establish Yiddish schools, to fund Yiddish cultural institutions and to establish standard Yiddish spelling. However, these agenda items received little attention, with much of the debate being focused on whether Yiddish should be considered the national language or a national language of the Jewish people. In 1925, YIVO, the Yiddish Scientific Institute, was founded in Vilna. It became the premiere institution for Yiddish scholarship and has been based in New York since 1940.

In the early days of the Soviet Union (1922 until the mid-1930s), the communist government supported Yiddish schools, theater, research and literature — as long as these were strictly cultural expressions without Jewish religious content. The extraordinary support given to Yiddish, and the respect initially shown to Yiddish writers, led many around the world to see the Soviet project as the true hope for the future of the language. However, the government soon began to censor Yiddish works, and eventually closed down most Yiddish institutions. During the purges of 1937, many Yiddish writers and leaders were arrested and executed at the increasingly paranoid orders of Joseph Stalin, who viewed Yiddish as anti-Soviet. In 1952, the remaining great Yiddish writers in the Soviet Union were brutally murdered in what is known today as the Night of the Murdered Poets (though not all of those executed were writers).

In pre-state Israel (1918-1948), and later in Israel, Yiddish was marginalized and, in some instances, outlawed. Until 1951, it was illegal for local theater groups to stage productions in Yiddish. Hebrew was the national language of the Jews in their land, and was considered the only legitimate medium of Jewish expression.

Post-Holocaust Yiddish

On the eve of World War II, there were roughly 13 million Yiddish speakers in the world.

The Holocaust destroyed most of this population. In America after the war, immigrant parents were often hesitant to speak Yiddish with their children. Though there were a few networks of Yiddish schools in the post-war period, after-school programs and camps could not compete with the intense pressures of Americanization. Yiddish began to take on a lowbrow image, and its use was associated with failure to climb up the American socioeconomic ladder of success.

But the last half century brought many positive developments for Yiddish. It has been seriously studied as an academic discipline, and Yiddish literature has been recognized as great world literature, exemplified by Isaac Bashevis Singer receiving the Nobel Prize for Literature in 1978.

The 1970s saw the beginning of a Yiddish and Eastern European cultural revival, particularly in music. Thanks to the work of highly-talented artists, at the forefront of which are groups like The Klezmatics, klezmer music is now a ubiquitous presence in American Jewish culture.

The Story of "Oy Vey"

Half Hebrew, half Aramaic, this classic lament is all Jewish.

BY MY JEWISH LEARNING

Oy vey! — also: Oy vavoy! Oy vey iz mir! Oy gevalt! Or quite simply: Oy! — is an iconic Jewish expression that conveys the weariness of a people overly familiar with hardship and oppression, as well as the resilience of a people that finds hope and sometimes even humor in catastrophe. It's both heavy and light. It's tragic and funny. It's so much better with a thick Yiddish accent. But where did it come from?

The word "oy" goes back thousands of years, all the way to the Hebrew Bible. In that classical biblical mode, there is nothing funny about it — "oy" is simply an expression of anguish, and may well be etymologically related to that English word "woe." Of all the biblical authors, the prophet Jeremiah uses it the most, a total of eight times. (Not for nothing has his name become synonymous with lament — giving us the English word "jeremiad.")

A few examples will give a sense of the way this word was originally used. In the Bible, "oy" can be wielded as a curse or at least a poetic barb thrown at one's enemies. For example:

Oy to you, O Moab!

You are undone, O people of Chemosh!

Numbers 21:29

Today we think of "oy" as a Jewish exclamation, but in the Bible it is used by all peoples. Another sworn Israelite enemy, the Philistines, have this to say when they realize that the Ark of the Covenant is back on the battlefield, protecting the armies of Israel:

Oy to us! Nothing like this has ever happened before.

1 Samuel 4:7

As with many onomatopoeic words, oy has variations — including in the Bible itself. Consider this line from Proverbs:

Who cries "oy!" and who "avoy!"?

Proverbs 23:29

Here, "oy" and "avoy" sound similar and clearly mean the same thing. Other variations of "oy" appear in Aramaic, a language closely related to Hebrew that was the lingua franca of Jews for many centuries in antiquity (and is also the language of the Talmud). So, for instance, the Talmud's Aramaic version of "oy" is the word "vay"— which may well give us the "vey" in "oy vey." As we saw from Proverbs, doubling the expression of woe was common even in biblical times.

Although "oy" seems to have been a nearly universal expression of lament, today the expression "oy vey" comes to us in English through Yiddish, where it feels very much a part of the Jewish character of that language. It is perhaps for this reason that Merriam Webster's dictionary traces "vey" not to the Armaic "vay" as suggested above, but to the Middle High German wē — which also means "woe."

Yiddish also gives us all the resonant variations of this lament, most notably oy vey iz mir ("woe to me!") and oy gevalt ("woe! violence!"). This last variant might seem the most disturbing, but it is usually the one used in the most comical way, employed to ruefully bemoan surprise disasters, such as: "He wore that? Oy gevalt!"

According to the Oxford English Dictionary, "oy vey" entered English usage in the 19th century, when the word was more commonly spelled "oi" before the more contemporary "oy" took over in the 20th century. In English, it exists alongside similar expressions of different origin — including a Scottish "oy" that means "grandchild" and an "oy" that is a variant of "hoy" and "ahoy," words used to call someone's attention.

According to an analysis run through Google Books, the word "oy" has been in steady decline in English since the 1980s. Nonetheless, "oy" and "oy vey" continue to be some of the most resonant and recognizable Jewish expressions. This was on literal display with Deborah Kass's devilishly simple bright yellow aluminum sculpture of the word. One side reads "OY" in capital letters, and the reverse side reads "YO," the Spanish word for "I" and also an English slang term that not only mirrors the original word but is nearly opposite in tone. Kass has explained that she loves the way these two letters, read in either direction, resonate in so many languages. Funnily enough, the English slang "yo" is pretty close to that older English "ahoy" that was also sometimes shortened to "oy."

What Does "Maccabee" Mean?

By Yehuda Shurpin

The word Maccabee has become synonymous with the small band of Jewish freedom fighters who freed Judea from the Syrian-Greek occupiers during the Chanukah saga in the Second Temple period. This originally applied only to Judah, who led the group following the death of his father, Matityahu, and is referred to in early writings as "Judah Maccabee" (Judas Maccabeus in Greek).1 What does it mean?

"Who Is Like Gd?"

Perhaps the best known explanation is that the word "Maccabee" is composed of the initial letters of a verse the Jewish people sang after Gd split the sea: "Mi kamocha ba'eilim Hashem , "Who is like You among the mighty, O Gd."2

It is said that this phrase was the battle cry of Maccabees, written upon their banners and shields.3

Mighty or Hammer

Some explain that the word "Maccabee" is related to the Greek word meaning "strong" or "fighter."4

Others explain that it comes from the Hebrew word for "hammer," makav, either because Judah was the "hammer of Gd," his features somewhat resembled that of a hammer, or because his earlier occupation was that of a blacksmith.

Extinguisher

Some suggest that it comes from the word Hebrew word mekabeh, which means "to extinguish." The Maccabees endeavored to snuff outthe fire of the Greeks, which spread death and desolation throughout the land of Israel.

Matityahu the Priest

The father and patriarch of the family was Matityahu the Kohen ("Priest"). Thus, some explain that the word Maccabee was actually an acronym for the the initial letters of his name, Matityahu Kohen Ben (son of) Yochanan.5

"Gd's Glory"

Rabbi Yeshaya Halevi Horowitz, known as the Shelah, writes that the word can be unscrambled to form an acronym for the words in Ezekiel: Baruch Kevod Hashem Mimkomo , "Blessed is the glory of the Lrd from His place."6

He explains this in the context of the sages' statement that "whomever disputes the reign of the House of David, it is as if he has a dispute against the Divine Presence." The Maccabees had sinned because they took the kingdom for themselves, even though they were not of Davidic stock. Nevertheless, they were called Maccabees, an allusion to the verse "Blessed is the glory of the Lrd from His place," implying that they didn't cause any blemish in the Divine Presence, since the original intention of Judah and his siblings was for the sake of heaven.7

Bringing Gdliness into the World

The mystics explain that the word Maccabee has the numerical value of 72 , alluding to the 72-letter Divine Name.

The Chassidic masters further explain that both verses connected with "Maccabee" denote drawing Gd's presence into the world. "Who is like You among the mighty, O Gd" refers to Gd as both "mighty" and "Gd." The first term implies the restraint needed to create a reality devoid of His overt presence. The latter represents the revelation of His presence. Placing the two words together represents a merging of the two dynamics.

"Blessed is the glory of the Lrd from His place" has a similar theme. The Hebrew word for "blessed" also means to "draw down." Thus, we are drawing His presence from "His place," a state of hiddenness, into our reality.

And that's ultimately what Chanukah is all about—bringing light and holiness into the darkness, a process that will be completed with the coming of Moshiach. May it be speedily in our days!

Lighting Shabbat Candles

Everything you need to know about kindling the Sabbath lights.

BY MY JEWISH LEARNING

Shabbat is ushered in every Friday night with the lighting of Sabbath candles, referred to in Yiddish as *licht bentschen*. In this article, we'll answer practical questions about candle-lighting, look at the origin of the custom and give you all the information you need (including a video tutorial) to confidently light your Shabbat candles.

When are the candles lit?

It is traditional to light the Shabbat candles during the 18 minute window right before sundown on Friday, which marks the beginning of Shabbat. Some cities have a tradition of offering a larger window for candle-lighting, most notably Jerusalem whose window begins 40 minutes before sundown. (In Jerusalem, a siren that can be heard throughout the city is blown at this time on late Friday afternoon to alert citizens that candle-lighting time is upon them.) The earliest one may light Shabbat candles is 75 minutes before sundown.

After sundown, whether candles have been lit or not, Shabbat has begun and one may not kindle a flame. The timing of this window of course varies from location to location and throughout the year. There are many online tools to look up the Shabbat candle-lighting time in your area this week.

Are any candles acceptable?

Shabbat candles must burn at least until you recite Hamotzi, the blessing over bread, and some sources say that they should burn for two to three hours. For this reason, birthday candles and Hanukkah candles, which burn down quickly, are not recommended. There are specially-made Shabbat candles that will fit in a regular-sized taper holder but are shorter than taper candles (and therefore will not burn all night), but a regular tea light will also work perfectly well. Many people choose neronim, candles in glass cups, that look especially beautiful and are a way to perform *hiddur mitzvah*, beautifying the commandment of lighting Shabbat candles. For the same reason, if you have a beautiful pair of candlesticks, this the time to use them. It is customary to light white candles, though this is not a hard and fast rule.

How many candles?

It is traditional to light a minimum of two candles in each household. Indeed, the pair of Shabbat candles is one of the most iconic images of the Holiday. Many reasons are given for the number two. Some say that it indicates the candles are special — holding a purpose one candle alone cannot. Some say that it represents the two instances of the commandment of keeping Shabbat given in the Torah, one found in Exodus 20:8 that says "*Zachor* (remember) the Sabbath," and one found in Deuteronomy 5:12 that says "*Shamor* (keep) the Sabbath." Others hold that the number two underlies the two major themes of Shabbat: creation and revelation.

However, many households have a tradition of lighting more candles, often one for each member of the household.

Who lights the candles?

Traditionally, lighting Shabbat candles was the obligation of the woman of the household. In households with no adult woman, a man would take over the responsibility. In many contemporary egalitarian families, lighting candles may be done by any adult in the house — and it is often done by the family all together.

Should I blow out the candles before I go to bed?

No, Shabbat candles should not be extinguished but allowed to burn all the way down. If you anticipate that your candles will still be burning by the time you are ready to hit the hay, it is especially important to light them in a safe place, far from any paper, textiles or other flammable items. It is traditional not to move the candles after they are lit.

What is the origin of the candle-lighting?

The Torah says nothing about lighting candles to welcome Shabbat; the practice first appears in rabbinic literature. It seems to have originated as an extension of the practice of lighting a flame before Shabbat precisely because flames may not be kindled on the Sabbath. This flame was a source of light after the sun went down. However, the Shabbat candles evolved into an important part of the ritual and it became forbidden to use them for any practical purpose, including as light to read by (this is why some people do not move the candles after they are lit — to avoid the temptation of using them for some practical purpose).

The Talmud records that lighting Shabbat candles is a mitzvah, a commandment, but does not record a blessing attached to them. The first recorded instance of a blessing said for lighting the Shabbat candles is found in the Siddur of Rav Amram (9th c.), and it is the blessing we say today, apparently modeled on the blessing for lighting Hanukkah candles.

How do you light Shabbat candles?

Normally, in Jewish tradition, blessings are said before the act. We say Kiddush before drinking wine and Hamotzi before eating bread. However, because saying the blessing over the candles brings in Shabbat, and candles may not be lit on Shabbat, the order is in this case reversed: candles are lit first, and the blessing is recited afterward.

Instructions: First, light the candles. Then, many people wave their hands around the flame three times and then bring their hands over their eyes, keeping their eyes covered while they recite the blessing. Then, they open their eyes and experience the candles anew after the blessing is said (a substitute for the fact that the candles cannot actually be lit after the blessing is recited).

The Blessing:

Barukh atah Adonai Eloheinu melekh ha'olam asher kid'shanu b'mitzvotav v'tzivanu l'hadlik ner shel Shabbat.

Blessed are You, Lord our God, Ruler of the Universe, who has sanctified us with commandments, and commanded us to light Shabbat candles.

The Hanukkah Story

The Maccabean revolt and the miracle of the oil.

BY LESLI KOPPELMAN ROSS

In 168 BCE, the ruler of the Syrian kingdom, Antiochus Epiphanes IV, stepped up his campaign to quash Judaism, so that all subjects in his vast empire — which included the Land of Israel — would share the same culture and worship the same gods.

Note: *There is some dispute about the exact dates of the Maccabean revolt and its various battles. The dates in this article differ from sources consulted in creating the map below.*

He marched into Jerusalem, vandalized the Temple, erected an idol on the altar, and desecrated its holiness with the blood of swine. Decreeing that studying Torah, observing the Sabbath, and circumcising Jewish boys were punishable by death, he sent Syrian overseers and soldiers to villages throughout Judea to enforce the edicts and force Jews to engage in idol worship.

When the Syrian soldiers reached Modin (about 12 miles northwest of the capital), they demanded that the local leader, Mattathias the Kohein (a member of the priestly class), be an example to his people by sacrificing a pig on a portable pagan altar. The elder refused and killed not only the Jew who stepped forward to do the Syrian's bidding, but also the king's representative.

With the rallying cry "Whoever is for God, follow me!" Mattathias and his five sons (Jonathan, Simon, Judah, Eleazar, and Yohanan) fled to the hills and caves of the wooded Judean wilderness.

Joined by a ragtag army of others like them, simple farmers dedicated to the laws of Moses, armed only with spears, bows and arrows, and rocks from the terrain, the Maccabees, as Mattathias' sons, particularly Judah, came to be known, fought a guerrilla war against the well-trained, well-equipped, seemingly endless forces of the mercenary Syrian army.

In three years, the Maccabees cleared the way back to the Temple Mount, which they reclaimed. They cleaned the Temple and dismantled the defiled altar and constructed a new one in its place. Three years to the day after Antiochus' mad rampage (*Kislev* 25, 165 BCE), the Maccabees held a dedication (*hanukkah*) of the Temple with proper sacrifice, rekindling of the golden menorah, and eight days of celebration and praise to God. [Proper] Jewish worship had been reestablished.

Perhaps the most famous part of the story is what happened next: a tiny jar of oil kept the candles burning for the full eight days. However, this detail does not appear in any Jewish texts until 600 years later in the Talmud, mentioned in a larger discussion of why Hanukkah observance is so important.

Reprinted with permission from Celebrate! The Complete Jewish Holiday Handbook

Bereishit: The World Needs a King

The Torah opens with the word "*Bereishit*" (In the beginning) but doesn't tell us in the beginning of what. There are commentaries that write that this is an abbreviated form, because it is clear that the Torah is referring to the beginning of time. Another approach is to look at how this word is used elsewhere in the Bible.

As it turns out, the word '*Bereishit*' appears another four times in the Bible, and in each case, it refers to sovereignty (or, kingdom), specifically, to the beginning of the reign of a king: "In the beginning of the reigns of Yehoyakim," "In the beginning of the reign of Yehoyakim," "In the beginning of the kingdom of Tzidkiyah," "In the beginning of the reign of Tzidkiyah." It is fitting to say that the opening verse of the Torah, "In the beginning," is also referring to the beginning of kingdom, '*malchut*' in Hebrew.

Kabbalah teaches that malchut is the root of time and the ultimate goal of creation is to make God king. The world that had just been created was in a chaotic and unstable state. The threat of collapse and chaos hovering over the world portended the danger of disintegration. The law of entropy threatens to slowly break up the foundations of the world so that over time, from generation to generation, reality degenerates and returns to chaos.

In order to prevent that degeneration, the world needs a king, whose first role is to support and gather the people– and stop the disintegration into tribes and individuals.

The essential need for a king to prevent reality from degenerating is at the very opening of the Torah. Based upon this, the Zohar teaches that the rectification of the nation is contingent upon the king. A society that does not have a worthy king at its head – even if it is comprised of completely righteous people – will eventually degenerate and fail.

The void at the center of society – at the point that unites the people around it – must be filled by a leader. When a worthy leader does not step up, "the other side," i.e., the negative, fills the void. Then it is not a king who leads the nation, but rather, a person who is motivated by his craving for control. He conducts himself according to opinion polls and public trends (as the sages said, that before Mashiach comes, "the face of the generation will be like the face of a dog." The metaphor means to say that just as dog runs before his master, as if he was the leader, but when they reach a junction, he waits to see which way the chariot will turn, and then again takes his place at the head of the entourage), so the leaders will not really lead the people but constantly look back to see what "public opinion" says, and then make their next decision. An unworthy leader like this does not prevent the degeneration of the nation. Instead, he attempts to get along with everyone and rule the nation by juggling between the different interest groups. This lack of leadership combined with the lust for control compromises the leader's ability to act solely for the good of the nation. It even creates situations in which he will endanger the nation in order to preserve his control, exposing the nation to precarious situations. In this state, even if all the individuals of the nation will attempt to work on their individual rectification, there is no chance for the people as a whole (and thus, not for the individuals, either) to achieve rectification and stability.

As long as the Nation of Israel (for whom the world was created, "for Israel, are also called '*reishit*' – the beginning" does not produce a just king who conducts the nation according to the Torah (for which the world was created – "for the Torah that is also called '*reishit*' – the beginning there is no chance for the rectification of the nation, and thus, no chance for the rectification of the entire world.

Chassidut teaches that one of the reasons for creating the world, is God's will to manifest His kingship. As the sages say, "there cannot be a king if there are no people." Conversely, just as "there cannot be a king if there are no people," so "there cannot be a people if there is no king." The essence of the nation is in the fact that it accepts the rule of the king. Thus, when the Nation of Israel is not rectified, when there is not the stable reality of a united nation that relies on the king, then there is no one to properly take upon himself the yoke of the kingdom of Heaven, and thus, the ultimate purpose of the creation of the world – so that God will have a nation to rule over – is not realized.

Judgement and Compassion

When contemplating the rectification of the kingdom, we must consider the essence of the worthy king and his personality. The world needs kingdom and a regime in order to maintain reality. But the kingdom itself is contingent on the king. The king is the head of the nation and his persona brings about the rectification of the kingdom, the nation and all reality. At the beginning, the King upon whom all of reality is contingent is God. The rectified king must be like his Creator, as He appears at the beginning of creation [for the entire kingship of the rectified king stems from the kingdom of God and draws it down into reality, as the Zohar says of the mitzvah to appoint a king: "Appoint, you shall appoint a king over you": The first "appoint" refers to Above (making God king). The second "[you shall] appoint" refers to below (appointing a human king).

The Torah describes God's "personality" and His conduct in the first story of creation, referring to Him as *Elokim*, the Divine Name of judgement, while in the second story of creation, the Torah refers to God as *Havayah Elokim*, in which the Divine Name of compassion precedes the Name of judgment. Based on this, the sages say that, "Initially God thought to create the world with the trait of judgment, and saw that the world would not be able to exist, so He prefaced it with the trait of compassion and partnered it with the trait of judgment."

It is explained in Kabbalah and Chassidut that the construction and rectification of all the traits of the heart [from *chessed* (lovingkindness) to *malchut* (kingdom)] begins with the right axis, with loving-kindness, while only the construction of kingdom and its rectification begin with the left axis, with judgment (or might, as it is usually called).

The rectification of the traits of the heart is the core ingredient in the internal rectification of every individual. It prefaces the rectification of external reality and is a prerequisite for the ability to rectify others. In this rectification of the heart, loving-kindness comes first. Despite the fact that when we are motivated to rectify a situation, thoughts of judgment come first – the assumption that it is necessary to rectify the individual with assertiveness and criticism – in actual practice, the rectification of the individual must begin with love and positivity. By contrast, the rectification of the kingdom, the rectification of reality in general and a political body like a state, in particular, must begin with might and assertiveness: "A king uses justice to establish a country."

Kingdom is based on definition of borders, on order and on discipline. The foundation of all the above is judgement. These traits are necessary for internal leadership of a state, but are even more necessary when the kingdom faces its external enemies. Kingdom is established in order to unite the nation and to safeguard it from evil. The king must be brave and very assertive against the enemies of his nation. (In the Bible we see that the request for a king and his actual appointment is always connected to the need to fight Israel's enemies and to the king's success at doing so).

It is only after the construction of the kingdom from judgment, after the king has established himself with the proper might and assertiveness, that the objective for which the kingdom was established: benefit and kindness for the nation – can be actualized. (The goodness that the king showers upon his nation, the nation of Israel, overflows to all the nations of the world). After the kingdom is built with might, it becomes a vessel to draw down loving-kindness – when the king manifests his great compassion over his people.

The king for whom we hope and yearn in our generation – the king Mashiach – reaches the summit of unification between judgment and compassion. The King Mashiach is described as, "*chadrach*" because he is "*chad*" (sharp) toward the nations of the world and afterwards "*rach*" (soft) toward Israel. Moreover, just as with the king, the might precedes the loving-kindness – and the Divine Name of judgement, *Elokim* precedes the Name of loving-kindness, *Havayah*, in the account of creation – so it is in history. In the first generations, the kingdom of Israel was founded principally on might. But the last king, the King Mashiach, turns much more toward loving-kindness so that his judgements are sweetened from the very start. His action to, "compel all of Israel to walk in its ways (of the Torah) and to rectify its breaches in observance... and fight the wars of God" will be accomplished with pleasantness and light that will repulse the darkness.

How to Pray for Happiness

The prayer Eilu Devarim reflects the seeming paradox that focusing on others more than ourselves makes us happier.

BY RABBI EVAN MOFFIC

Should we pray for happiness? On the face it, of course we should. Who doesn't want to be happy?

But something about word "happiness" strikes Jews in the wrong way. There's the old joke about the Jewish telegram: "Start worrying… details to follow." Our default is often guilt rather than happiness. It is as if we have been programmed to see anxiety around every corner, to be more comfortable in the familiar "oy" over the risky "joy."

Happiness is also an odd English word. It comes from the Middle English hap, as in happenstance and haphazard. This origin suggests that a happy life is a result of randomness and luck. Prayer has nothing to do with it.

In our consumerist culture, happiness is also frequently confused with pleasure, and praying for pleasure can feel self-indulgent. But happiness and pleasure are different.

Pleasure is short-term, like getting a massage or eating a sumptuous meal. Happiness is long-lasting. It is flourishing, which is a word preferred by the founder of the scientific study of happiness, Professor Martin Seligman. According to Seligman, flourishing contains five key components: positive emotion, engagement, relationship, meaning, and accomplishment. An easy way to remember them is the acronym PERMA.

The Jewish happiness prayer, as we will see below, promotes flourishing. It is the happiness experienced through a life of meaning and purpose.

What is the happiness prayer? It is a series of verses from the Mishnah we recite as part of the morning worship service. It is found in many prayer books as part of the traditional series of morning blessings.

The prayer begins with the words Eilu Devarim ("These are the Words"). The Hebrew word devarim also means actions or deeds. So the happiness prayer is a series of words describing actions that promote happiness.

The prayer contains ten actions in total, which I have translated as follows:

These are the deeds with infinite benefits.

A person enjoys their fruit in this world,

and in the world to come. Guide me in embracing these sacred practices:

Honor those who gave me life

Practice kindness

Learn Constantly

Invite others into my home

Be there when others need me

Celebrate life's sacred moments

Support others during times of loss

Pray with intention

Forgive those who hurt me and seek forgiveness where I have others

Commit to constant growth.

This translation is not literal. For a few of the practices, I chose to convey the value expressed in the specific practice itself. For example, the Hebrew phrase that literally means "provide for a bride" I have rendered as "celebrating life's sacred moments." Providing for a bride reflects the importance of marking sacred moments with ritual, and these moments are not limited to weddings. Today they include anniversaries, baby namings, even graduations. Finding ways to participate in and create communal celebrations around those life events makes us happier.

The academic discipline of positive psychology has reinforced the message of the happiness prayer. Indeed, even though the rabbis who wrote this prayer were not familiar with positive psychology, their teachings intuit it. The actions this prayer calls upon us to take fit squarely within the PERMA framework noted earlier.

For example, celebrating life's sacred moments incorporates positive emotions, relationships, and meaning. Praying with intention is a act of engagement, and prayer itself encompasses a worldview that life has meaning. Knowing how to pray — the words, the rhythm, the melodies — gives us a feeling of accomplishment. When we look at the Eilu Devarim prayer as a guide to happiness, we can see each of its practices as an expression of some aspect of PERMA.

Saying the prayer also promotes happiness in other ways. First, it pushes us outside of ourselves. Almost all of the ten practices involve other people. Inviting others into our lives, practicing kindness, and comforting mourners, are just the most direct examples. The rabbis understood the seeming paradox that focusing on others more than ourselves makes us happier. As Victor Frankl put, "the door to happiness opens outward."

Frankl's observation helps us see a second source of happiness in this prayer. It roots us in a religious worldview. Its opening verses remind us that we are reading more than a list of good deeds. They are a series of practices that echo through eternity. We feel their effects in this world and in the world to come.

Put differently, embracing a religious worldview makes us happier. We can speculate on why this is true. But I suspect part of the reason is that faith is a mindset that pushes us — in some cases, even obliges us — to do things that may not feel great in the short term, but that enhance our lives in the long term. These are the things we do that we can look back on a year later and feel happy to have done.

Every year, I fast on Yom Kippur, the Jewish Day of Atonement. To do so is a commandment found in the Torah and has been a Jewish tradition for more than 4,000 years. Since I am working all day — delivering sermons and leading my congregation in eight hours of prayer — fasting is the last thing I want to do. Yet it enhances my experience of the day and my connection to others. It does not feel pleasurable in the moment. But when I look back, I know I experienced the power of the day.

This is the kind of commitment faith has always nurtured, and ignoring the role of faith in the search for happiness is like going to search for a treasure and throwing away an old map leading directly to it. The Eilu Devarim prayer is such a map. May it guide us on our journey.

Rabbi Evan Moffic is the spiritual leader of Congregation Solel in Highland Park, IL. He is the author of the "The Happiness Prayer: Ancient Jewish Wisdom for the Best Way to Live Today."

What is Sigd?

An Ethiopian Jewish Holiday held 50 days after Yom Kippur.

BY MY JEWISH LEARNING

Sigd is an Ethiopian Jewish Holiday celebrated on the 29th of Cheshvan, exactly 50 days after Yom Kippur.

When is Sigd 2021?

The Ethiopian Jewish community lived in complete isolation from other Jewish communities for many centuries, until the mid-20th century when many Ethiopians were air-lifted to Israel. For this reason, the Ethiopian Jewish community, called the Beta Israel, developed many Holidays and celebrations that do not exist in other Jewish communities.

The name "*Sigd*" means "prostration" in Ge'ez, an ancient Ethiopian liturgical language, but it is related to the word sged (same meaning) in Aramaic, one of the languages of the Talmud.

Sigd is about accepting the Torah and yearning for Israel and the Temple. It is thought to be the date on which God first revealed himself to Moses.

Traditionally, members of the Beta Israel community fast on Sigd, read from their scriptures (which are called the Octateuch, the five books of Moses plus Joshua, Judges and Ruth), recite psalms, and pray for the rebuilding of the Temple. It is also a time for renewing the Israelite covenant with God. The fast ends mid-day with a feast and dancing. For this reason, though it is connected to Yom Kippur, it shares many resonances with Shavuot.

Since 2008, Sigd has been recognized as a state Holiday in Israel. In Israel today, it is celebrated for an entire month leading up to the 29th of Cheshvan, and it is an opportunity to raise Ethiopian Jewish visibility and educate Israeli Jews about Beta Israel customs.

Tzom Gedaliah

The history and observance of this minor fast day right after Rosh Hashanah.

BY DANIEL KIRSCH

The Fast of Gedaliah is a day set aside to commemorate the assassination of Gedaliah, the Babylonian-appointed official charged with administering the Jewish population remaining in Judah following the destruction of the Temple and exile in 586 B.C.E. It is observed on the third of Tishrei (the day after Rosh Hashanah) with a fast from sunrise to sundown, and like on other fast days, the recital of special prayers ("Anenu") and the reading of selected biblical readings (Exodus 32:14; 34:1-10). In years when Rosh Hashanah begins on Thursday, the fast is postponed until Sunday, as fasts other than Yom Kippur are not permitted on Shabbat.

Remembering Gedaliah

The earliest commemoration of Gedaliah's death might be said to have occurred immediately after his assassination, with the pilgrimage of those who had come to mourn him only to be stricken down by Ishmael.

We next hear of this as a day of mourning connected with three other fast days in the Book of Zechariah. In an oracle dating to the end of the sixth century B.C.E. in Zechariah 7-8, we find a group coming to the prophet to ask whether it is still necessary to solemnly commemorate the destruction of the Temple now that the people have been permitted to return to their homeland and rebuild the Temple. In an extended response that never directly answers the question, but does assure them that God has plans for their future prosperity, Zechariah informs them that these four Holidays will one day be celebrated with joy and gladness. Perhaps Zechariah's response was intended to mean that these solemn commemorations were still necessary, but would not be so forever.

It should also be noted that Zechariah makes reference to four fast days associated with the demise of Judah (Zechariah 8:19), but he is only asked about one fast, the one commemorating the destruction of the Temple (Zechariah 7:3). In his response, Zechariah refers to all four fast days. This may suggest that not all Jews observed the other three fast days.

The next reference to the Fast of Gedaliah comes in the Babylonian Talmud. In Tractate Rosh Hashanah 18b, the rabbis assign the third day of Tishrei as the date the Fast of Gedaliah is to be observed; the biblical text (Zechariah 7:5; 8:19) simply refers to the month of its observance but not the date. The rabbis add that the fact that a fast day is designated to commemorate Gedaliah's death suggests that the death of a righteous man was just as tragic as the burning of the Temple.

A Guide to Jewish Acronyms and Abbreviations

Common Hebrew (and Aramaic) shorthand translated and explained.

BY MY JEWISH LEARNING

For centuries before text-messaging and emailing birthed ubiquitous linguistic shorthand terms like LOL, TTYL and IMHO, Jews were not just the People of the Book, but the People of the Acronym.

Acronyms — in Hebrew, Aramaic and transliteration — appear frequently in Jewish correspondence, books, spoken conversation and even on gravestones. Famous rabbis are frequently referred to by their acronyms. Even books themselves, like the Hebrew Bible are often identified in this abbreviated manner.

Modern Hebrew has its own ever-growing roster of acronyms, such as its FBI equivalent, *Shabak*, also known as the *Shin Bet*. (Stands for for *Sherut Habitakhon Haklali*, or General Security Service.)

Below are some of the most common acronyms and abbreviations organized alphabetically (in English transliteration) by category. If no English initials appear, that means English initials aren't used for this term. Did we miss an important one? Leave it in the comments below or email us at community@myjewishlearning.org.

General Acronyms and Abbreviations

A"H

Stands for: *alav hashalom, aleha hashalom or aleihem hashalom*

Pronounced: ah-LAHV hah-shah-LOHM, ah-lay-HAH hah-shah-LOHM

What it means: Hebrew for "peace be upon him." Alternately "upon her" or "upon them."

When it's used: Following the name of someone who is dead.

BD"E

Stands for: *Baruch dayan emet*

Pronounced: bah-ROOKH dah-YAHN eh-METT

What it means: Hebrew for "blessed is the true judge."

When it's used: Commonly said to a mourner upon learning of their loss.

B"H

Stands for: *B'ezrat hashem*

Pronounced: b'ez-RAHT hah-SHEM.

What it means: Hebrew for "with God's help."

Note: This acronym also stands for Baruch HaShem or Blessed is God.

BS"D

Stands for: *B'siyata dishmaya*

Pronounced: bah-SAHD.

What it means: Aramaic for "with the help of Heaven."

When it's used: Some traditional Jews put these letters on the upper corner of every piece of written material.

IY"H

Stands for: *Im yirtzeh hashem*

Pronounced: eem yeer-TZEH hah-SHEM

What it means: Hebrew for "if it will be God's will" or "if it is God's will."

N"Y

Stands for: *Nehro or nehrah yair*

Pronounced: noon yood (the two Hebrew letters), orvneh-ee-ROH yah-EER (for a man), neh-ee-RAH yah-EER (for a woman)

What it means: Hebrew for "his/her candle should burn bright."

When it's used: When writing a letter to someone who is alive. As in, "Dear David N"Y, How are you?…."

Shlita

Stands for: *Sh'yichyeh l'orekh yamim tovim amen*

Pronounced: SHLEE-tuh

What it means: May he (or she) live for many good days, Amen.

When it's used: Often said after the name of a prominent living rabbi.

Shotz

Stands for: *Shaliach tzibur*

Pronounced: SHAHTZ or shah-LEE-ahkh tzee-BOHR

What it means: Hebrew for the person leading a prayer service (literally "public emissary").

Tanach

Stands for: *Torah, Nevi'im, Ketuvim* — known in English as Torah (also Five Books of Moses), Prophets and Writings

Pronounced: tah-NAKH

What it means: The Hebrew Bible, which Christians refer to as the Old Testament.

Z"L

Stands for: *Zichrono* [for a man] or *zichrona* [for a woman] *l'bracha*

Pronounced: zahl, or zee-chroh-NOH luh-brah-KHAH or zee-chroh-NAH luh-brah-KHAH

What it means: Hebrew literally for "memories for blessing," usually translated to "may his or her memory be a blessing."

When it's used: Usually appears in parentheses after the name of a person who is deceased.

On Gravestones and in Cemeteries

N"E

Stands for: *Nucha* [for a woman] or *nucho* [for a man] *eden*

Pronounced: noon ayin (the names of these two Hebrew letters) or noo-KHAH EH-den (for women) or noo-KHOH EH-den (for men)

What it means: Hebrew for "Let his/her rest be paradise (Eden)."

P"N

Stands for: *Po nikhbar*

Pronounced: *pay noon* (the two Hebrew letters) or POH neek-BAHR

What it means: Hebrew for "here lies" or "here is buried." A variation on this is pay tet, which stands for po tamun, "here is hidden."

TNZBH

Stands for: *Tehi nishmato tzrura btzror hachayim*

Pronounced: tuh-HEE neesh-mah-TOE tzroo-RAH beh-TZROHR ha-khaye-EEM

What it means: Hebrew for "May his/her soul be bound up in the bond of life."

Rabbis and Sages

Maimonides (Rambam)

Besht

Stands for: Ba'al Shem Tov

Pronounced: Besht

What it means: Hebrew for "the owner/master of a good name," this was the title given to Israel ben Eliezer (16981760), the founder of Hasidic Judaism.

Rambam

Stands for: Rabbi Moshe (Moses) Ben Maimon, also commonly known as Maimonides, the prolific and influential 12th-century scholar originally from Spain.

Pronounced: RAHM-bahm

Modern Hebrew

Motzash

Stands for: motz-AY sha-BAHT

Pronounced: moh-TZASH

What it means: Saturday night, after Shabbat officially ends.

Ramat Kal

Stands for: ROHSH ha-mah-TEH ha-klah-LEE

Pronounced: RAH-mat KAHL

What it means: Chief of staff, or commander-in-chief of the Israel Defense Forces (IDF)

Sofash

Stands for: sohf shah-VOO-ah

Pronounced: soh-FAHSH

What it means: Weekend

Tzahal

Stands for: *Tzava hahagana l'Israel*

Pronounced: TZAH-hall

What it means: The Israel Defense Forces (IDF)

Hebrew Letter Vowels

The Midrash Talpiot explains that the letters have their source in the Sefirah of Binah. The vowels have their source in the Sefirah of Chochmah. And the Trope marks have their source in the Sefirah of Keter.

This means that the vowel is more spiritual than the letters and that is why they are smaller and occupy less spiritual space and also less physical space on the scroll or page. It also explains why the vowels can not be comprehended on their own. They need to be revealed by the letters in the lower Sefirah. We call the vowels the soul and the letters the body.

Letters need vowels for their power. The letters have a sound without the vowels but it is too spiritual to be effective. It is like a ghost who desires to make things move in the physical world. He tries to pick the things up and goes right through that thing. When the ghost puts on a body he can pick up the material thing. When the vowel is near a letter it causes the letter sound to expand and become effective in the physical levels.

There are different ways to categorize the vowels. One system of categorization says there are 12 vowels which are put into 4 categories. Another system says there are 12 vowels which are put into 3 categories. In my opinion there are 13 vowels or 14 vowels. I add a "no vowel" vowel to these 12 vowels to arrive at this. I also categorize the Dagesh as a vowel. I have not seen this anywhere else. Does this truly matter? I will let you decide. When? At the end of the class(es) on vowels.

A vowel consists of a point, a line, or a combination of a point with a line. Vowels have three possible locations. 1) Below the letter; 2) To the left of the letter; 3) Above the letter. This is not used as a categorization technique. Why do you think that is?

Here is a little known aspect of vowels. **Vowels have a gematria value which changes the gematria of the word.**

One example of this is the letter Gimmel. When it is spelled out it is gimmel mem lamed. These same letters in the same order also spell the word gomel. So we have three meanings of the word that is spelled gimmel mem lamed.

One final note about vowels or actually non vowels. The dot that lets us know if the Shin is a Shin or a Sin is not considered a vowel since it relates to the body and sound of the letter itself. To help clarify this point lets understand why a dagesh is a vowel but the dot determining the sound of the Shin is not. One reason that is easy to understand is the Dagesh is uses for dealing with the 7 double letters. it is necessary to teach us if this letter is coming from Chesed or Gevurah as the source changes the sound. The dot regarding the Shin is only dealing with the one letter which is a Mother letter and above the idea of the vowels.

The relationships to the Sefirot are from the system of the ARI. Please note that each Sefirah mentioned above have the following additional Sefirah added to it, Keter of Chochmah of the Letters. Therefore each vowel becomes three levels of Sefirot.

Cholam

In addition to the Kabbalistic Metaphor of the Sefirot, there is a metaphor of "spheres of creation." The Highest sphere is occupied by Divine Angels that corresponds to the Cholam.

The Cholam is always placed above the letter, yet does not always need the vowel holding place of a Vav. When the Cholam lacks the Vav it is called incomplete. It is taught that the word will become complete by rearranging the letters of the Torah. This means the letters of the Torah are complete but the words they create are not the same for the World that is Coming (Olam Habah) and the World of Tikune (Our present physical world).

The gematria of Cholam is 78. This is 3 times the gematria of the Tetragrammaton. It represents HaShem on the Right, HaShem on the Left, and HaShem in the middle. As explained, when we will discuss the Caf, Lamed, and Mem letters which spell Melech meaning King, the order relates to the verse HaShem Melech, HaShem Malach, HaShem yimloch LeOlam Vaed. One of the meanings of this verse is the unification and correction of the essence of time. Melech is the past, Malach is the present, and Yimloch is the future. The Tikune of time is to be unified. The past is a cause for the present which also includes the future. This is the true meaning of the Buddest and Kabbalistic teaching "Live in the Now".

The Cholam reinforces its regal nature by always being on top of the letters, as the King wears a crown. Since this is true Why is the Cholam not the Keter in the system of the ARI?

Every Shabbat we read/sing Psalm 136 which has 26 verses all ending with the words Ki LeOlam Chasdo. This phrase translates as "For his kindness endures forever". The word Chasdo meaning His Kindness has a gematria of 78. We learn from the gematria relationship that the Cholam and the highest nature of HaShem is Kindness or Loving Kindness as it has come to be translated.

When we permutate the word Cholam we get the following:

Dream as well as the name of the vowel

Forgiveness

Pity

Circle

All of these words connect to the end of days (a term that refers to the Birthpangs of Mashiach) as follows: At the time of Mashiach,

HaShem will have pity on His People and forgive them for all of their transgressions. World History will then commence a new cycle in the circle of Time.

Here are some other meanings included in the vowel as seen from additional permutations.

Bread

Salt

These two words also symbolize eternity as they were significant parts of the rituals of the Temple. The Table in the Temple held the 12 ShewBreads which stayed fresh and warm from Shabbat to Shabbat when they were replaced with the new ShewBreads. Also all sacrifices needed to be Salted. Can you answer the question Why did the sacrifices need to be salted?

Here is a Hint: Salt is white and represents the Right Column.

Shuruk

The Shuruk is connected to the middle sphere which corresponds and is occupied by the planetary orbits.

The Shuruk is always placed in the middle or central position representing the middle sphere as well as the energy of balance.

When we permute the word Shuruk we learn many things as follows:

Knot

Lie or Falsehood

Connecting word like just, only but, except, in reverse order it means cold or chilly. When connected to the letter shin it becomes 300 connections or the fire of the cold.

The Shuruk is the knot that connects the Cholam to the Chirik. The upper sphere to the lower sphere.

The first verse in the Torah: Beraishit Barah Elokim Et Hashamayim Vet HaAretz does not have the Shuruk or Kubutz vowel even though it has all of the other major vowels. This is because there is no room for falsehood in the Torah of truth.

Kubutz

The Kubutz vowel is a subsidiary of the Shuruk vowel. This is clear from the mutual sound of each. The question that needs to be asked is why is it necessary for there to be two different vowels with the same sound? Send me your answers to this question after you have time to think about it.

The shape of the Kubutz vowel is three dots below the letter shaped in a diagonal. The Kubutz is used when it is necessary to stress the idea of the connection between the upper and the lower spheres or the idea of balance the path of Judaism. It also represents the idea of a Vav as the three dots make a diagonal vav. The gematria of the Shuruk has a gematria of 600 which has the small gematria of 6 just like the Vav.

Chirik

The lowest sphere is our physical world. The vowel connected to this sphere is the Chirik. Can you guess why?

Let's permute the word Chirik as well.

Korach - Moses' cousin who strove with him over his nepotism. korach ends his life by being buried alive at the gates of Gehinom (always thought of as underground) After Noshe created an earthquake.

Distant

To Investigate and Question

The chirik always is written below the letter the most distant from the Cholam. Below the letter represents our physical world which is the most distant from HaShem. Our physical world is also where we constantly investigate and question always searching for Truth and Wisdom, various attributes of HaShem. This means we are searching for HaShem.

Tzerei

The Tzerei represents the high sphere as it is in process of being built to a higher, larger manner. The two dots standing side by side represent the lack of jealousy in the various races of angels. That is why they can be side by side.

The Tzerei, representing the highest sphere is never mixed with an other vowel as it represents the higher levels. An example of this is the word Aish spelled Aleph Shin. The Aleph has a Tzerei vowel because the idea of a flame is constantly ascending.

The Tzerei spelled Tzadi, Reish, Yood can be permutated to spell Yetzer which means inclination (usually thought of as evil inclination). The numerical value of both words is 300 which is the same as the Name of God Elokim spelled out and a transformation of the Tetragrammaton using the At Bash method. This teaches us that it is HaShem who helps us overcome our evil inclination when we follow the natural order of the Torah and its regulations. This form of the Tzerei vowel also demonstrates the equality of the two inclinations the good one and the evil one.

Segol

The segol is composed of the Tzerie being side by side and the shva being one atop the other. This builds the middle sphere. The shape of the Segol is an equlateral triangle. One of the dots of the Shva is concealed. The three dots of the Segol represents the three alphabetic structures, known as Al-Bam, At-Bash, and Ach-Bi. These letter substitutions for a triangular transformation ring. When one does a double substitution from one of the structures and then use another of the structures the result will form the third structure.

Shva

The Shva has two dots one above the other representing the lowest sphere and indicating the inability of man to get along yet. It also represents the manner of the physical world. In the physical world is the manner of building starting with a foundation below and the actual building above.

Patach

The Patach has the meaning of open as in the phrase "open your hands."

Kamatz

the Kamatz has the meaning of closing or gathering in. The Cohen would reach is open hand into the flour and close it and bring forth the Kamitzah the amount of flour needed in the Mincha offering used in the Beit Mikdash or the Temple.

Chataf Patach

Combination Patach and Shva.

Chataf Kamatz

Combination Kamatz and Shva

Chataf Segol

The Chataf Segol is formed from a combination of the Segol and the Shva. This represents a servant standing by his master ready to serve him. It also represents how the lower forms of creation fulfill their purpose by serving the higher forms of creation.

Vowel Gematria Examples

Ehchad

Gematria of letters only = 13; Since the word means One gematria of 13 represents unity.

Gematria of vowels is 86. 86 is the Name of God representing judgment which is Elohim. This demonstrates the subservice of judgment to mercy. Do you see how?

Together 13 + 86 = 99; when we add the Colel we get 100 representing 10 x 10 which is a complete structure of 10 Sephirot within 10 Sephirot.

Sounds of Letters and Vowels

Mogen David - Star of David

Mogen David are code words for Shield of David. It represents the Tree of Life for the lower 6 Sefirot with the Center of the star being used as the 7th Sefirot - Malchut. It is formed from two triangles which represent the idea of the two worlds being upside down from each other. This means we start with the unified point of HaShem and progress down to a base and then transfer to another base and progress down to a single point representing the negative force or ego. To go from one wide base to another we must cross the abyss and in so doing we make right left and left right. We can also see from this chart that the protection shield also includes all 27 letters of the Aleph Bet.

What Is Gematria?

Hebrew numerology, and the secrets of the Torah.

BY HILA RATZABI

Gematria is a numerological system by which Hebrew letters correspond to numbers. This system, developed by practitioners of Kabbalah (Jewish mysticism), derived from Greek influence and became a tool for interpreting biblical texts.

In gematria, each Hebrew letter is represented by a number (for example, aleph = 1, bet = 2, etc.). One can then calculate the numerical value of a word by adding together the values of each letter in it. In the realm of biblical interpretation, commentators base an argument on numerological equivalence of words. If a word's numerical value equals that of another word, a commentator might draw a connection between these two words and the verses in which they appear and use this to prove larger conceptual conclusions.

The Hebrew Alphabet in Numerology

1 Aleph	4 Daleth
2 Bet	5 Heh
3 Gimel	6 Vav
7 Zayin	90 Tzady
8 Het	100 Koof
9 Tet	200 Reish
10 Yud	300 Shin
20 Kaf	400 Taf
30 Lamed	500 Kaf (final)
40 Mem	600 Mem (final)
50 Nun	700 Nun (final)

60 Samech   800 Peh (final)

70 Ayin   900 Tzady (final)

80 Peh

Who Believes in Gematria?

While gematria was used periodically in the Talmud and Midrash, it was not central to rabbinic literature. The rabbis occasionally employed gematria to help support biblical exegesis, but did not rely on it heavily. They were much more invested in the use of logical reasoning and argumentation to support their positions.

However, gematria is essential to Kabbalah, the Jewish mystical tradition. The very basis of the kabbalistic cosmological system rests on the belief that God created the universe through the power of the Hebrew letters along with their numerical values. Indeed the many names of God and their permutations in Kabbalah have numerical values that are believed to contain potent power.

Gematria's Core Texts

The term "gematria" comes from the Greek "geometria," and the concept can be found in the writings of the Greek philosopher Plato. In rabbinic literature it first appears in the Baraita of the Thirty-two Rules, by Rabbi Eliezer in 200 CE. This text, which no longer exists except in references, elaborated 32 rules for interpreting the Bible. The 29th rule involved the use of gematria.

Sefer Yetzirah, the earliest kabbalistic text, believed to have been written in the 2nd century CE, was the first kabbalistic text to elaborate a system of gematria. This text is concerned with God's creation of the universe through the powers of the Hebrew alphabet, and with the permutations of God's name. The mystic practitioner could, it was believed, use this knowledge to harness the powers of creation. Sefer Yetzirah supposedly contains the instructions to create a golem, the legendary creature made out of mud, popularized by the Maharal of Prague in the 19th century.

In the 1200s the Hasidim of Ashkenaz ("German pietists," a group of rabbis who practiced a mystical and ascetic form of Judaism, not to be confused with Hasidism, which developed 500 years later) used gematria in their mystical writings. Their writings influenced Abraham Abulafia of the Castilian school of Kabbalah, whose meditation techniques included contemplating different names of God. The kabbalist Moses Cordovero of Safed, Israel, in 1542 compiled a handbook called Pardes Rimonim (Garden of the Pomegranates), which includes many sections that expound on and elaborate previous systems of gematria. The Sabbatean movement of the 17th century (the followers of which believed their leader, Shabbatai Tzvi, to be the messiah) and the Hasidic movement of the 18th century built on the kabbalistic tradition, employing gematria as a tool in their mystical writings.

Famous Examples of Gematria-Based Arguments

One famous example of gematria is in the interpretation of Genesis 14:14, which appears in the Baraita of the Thirty-two Rules and in other Talmudic and Midrashic references. This verse mentions the 318 men that made up the household of Abram (later in Genesis, God changes Abram's name to Abraham), whom he took with him to defeat the armies that had recently attacked his kinsman. The numerical equivalent of the name "Eliezer" (Abram's servant) is 318; therefore, the text suggests that in fact it was only Eliezer that came with Abram, not all 318 men. A Hasidic text, the Kedushat Levi, uses gematria to draw additional conclusions from this verse. This text observes that the numerical value of the word "siach" (Hebrew for speaking or conversing) is 318. Therefore, the text argues that it was through the power of speaking God's holy name that Abram defeated his enemies.

Much of gematria focuses on the various names of God and the powers of these names. The name Elohim adds up to the number 86, which equals the value of the word hateva (Nature). This equivalence leads to the conclusion that Elohim refers to the divine presence as it manifests in the physical world, as opposed to the name YHVH, which connects to the heavenly universe.

Modern Belief in Gematria

Throughout history, some people have believed that the Torah contains secrets that can be revealed by gematria and used to predict historical events. This belief continues to this day, and was popularized by Michael Drasin's best-selling (and much criticized) *The Bible Code*, published in 1997. Some Hasidic communities that are steeped in the study of kabbalistic literature believe that the Torah, as read through the lens of gematria, contains clues to current events.

Skeptics, however, have noted that gematria can be employed as "proof" to support diametrically opposing positions, depending on the words and phrases one chooses to highlight and calculate. A somewhat tongue-in-cheek illustration of this involved an attempt to predict the 2016 United States presidential election through the gematria of the candidates' names. The author of the article showed how this line of reasoning could be used just as easily to predict the victory of either candidate. Nevertheless, gematria continues to have an appeal in some quarters.

Hoshana Rabbah

The seventh day of Sukkot is called Hoshana Rabbah, and is considered the final day of the divine "judgment" in which the fate of the new year is determined. It is the day when the verdict that was issued on Rosh Hashanah and Yom Kippur is finalized.

The Midrash tells us that Gd told Abraham: "If atonement is not granted to your children on Rosh Hashanah, I will grant it on Yom Kippur; if they do not attain atonement on Yom Kippur, it will be given on Hoshana Rabbah."

Isaiah says,[1] "They seek Me day [after] day." The Talmud explains[2] that these two "days" refer to the day when the Shofar is sounded (Rosh Hashanah) and the day when we take the willow (Hoshana Rabbah)—the day when the heavenly judgment begins, and the day when it concludes.

In addition, on Sukkot we are judged regarding how much rain will fall in the upcoming year.[3] Thus, on Hoshana Rabbah, the final day of Sukkot, this judgment is finalized. Considering how much our wellbeing and economy depend on bountiful rainfall, it is clear how important this day is.

The Day of the Willow

The primary observance of Hoshana Rabbah is "the taking of the willow." In addition to the Four Kinds taken every day of Sukkot, it is a tradition, dating back to the times of the prophets, to take an additional willow on the seventh day of Sukkot. This commemorates the willow ceremony in the Holy Temple, where large eighteen-foot willow branches were set around the altar every day of Sukkot. Every day of Sukkot the altar was circled once, to the sounds of supplications for divine assistance; on Hoshana Rabbah, the altar was circled seven times.

Today, during the course of the Hoshana Rabbah morning services, all the Torah scrolls are taken out of the Ark and are held by people standing around the bimah (Torah reading table). The congregation then makes seven circuits around the bimah (instead of the one circuit done the other days of Sukkot) while reciting the Hoshaanot prayers, with the Four Kinds in hand. At the conclusion of the Hoshaanot we take a bundle of five willows (available for a nominal fee at most synagogues), and with it we strike the ground five times, symbolizing the "tempering of the five measures of harshness."

It is customary for all—men, women, and even small children—to perform this ritual. One should not use a willow bundle already used by another; a bundle should be purchased for every family member. After the bundle is used, many have the custom of throwing it onto the top of the Ark.

Other Hoshana Rabbah observances:

Night Learning

In consideration of the auspiciousness of the day, it is customary in many communities to remain awake on the night preceding Hoshana Rabbah. After joyous dancing, we recite the entire book of Deuteronomy, wherein the precepts to love and fear Gd are expounded at length. In certain communities, the entire book of Deuteronomy is read in the synagogue from the Torah scroll. After midnight, the entire book of Psalms is recited. In some congregations it is a custom for the gabbai (synagogue manager) to distribute apples (signifying a "sweet year") to the congregants. These apples are then taken home, dipped in honey, and eaten in the *sukkah*.

Morning Prayers

Because of the length of the day's Hoshaanot prayers, the morning service is a bit longer than the usual Chol Hamoed prayers. However, in many communities (though not in Chabad synagogues), the prayers are augmented with many standard Holiday prayers as well as additional liturgy composed specifically for Hoshana Rabbah—and as such, last for several hours. In fact, in certain communities it is even customary to sound the *Shofar*, as a call to repentance, during the course of the prayers.

The Hoshaanot prayers and circuits are done immediately before the reading of the Torah, or in some communities, after the Musaf prayer.

Lekach

The Rebbe would distribute *lekach* (honey cake) on Hoshana Rabbah, to those who had not received a piece before Yom Kippur.

Festive Meal

A festive meal is eaten in the *sukkah*. We dip the bread in honey for the last time. Many have the custom to eat kreplach—dough filled with ground beef or chicken, folded into triangles—on this day.

Hoshana Rabbah is also the last occasion on which we recite the special blessing for eating in the *sukkah*, since the biblical commandment to dwell in the *sukkah* is only for seven days (though it is the practice of many communities—and such is the Chabad custom—that outside of the Land of Israel, we eat in the *sukkah* also on the eighth day, Shemini Atzeret).

Eruv Tavshilin

In the event that Hoshana Rabbah falls on a Wednesday (so that Simchat Torah will be Thursday night and Friday), an *eruv tavshilin* must be made on Hoshana Rabbah, to allow cooking and other necessary Shabbat preparations to be done on Friday.

Jewish Death and Mourning 101

What you need to know about Judaism's death, mourning and burial practices.

BY MY JEWISH LEARNING

Judaism does not shy away from close encounters with death, but frames them ritually. Much attention is paid to treating the dead (and even a dead body) with respect (*k'vod ha-met*) and to comforting mourners (*nichum aveilim*).

History and Development

Many practices surrounding death that continue to this day–such as tearing one's clothes, burial, and mourning the deceased–find their origins in the biblical text. There is both a remarkable consistency and fascinating differences in Jewish burial and mourning practices around the world.

Dying

Long before death, one may write an "ethical" will, recording values and guidance for one's descendants. Individuals who may be dying are encouraged to recite the traditional deathbed *viddui*, or confession of sins.

Before the Funeral

Until the burial, a person who hears of the death of a first-degree relative (a parent, spouse, sibling, or child) is an onen (literally "someone in between"). Traditionally, the enigmatic yet powerful phrase "*baruch dayan ha-emet*" ("blessed is the judge of Truth") is uttered upon hearing the news, and a garment is torn. The body is prepared for burial with great care by the hevra kaddisha (the sacred burial society), including ritual purification (*tahora*), and dressing the body in shrouds (*tachrichim*).

Funeral and Burial

Mourners are greeted by those attending the funeral, and tearing (*kriah*) of a garment or ribbon is repeated. The funeral has a small number of fixed liturgical elements, including the short prayer *El Maleh Rachamim* ("God full of compassion"), and usually includes psalms and a *hesped*, or eulogy. The service may take place in a funeral home, in a synagogue, or at the graveside. The burial is framed by other liturgical elements, including the recitation of a special version of the Kaddish prayer, often thought of as the "mourner's prayer." Mourners and others participate in covering the casket with dirt. Mourners leave the graveside first, and others say to them the traditional words, "May God comfort you among all the mourners of Zion and Jerusalem."

The Mourning Period

The Mourning period is successively less intense; many Jews and non-Jews view the Jewish process of mourning as psychologically wise. Its traditional elements are: *shiva*, seven days during which mourners are visited at home by family and community, and participate in prayer services held at home; *sheloshim*, the first 30 days of mourning, during which mourners return to their normal routine but refrain from many customary pleasurable activities; and, for those who have lost a parent, 11 months of *aveilut* (mourning), during which Kaddish is recited daily.

A tombstone may be erected or uncovered at any time; an "unveiling" is often done a year after the death. The anniversary of death, or *yahrzeit*, is observed each year, and the deceased is remembered four times annually during *Yizkor* services.

In Practice

Jewish funerals often take place almost immediately after a death. Outside of Israel, it is not customary to send flowers, but charitable donations are a common and meaningful practice. A person paying a "shiva call" on a bereaved individual or family can easily learn the basic customs of this unusual yet comforting visit.

Issues

Suicide is forbidden in Jewish law; an individual who takes his or her own life is usually presumed to have been suffering from mental illness. Traditionally, cremation is forbidden because of the sanctity of the human body; similarly, autopsies are, with some exceptions, traditionally not permitted. Organ donation is permitted in order to save another individual's life. Law and custom mandate special cemeteries for Jews, but many contemporary Jewish cemeteries will arrange to bury non-Jewish spouses. Many converts to Judaism follow traditional mourning practices (including saying Kaddish) for their non-Jewish family members. And while Jewish tradition frowns on things which can be construed as mutilation of one's body, like tattoos and body piercing, none of these things represent a barrier to burial in even the most traditionally-run cemetery.

5782: Numbers and Meanings for the New Year

Rabbi Yitzchak Ginsburgh

Elul 5, 5781 • Kfar Chabad

As per the Alter Rebbe's metaphor capturing the essence of the month of Elul, the king is now in the field and everyone is able to approach, speak with him and ask for what they need. The most important need is the coming of Mashiach immediately.

We have a custom to begin the year with the different allusions of the number of the year—specifically focusing on these *gematriot* (numerical allusions) that pertain to our inner service and that enhance our ability to approach Hashem now and during the coming year.

The phrases representing the year 5782

The year we are about to enter is 5782, but as is well known, the custom is to refer to the year as 782, sans the millennia. This is the number we will contemplate and reveal important allusions regarding. Before beginning to look at the numerical hints associated with the new year, we like to give a phrase or idiom that captures the letter-representation of the year . The first two letters, which are the same for an entire century, customarily stand for "May it be a year of".

30 years ago in 5752 , the Lubavitcher Rebbe explained that the letters representing the year stood for the phrase, "May it be a year of wonders in all things". Wonders can be written as either with or without the prefix letter *nun*. So actually, the phrases used in the entire present decade (5780 through 5789) can just be copied from those used three decades ago (from 5750 to 5759). For our particular upcoming year, 5782, we could then use the phrase, "May it be a year of wonders in all things". Wonders in all that we do and in all that God does with us.

Another beautiful idiom that uses the letters is "face to face" and so this year can stand for the phrase, "May it be a year of face to face". God gave us the Torah face to face. Face means inner in Hebrew, and so God gave us the Torah from His inner essence directly to ours. The idiom, "face to face," applies both to the relationship between man and God and between man and his fellow man. Thus, the coming year is for uniting and relating to other souls in a manner of face to face, from my inner essence to yours and back again. When we approach someone with direct light (or *yashar*) it causes them to reflect back to us with what is called reflected light (or *chozer*).

Building a *partzuf* for 782

These were two examples using the initials of the year. But this is not the technique we normally employ, because we usually focus on the numerical value of the year, which once again is 782. We are going to choose from a multitude of possibilities—many different words, idioms, and phrases, whose value is 782—six different phrases, which are very significant and also have a common denominator to them. In each case, the phrase that equals 782, will refer to two or more concepts that go together naturally. Together, these six different expressions from the Torah, form a partzuf, or a model that reflects the human form which is based on the ten *sefirot* with which God creates reality.

The *sefirot* and their inner experiential dimension from above to below begin with the super-consciousness of the soul—usually divided in two (pleasure and will). Then the intelligences of the soul divided into the three faculties of the mind: wisdom, understanding, and knowledge. Then the emotions of the heart, loving-kindness, might (or courage) and compassion. Then the powers of the soul to enact itself in reality, to impress itself upon reality: confidence, sincerity, and the power of self-fulfillment of the soul, which correspond to the sefirot victory, thanksgiving, and foundation. Finally, we have the external reality of the soul, the kingdom, the purpose of creation, which is described by the verse, "God will be King over the entire world, on that day [the day of the Mashiach], God will be one and His Name will be one." This is just to remind us of the model and the flow of all the *sefirot*, which are also the powers of the soul, the way God created man in His image.

Crown: "May He give you peace"

We will now begin from above and descend downward. The first allusion of 782 is the climax of the Priestly Blessing, which is one of if *not* the numerical gem of the Torah. It is comprised of three verses. The priests say, "May God bless you and guard you. May God shine His countenance upon you and give you grace." And the third and final verse and blessing is, "May God lift His countenance upon you and give you peace." The final three words, are the climax, "May He give you peace". There is a very important intent in these words, which we say every day, that the ultimate blessing is peace—peace in the world, peace of mind; peace in Hebrew also means consummate perfection or soundness, even good health, anything that needs to be complete is peace.

The sages say that there is nothing greater than peace. This is the ultimate blessing that the Torah blesses us through the priests who are the messengers that bring the word and blessing of God to us, and we send them to receive this message and channel it through them to us. The ultimate blessing are the final three words.

In the sages, they teach us that each part of the three blessings is about something specific. The *Sifrei*, the anthology of interpretations of the words of the Torah according to the oral tradition received from Sinai, explains that "May He give you peace" means "the peace of the Torah". The explanation is that there is something unique about the Torah since it has the power to make peace between opposite opinions.

This is very prominent throughout the rabbinic literature. Even though one sage says so and the other says the opposite and they contradict one another, "these and these are both the words of the living God." There is something intrinsic about the Torah that the peace of the Torah is the true ultimate union of opposites that will be revealed in the future by the Mashiach. In this world we cannot yet fully understand what it means that two opposite opinions can be one. This is why this allusion belongs to the realm of the crown, to the supernal super-conscious realm of the soul. There the Torah makes peace between the people that express these opposite opinions—everything that a rabbinic sage says expresses his soul root. In our world, these opposite soul roots even seem antagonistic, but in the crown, they are ultimately in a state of perfect peace. As the Torah says, "In Vaheb in Sufah," which the sages allegorically interpret as meaning, "love in the end," meaning that the dispute between the different opinions clarified through the study of Torah, which is like a war, ends with love. In the crown it is revealed how all different people are actually one and the same in their Divine essence; that every Divine soul of Israel is an actual part of the Divintiy of God. Divinity does not split into parts, so each soul is a reflection of the entire whole. Every part is the whole, except that you only see one aspect of the infinite dimensions of the whole.

This phrase, "May He give you peace" equals 782. If I add the interpretation of the sages, "the peace of the Torah" to 782, the sum comes to 1781, which is 13 times 137, where 13 is the value of "one", or "love" —peace is a revelation of love and oneness—and 137 is a very important number, the most important number in modern physics, it is the value of the word "kabbalah". So, this is a very beautiful number.

One more point about this. As we said before that peace means perfection in Hebrew. To give peace is the peace of God. What does this mean. The Torah and God are one and the same. The peace of God is an expression explained in the early texts of Kabbalah, that God is complete (peace) inasmuch as, although He is infinite, He possesses the power of finitude in His infinity. He is without boundaries, but to be complete He cannot be lacking anything, not even the opposite of what He appears to be. Before the contraction of His infinite light, He is infinite. But to say that He is just infinite and does not possess in His essence finitude, is to take away His completeness. Therefore, the completeness of God, which is also the completeness of the Torah, is that it also includes details. Everything in the Torah has a limit, it is limitless together with being limited, simultaneously. Since all the different details come from the same infinity, for that reason itself, different sages, which are representative of different soul roots, each has his affinity—they are all part of the infinite one. There is both a limit (like in mathematics) and sometimes there is no limit. The unity of the limitless and the limit is the peace of God, which is also the peace of the Torah. This is the first meditation of 782.

Crown: "To dwell in the mist"

The second meditation, which we will call the transition stage between absolute infinity and the manifestation in reality, which is finite—because the power of limits is part of the infinity. When king Solomon inaugurated the first Temple, he said a very important prayer to God and in this prayer, he began with a phrase that equals 782. The Book of Kings describes, "Then Solomon declared, 'God has chosen to dwell in a mist'. The word "then" precedes the songs of the Torah. God desired to dwell in the mist or the fog. This mist is also referred to as "the thickness of the cloud". The first time this word appears is when Moses went up to the mountain to receive the Torah, "Moses approached the mist in which God was". This word, "mist" appears 3 times in the Torah and altogether 15 times in the Bible. It is unique because it is a four-letter root, not very common in Hebrew. What King Solomon is telling us is that the secret of the Temple is the purpose of all of creation, that the entire world becomes a dwelling place for God and God says and chooses to dwell in the mist, which equals 782. The initial letters of this phrase spell "heart". This is another straightforward allusion for the coming year.

What can we learn from this phrase? Sometimes it is explained that the spiritual meaning of the word mist is "uncertainty." Just like before we talked about limits and unlimited, obviously our faith is certain, God is certain and the Torah is certain, but God chooses to dwell in uncertainty, in the fog, in the mist. Solomon in these first words is explaining what this temple that he built for seven years is in a sense, a fog. It is the thickness of the cloud has a direct and exact translation into English: condensation Condensation means that vapor condenses into droplets of water. This is one of the most fundamental teachings in Kabbalah: "From the thickening of the lights, the vessels were made". Everything is made of light and vessels. They seem to be opposite states of being. But actually, the vessels come into existence from the light. Light represents the infinite. The value of the word "light" itself equals "infinity". That infinity, which is sometimes called the primordial atmosphere, condenses into droplets, like the condensation of vapor into droplets. What does this mean spiritually? It means that the mist, the uncertainty is the transitory stage between two definite states of being; uncertainty is relatively a state of nothingness, because it is uncertain what exactly will come into being after the transition is over. In English this is called metamorphosis. This is just a broader term for the physical process of the condensation of water, which in Kabbalah is called "light, water, firmament". First light, which is the atmosphere, the air becomes water and then it becomes the firmament—which is the vessel. It is like the transition from the egg to the chick, the uncertainty is the state in between where it is not clear what will become. This sounds very deep and indeed is a very deep and important concept.

It is said that Moses is the first redeemer, and he is also the final redeemer. Moses is certain just as the Torah he gave is certain. The *Rambam* writes that nothing will be new by the Mashiach, he has less prophecy than Moses, yet he also has more holy spirit. What is the difference between prophecy (which Moses has more of) and Divine inspiration or Holy Spirit (that the Mashiach has more of)? Moses is the epitome of certainty, and that is the infinite of God. If there is no limit, there is no doubt. No limit means that the mind of God as it were, is not limited in knowing. When knowledge has no limit, then everything is certain. But, if there is a limit to knowledge—like in the case of the human mind—we have a limit to our knowledge, then there is uncertainty and that is why we have uncertainty. The sages say in the Talmud that there are seven things that are concealed from man. Two of them are: what will be one's livelihood—the source of his physical sustenance in this world—and when Mashiach will come. The Alter Rebbe says that from this we learn that these two things are commensurate. They are identically uncertain. There is something certain about Mashiach—that he is uncertain. The ultimate certainty in our realm of consciousness is uncertainty. In the Tanya it says that these two are equal (actually all seven, but he only quotes these two). But, there are other places in Chassidut that says that the source of one's livelihood is even more uncertain than when Mashiach will come. Maybe that's why the Rebbe could say that Mashiach was here already and yet it was still uncertain how you would make your living. Something that is uncertain is the secret of the fog in which God has chosen to dwell.

It is worth doing all of these *gematriot* for the New Year just in order to understand all these important concepts. So, we said that Moses is the first redeemer and he is the final redeemer, what then is the difference? As Moses and as a prophet the first redemption is about certainty, about being in tune with God's unlimited total knowledge of all, that He and His knowledge are one. But, Mashiach and the final redemption are the epitome of uncertainty—he is and always remains about uncertainty. Even when he is here, Mashiach is about metamorphosis. The world has to go through transition, through change, it has to undergo condensation.

Every word in Hebrew derives from roots, two letters than three letters than the rest. The strongest letter in the sub-root of "mist" is the pei. We are now explaining the etymology of "mist" using an inner methodology. The root is the same root of the word, those who after the sin of the spies wanted to take the initiative and the self-confidence to enter the land of Israel even though Moses told them that God was not with them, "and it will not be successful". And indeed, the attempt to take the initiative without God's certain support certainly led to them being killed. But Rabbi Tzadok of Lublin writes that in the future, they will succeed, people who take initiative to bring Mashiach, just as the Rebbe said, do everything in your power to bring Mashiach, a new think, a new plan. It will be successful in the future. In the process of metamorphosis of the egg becoming a chick, sometimes it works and sometimes it does not; there is uncertainty. In the past it was a negative transition, but in the future that metamorphosis which depends on taking initiative and having self-confidence will be successful in bringing Mashiach and this is actually the only one way to bring Mashiach, since Mashiach is uncertain. The idiom for change in Hebrew is meeting someone in the corner, which implies moving through a 90 degree change, moving one way and then turning the corner to go in a different direction altogether. The corner itself is nothing—it has no definition; it is also a fog or mist.

Rosh Hashanah is also a corner. It is the corner that we turn; the corner is the light that surrounds all worlds. This itself is a great thought in itself, the secret of the mist and God's desire and choice to dwell there.

The simple derivation is different. According to grammar, "mist" comes from the word meaning, "the small back of the neck" and it represents the stiff neck of the Jewish people. Being stubborn to believe in the certainty of the uncertainty. We are stubborn to believe that the caterpillar we are looking at now will turn into the most beautiful butterfly imaginable. From a worm the world is going to transform into the most beautiful phenomenon possible.

These first two allusions are related to one another.

Wisdom, Understanding, and Knowledge: The God Abraham, the God of Isaac, and the God of Jacob

The next allusion is the phrase we say at least three times daily at the beginning of the *Amidah*, the silent devotion. In the first blessing, we refer to God as "the God of Abraham, the God of Isaac, and the God of Jacob" a phrase that also equals 782. The three patriarchs themselves correspond to the three emotive faculties of the heart—loving-kindness, might, and beauty. But, when we speak of the "God of," each of the patriarchs we are referring to the intellectual faculties that lie above the emotive faculties. Thus, the God of Abraham refers to wisdom , the God of Isaac refers to understanding, and the God of Jacob refers to knowledge.

This is something that we can and have in mind this coming year. This coming year is the year of devotion and prayer to the God of our fathers.

So, we had two allusions above the mind: the ultimate above the mind is the peace of God and the peace of the Torah. Then we had the transition from light to vessel, the metamorphosis the state of uncertainty the fog. Then comes the mind, which is the God of Abraham, Isaac, and Jacob.

Loving-kindness, might, and beauty: The Binding of Isaac

The next allusion is a phrase that is just two words, which we also say in our prayers many times, the binding of Isaac which also equals 782. What does this represent? God gave Abraham an infinitely difficult test—to sacrifice his only son which God had promised would be the seed after which Abraham's name would be known. All tests, especially this one even more than others, can be surmounted through faith (everything begins in faith). The secret of the binding of Isaac is that the two opposites (like the opposite opinions of the sages which lead to peace and love between them), the ultimate duality of the right (Abraham) and the left (Isaac) at the moment of the binding, when Abraham is ready to sacrifice his son, and Isaac knows that he is about to be sacrificed and accepts it lovingly, their attributes metamorphosized. The love of Abraham became awe or fear and the awe of Isaac became love. The power to unite them comes from the "perfection of all" which comes about through the blessings, "May He give you peace." When we mention Isaac's binding on Rosh Hashanah, we do so as part of the additional blessing in the Amidah known as "remembering the covenant." The conclusion of this blessing is "May you remember Isaac's binding with mercy." Thus, not only are Abraham and Isaac who represent loving-kindness and might involved in Isaac's binding, but they bring about the revelation of God's mercy on the Jewish people—more than anything else, it is the Binding of Isaac that brings about the revelation of mercy or compassion, the inner aspect of the *sefirah* of beauty—the third emotive faculty. That is why we ask God to remember it on Rosh Hashanah and this will arouse mercy on our souls.

So in the Akeidah, Isaac's binding, we have the unity of the love and fear and this union brings down compassion, which is the third emotional attribute. So now we have all three emotional attributes.

Victory and thanksgiving: Gerizim and Eival

Again, in each of these numerical equivalencies we find two or even three different concepts interlinked. The next pair that equals 782 is the two mountains that we read about last week in the Torah, "Mount Grizim [and] Mount Eival" . When we entered the land of Israel, we were commanded to go to Shechem, which is situated between these two mountains. Six of the tribes were on one mountain and six on the other and the Levites were in the middle speaking the blessings and the curses to Gerizim and Eival, respectively. They are thus a pair.

What is the source in Kabbalah for these two mountains? There are number of different explanations. But one of them is that they are the secret of the two pillars that Solomon built in the Temple—a feature that didn't exist in the Tabernacle. These two pillars correspond to self-confidence and sincerity, the two feet of the soul that together walk. Pillars are like legs. They correspond to these two mountains. The blessings were given on Gerizim, the self-confidence of victory of eternity, and the curses on Eival, not something negative for there has to be a transition. The curses are expressed explicitly in the Torah—there is something more necessary about Eival than with Gerizim—believing that everything is for the good and that itself transforms the curse into a blessings. So, the coming year is about drawing in one's mind these two mountains. We also wish this be a year in which we return to Shechem.

Foundation and Kingdom: the image of God, the likeness of God

The final of the six allusions—the last one has to also be a pair that will correspond to foundation and kingdom, the truth of self-fulfillment and the final manifestation of the entire flow of energy and revealing that God is one and His Name is one.

There are two phrases describing how man's creation mirrors God. The first is that man was created in God's image, the second is that man was created in God's form and together, "God's image [and] God's likeness" equals 782. The first is more familiar. The second appears in what is sometimes considered the third account of creation. In the first account of creation it says, "Let us make God in our image and our likeness." Then man is created in God's image. But, later on it says that man was created in God's likeness.

What is the difference between them? *Tzelem* (translated as "image") represents the *tzaddik*, who is the foundation of the world. This is the ability man has to fulfill his potential, to fulfill himself. [missing…] *Tzelem* is masculine and the "likeness" is feminine. Every male is an image of God and every female is a likeness of God. Likeness is the ability to receive. The female aspect is to receive and reflect Godliness. Image is the ability to project. Likeness is a reflection. Both *tzaddik* and *tzelem* begin with. In fact, *tzelem*, is a shortened form of, "*tzaddik* the foundation of the world". The female aspect is the likeness.

How is this word likeness used in the Torah? It is not a *mitzvah* to be an image of God. But there is a *mitzvah* to be like God. The sages explain that to "walk in His ways". You should be like God—just as He is compassionate you should be compassionate, etc. So the female aspect of man is one of the fundamental *mitzvoth* of the Torah. But the ability to project Godliness into the world is not a commandment it is a state. The male state is not a commandment, but the female state is a commandment. Kingdom is an active reflection. So, 782 captures these two aspects of man's relationship with the Divine.

To summarize: we have seen how 782 is related to the ultimate union of opposites. To the secret of the Temple itself the secret of transition and existential uncertainty, the secret of Mashiach. Then, to the prayer to God as the God of the patriarchs, the mind of the soul. To the union in the heart itself the right and the left and their interchange in the Binding of Isaac. To remember it arouses mercy. Then to the blessings and the curses at the two mountains. Both are necessary. The ability to walk in the world. The two pillars and finally, to the two aspects of man.

This is our meditation upon the number 782. May it be a year of revealed good, revealed Mashiach, that we certain of the uncertainty, infinitely happy uncertainty

Unedited transcript written by Moshe Genuth

Elul: The Month of Self-Discovery

Elul is not just the pre-festive month. If you skip Elul and don't give it any special attention, you might suddenly find yourself unprepared at Rosh Hashanah. Just like Friday prepares for the coming Shabbat, so too, Elul, the sixth month from Nisan, is an essential preparation for the seventh month of *Tishrei* in particular, and for the coming year in general.

I Am for My Beloved

It is a well-known fact that the initials of the phrase, "I am for my Beloved, and my Beloved is for me" spell out "Elul". This means that it is an appropriate time to arouse ourselves to approach God. If "I am for [i.e., towards] my Beloved" by doing *teshuvah* (repentance) and good deeds then, "my Beloved [will be] for me." A lesser known fact is that the rest of the allusion is that the final letters of that very same phrase are four letters *yud*, which hint at the forty days (4 times 10, the numerical value of *yud* of compassion and forgiveness that begin on the first day of Elul and conclude on Yom Kippur, when "I" and "My Beloved" unite as one. These were the final set of forty days that Moses spent on Mt. Sinai, at the end of which he descended with the second Tablets of the Covenant.

This allusion brings us to the letter with which the month of Elul was created, which indeed, is the letter *yud*, in whose path we will now step out towards the coming month.

In the verse "I am for my Beloved and my Beloved is for me," it all begins with "I." The month of Elul is the most appropriate month for personal soul-searching and trying to present our personal "balance-sheet" towards the end of the Jewish year. Yet, beyond all of our personal accounts—regarding what we have done during the past year—we are liable to reveal that we have gotten lost in the overall tally… there are so many things that we have dealt with, we have scattered in every direction, but where were we really, where is our "I"? The urgent task of Elul is to find our lost "I," to rehabilitate our personality and to take it to a renewed meeting with God, "I am for my Beloved." But, how do we do that?

Flee to a City of Refuge

In Chassidic writings it is explained that Elul is the "city of refuge" of the year. What is a city of refuge? When someone commits involuntary manslaughter, he is obligated to flee from his regular location and reach a city of refuge, where he must now settle. Outside the city of refuge he lives in fear of his life (exposed to possible injury and death at the hands of the "blood avenger"). This is how every one of us should feel, to a certain extent, when the month of Elul arrives. We look in all directions in shock: Oh my goodness, what have I done? Who have I (almost) killed? Myself. I must immediately find myself a protected space where I can hide out, renew my proper way of living, and rediscover my true self.

But, where is the soul's city of refuge? We need to reach the root of the soul. The verse states, "Flee to your place"—i.e., to one's initial starting point. This point is represented by the letter *yud*, the smallest of all the letters of the *alef-bet*, whose form is exactly like a concentrated point. One might do a "guided imagery" exercise: begin by peeling away all the layers of one's personality, all the unwanted baggage that has accumulated over the years, until we return to our mother's womb. But, that's not enough, we need to go even further back in time, until we reach the seminal point from which we were born (more precisely, the fetus is created from the meeting between the father's seed and the ovum, but for the time being we are focusing on the fertilizing power of the seed, which represents the essence of the soul, according to Kabbalah)—this drop of seed is represented by the letter *yud*. If we continue further, we can identify the source of that drop itself as, "the drop of the son in his father's mind" (as Chassidut phrases it This point is the most fundamental root of a child, even before that drop becomes a separate entity that leaves on its long journey to create a fetus and a complete human being.

Physical reality is parallel to spiritual reality. Even our soul follows a similar journey until it appears in our familiar personality. The fundamental kernel of our soul is also in "the mind of the father"—i.e., in God, the Creator's thought (where even the term "thought" is a borrowed expression and is not the same as what we know as "thought"). This root is the letter *yud* of the soul, and there is the city of refuge where we escape to. However much we have diverted from the path of life and have gotten lost, once we reach the source of our soul we can renew our "I" from it.

Compassionate Father

Our journey to the source to the root of our soul has brought us to a rendezvous with our Father, "Our Father; compassionate Father." As deep as we might dig into ourselves, we will never find our lost identity until we recognize the existence of our most fundamental soul root that is incorporated within the Almighty. Indeed, we usually approach God as "King" (as in the formulation of the blessings, "Our God, King of the universe"). But, in Elul we meet Him first and foremost as a good Father. There is a famous allegory that states that in Elul "the King is in the field"—however, the special thing about this state is that when the king is in the field, he does not appear with his usual formal attire, rather he shows a smiling face to everyone, allowing all to approach him without any special preparation—exactly like a compassionate father. Only when we arrive at Rosh Hashanah, will God be revealed as a king in his palace (and then we stand before Him in awe, accepting upon ourselves the yoke of His sovereignty). The relationship reaches its climax on Yom Kippur when we are most like a married couple, as we say in the Yom Kippur prayers, "We are Your [beloved] wife and You are our [darling] husband."

The month of Elul directly follows the month of Av . In Av (especially at the beginning of the month) we cannot sense God's revealed compassion, but in Elul, God is revealed to us "Like a Father, who has mercy on His children." This is how Elul bridges between Av and Tishrei, and with its energy we can begin the new year from the beginning; indeed, the word "In the beginning" is a permutation of the letters "Av-Tishrei" . In other words, in Elul we begin to hear the roar of the lion that is the mazal (zodiac sign) of the month of Av, of which the verse states, "A lion roars; who does not fear?" The word "lion" is an acronym of "Elul" , "Rosh Hashanah" , "Yom Kippur" and "Hoshanah Rabbah" , the four days of judgment on which we are in awe of God.

"I" from "Nothing"

The letter *yud* has the great honor of being the first letter of God's Essential Name; in fact, when each of the letters of the Name are spelled in full, there are also ten letters to the Name, where 10 is the numerical value of the letter *yud*. As such, the letter *yud* represents the *sefirah* of wisdom, which is referred to as "Father", in the same way as an individual's soul represents the *yud* of the soul's source within their father.

The significance of the *efirah* of wisdom is not identical to wisdom as we usually understand it as intellectual talent or one's total knowledge. Wisdom is not intellect, but a higher plane of the soul where we experience the actual flash of innovation, the general energy that later becomes a well-defined and conceivable idea in our intellectual comprehension (and since wisdom is a plane of the psyche that is not intellectually tangible, it is in fact a vessel for the appearance of the light of faith, and also the amazing and incomprehensible ability for self-sacrifice).

The letter *yud* is the only letter that hangs in the air (i.e., above the line of text), and does not rest on stable ground like all the other letters of the *alef-bet*, because wisdom appears from above as if it hovers in the air, until it descends and materializes below. In this form one can envision the entire world as hanging in the air and beginning to be created from above downwards, as in the verse, "He suspends the earth on nothing".

[More precisely: in the script of the Torah the letter *yud* is not just a plain drop of ink, but a "drawn point," with its upper part the "cusp of the *yud*" turning upwards. This cusp indicates the hidden root of wisdom itself, before it is revealed. In Kabbalistic terms, the root of wisdom is in the "latent wisdom of the crown." In the human psyche, in Chassidic terms, this is the "power of the intellect," from which the lightning-like flashes of wisdom exude, above which is "the primordial intellect." Latent wisdom is an "undrawn point," that completely lacks dimensions.]

In order to expose the root of our souls, which corresponds to the *sefirah* of wisdom and to the letter *yud*, an inner power of the soul is required—the power of selflessness, which relates to standing before God feeling like a zero-dimensional point. In great righteous individuals, their selflessness is at a very high level, like Moses, who said of himself, "And we are what [i.e., 'nothing']." We too can "savor" something of the level of the righteous (mainly by just learning about it), but the main service of the average individual is to reach "selflessness" at the basic level that everyone can achieve—recognition of the fact that I am created anew, ex-nihilo, at every moment, and without the Divine "nothingness" that flows through me and vitalizes me, I am nothing (and the more one meditates on this, the more tangible this recognition becomes). In short, in order to find our genuine, rectified self, we need to nullify our egos and sense the Divine "nothingness"; this is how our new self is born from the hidden root of the soul that is within our compassionate Father.

From the Head to the Arm

So far, we have delved into the hidden root of the soul as if we had entered the incomprehensible point of the letter *yud*. But, our journey must not end here. Of course, the letter *yud* is just one point that hangs in the air, but this point gradually develops. The fundamental development of every letter is revealed in its "filling"; in this case, the filling of the letter *yud* is *yud-vav-dalet*. These three letters represent the development of the *yud* from a zero-dimensional point (practically speaking, every point we see on paper has dimensions, otherwise we wouldn't see it, but the *yud* represents a dimensionless abstract point). The *vav* is that very same point when it is elongated downwards (until it reaches the earth, at long last), becoming a longitudinal line. The letter *dalet* has a longitudinal line and a latitudinal line, which together form a two-dimensional area. This development of "point, line, area" is the basic outline for any process of realizing an idea from potential into actuality, and in our psyches too, we must break out of the root point (*yud*), strive for contact with reality like a dispatched arrow (*vav*), and realize it in practice in all of space (*dalet*).

There is a clear phenomenon of this three stage structure of *yud-vav-dalet* in the way someone expresses themselves (via the "vestments of the soul"): the point of the *yud* is thought, the line of the *vav* is the voice of speech (which expresses thought), while the area of the *dalet* is concrete action. However, if we look closely at the name of the letter *yud* we will see that it contains the word "hand". The form of the letter *yud* is like a head, the wisdom and thought in the mind, but the head needs to collaborate with the hand's power of action and to the ten fingers of the hand (like the numerical value of the *yud*) that grant us our amazing power of creativity. This is how Kabbalah interprets the verse, "Open your hands…": open the letter *yud* and turn it into an active hand. Indeed, the special talent of the month of Elul is the sense of action, which is also referred to as the sense of rectification—to teach us that wisdom must be expressed by rectifying the world through concrete actions and it cannot suffice with abstract philosophical ideas. Similarly, to the other extreme, only by connecting to the point of pure wisdom can one clarify reality and correctly utilize the power of action.

If the *yud* corresponds to the *sefirah* of wisdom, the initial core of revelation, then after wisdom has been developed and revealed, the *yud* itself is filled, eventually reaching the practical *sefirah* of kingdom (the tenth in line of all the *sefirot*).

Operation *Tefillin* for a Good Year

The correct connection between the head and the hand is explicitly expressed in the mitzvah of *tefillin*, which we attach to our hands and heads, thus joining our thought-filled heads with our hands that itch for action. We attach the hand *tefillin* to the left arm; indeed, the body limb that "regulates" the month of Elul is the left arm. The left arm is nearest the heart (so that the hand *tefillin* actually sit upon the heart) – because just as we speak through the point of wisdom that rests in the mind, so too there is the inner point of the heart (and these two points "compete" with each other to determine which is more essential and innate). The *tefillin* also connect this point to the sense of action in the hand. The letter *yud* itself appears in the *tefillin* in the special knot in the form of a *yud* that is made in the strap that is closest to the hand *tefillin*, so that the hand is close to the *yud*.

The word "*tefillin*" is in the plural and its singular form is "*tefillah*" which is identical to the word for "prayer." Indeed, there is a strong connection between *tefillin* and prayer, since there is an emphasis on wearing *tefillin* especially during prayer times. In depth, *tefillin* alludes to two types of prayer: "hand prayer," which is a natural type of prayer that stems directly from the heart (perhaps our hands will move of their own accord during such a prayer). Usually, this is a short, direct prayer, like the shortest prayer in the Torah, "God, please heal her, please." And there is a "head prayer," a prayer that stems from long in-depth mindful meditation (as generally encouraged in Chabad Chassidut; the prayer of a true, profound servant of God). But, even the "head prayer" does not ignore the heart, since the aim of mental meditation is eventually to touch and "move" the innermost point of the heart (just as the law is that one should take care that the hand *tefillin* should always be worn when the head *tefillin* is worn. The strong connection between the head and the hand is alluded to in the numerical equivalence of "head hand", which equals "prayer", the singular of *tefillin*, as mentioned above.

When attaching the *tefillin*, the order is that first we attach the hand *tefillin* and afterwards the head. In our context, first comes Elul, whose principle service is action, i.e., the talent for rectification (rectifying my ego), corresponding to the left hand, an aspect of the hand *tefillin*. Afterwards, comes the month of Tishrei, which begins with the "Head of the Year", which represents the head *tefillin*. However, even during Elul we prepare ourselves for the head tefillah, by connecting to the point of wisdom and selflessness of the letter *yud*. In this way, *tefillin* is not just an external accessory that is placed upon the head, but it penetrates, as it were, into the head, becoming the Jewish royal crown, of which is said, "And all the peoples of the world will see that God's Name is called upon you and they will be in awe of you—this refers to the '*tefillin*' in the head."

The *tefillin* campaign was the first campaign initiated by Rabbi Menachem Mendel Schneerson, the Lubavitcher Rebbe, and there is no better time than the month of Elul to go out in the street and give more and more Jews the opportunity to participate in this mitzvah. The Rebbe emphasized the special importance of the mitzvah of *tefillin* in guarding our soldiers and granting them victory over the enemy, as indicated in the verse, "And of Gad he said: "Blessed is He Who grants expanse to Gad; he dwells like a lion, tearing the arm [of his prey, together] with the head"—this is in merit of the *tefillin* which are placed on the arm and the head. Indeed, the tribe of Israel associated with Elul is the tribe of Gad!

After a good dose of prayer and *tefillin*, in the head and in the heart, we will accept God's yoke upon us this coming Rosh Hashanah, and we can already wish you all, ketivah vechatimah tovah— May you be inscribed and sealed for a good year.

The Arizal teaches that, "The initial letters of the words [referring to a case of involuntary manslaughter], '[God] brought it about by his hand, I will make [a place for you to which he shall flee]' are Elul, to allude to the fact that God in His loving-kindness has made and ordered the month of Elul, for all those who have sinned throughout the year to return then and to do *teshuvah* (repentance)" (*Sha'ar Hapesukim, Parashat Mishpatim*).

9 Jewish Things About Pomegranates

Why this ancient fruit is a Jewish symbol.

BY MJL

9 Things You Didn't Know About Rosh Hashanah

ROSH HASHANAH

Images of pomegranates are mainstays of Rosh Hashanah cards, Jewish jewelry and a range of Jewish ritual objects, and the fruit itself makes frequent appearances in Jewish cuisine. But what's so Jewish about this ancient treat? Quite a lot!

1. The Pomegranate Is One of Israel's "Seven Species."

The pomegranate is one of the seven species of Israel (along with wheat, barley, grapes, figs, olives, and dates) listed in the Torah in Parashat Eikev (Deuteronomy 7:12-11:25).

2. Pomegranates Traditionally Symbolize Fertility and Love.

In Jewish tradition, pomegranates are a symbol of fertility and love, winning them frequent mention in, among other biblical texts, the Song of Songs. For example (Song of Songs 4:3): "Your lips are like a crimson thread; your mouth is lovely. Your brow behind your veil [gleams] like a pomegranate split open."

3. Pomegranates Decorate Many Torah Scrolls.

Rimonim (pomegranate-shaped ornaments) top this Torah scroll. *(Israel Defense Forces/Flickr)*

The decorative ornaments at the top of many Ashkenazi Torah scroll covers are often shaped like pomegranates and are called rimonim, the Hebrew word for pomegranate.

4. Pomegranates Are Part of the Sephardic Rosh Hashanah Seder.

The pomegranate is one of several symbolic foods incorporated into the Rosh Hashanah seder, a Sephardic ritual. Before eating the pomegranate seeds, Jews traditionally say, "May we be as full of mitzvot (commandments) as the pomegranate is full of seeds."

5. A Pomegranate Is Often the "New Fruit" on the Second Night of Rosh Hashanah.

Many Jews use pomegranates on the second night of Rosh Hashanah, for the custom of saying a blessing over a "new fruit," one that people have not eaten in a long time.

6. Pomegranate Seeds Are Associated With the 613 Mitzvot (Commandments).

The pomegranate is often said to have 613 seeds, corresponding to the 613 mitzvot (plural of mitzvah) derived from the Bible. While this is not actually true (the number of seeds in each pomegranate varies widely), some have theorized that this belief stems from a misinterpretation of a passage in the Gemara (Berachot 4), which concludes that even "the empty ones among the Jews are full of mitzvot like a pomegranate is [full of seeds.]"

7. Pomegranates Continue to Grow in Israel.

Pomegranates have been cultivated in Israel (and throughout the Middle East) for thousands of years, and they continue to grow there in abundance. When pomegranates are in season, fresh-squeezed pomegranate juice is available in kiosks throughout the country.

According to the Israeli Agriculture International Portal, Israel harvests approximately 60,000 tons of the fruit annually, of which about half are earmarked for export.

8. Pomegranates Are Frequently Mentioned in Jewish Texts

Pomegranates make frequent appearances in the Bible and Talmud, including:

- In Parashat Sh'lach (Numbers 13:1-15:41) in the Torah, a pomegranate is one of the items brought back by the 12 spies when they return from scouting out the Land of Canaan.
- Images of pomegranates adorn the robes of the high priest, as described in Parashat Tetzaveh (Exodus 27:20 – 30:10) of the Torah.
- In one story in the Talmud, the wife of a rabbi (Hiyya Bar Ashi) tests him by disguising herself as a prostitute and then seducing him, demanding he pay her with a freshly picked pomegranate. (Kiddushin 81b)

9. Pomegranates Are Found on Ancient Judean Coins.

An image of a pomegranate decorated some ancient Jewish coins, including a recently discovered one from the era of the Bar Kochba revolt (second century CE).

Funny Jewish and Yiddish Sayings

- Ask about your neighbors, then buy the house.
- Don't live in a town where there are no doctors.
- If God lived on earth, people would break his windows.
- If the rich could hire the poor to die for them, the poor would make a very nice living.
- He has more in his head than in his pocket.
- Rejoice not at thine enemy's fall - but don't rush to pick him up either.
- Worries go down better with soup than without.
- You can't sit on two horses with one behind.
- They are both in love: he with himself and she with herself.
- With horses you check the teeth; with a human you check the brains.
- The hat is fine but the head is too small.
- He's meditating on whether a flea has a belly-button.
- Thieves and lovers like the dark
- All is not butter that comes from a cow.
- If he were twice as smart, he'd be an idiot!
- If a girl can't dance, she says the musicians can't play.
- Dress up a broom and it will look nice too.
- Even a bear can be taught to dance.
- Don't give me the honey and spare me the sting.
- A black hen can lay a white egg.
- Man plans and God laughs.
- If you sleep with dogs, you get up with fleas.

Wise Proverbs

- A bird that you set free may be caught again, but a word that escapes your lips will not return.
- A mother understands what a child does not say.
- A pessimist, confronted with two bad choices, chooses both.
- As he thinks in his heart, so he is.
- As you teach, you learn.
- Do not be wise in words - be wise in deeds.
- Don't be sweet, lest you be eaten up; don't be bitter, lest you be spewed out.
- Don't look for more honor than your learning merits.
- First mend yourself, and then mend others.
- He that can't endure the bad, will not live to see the good.
- If charity cost nothing, the world would be full of philanthropists.
- If not for fear, sin would be sweet.
- Make sure to be in with your equals if you're going to fall out with your superiors.
- Not to have felt pain is not to have been human.
- What you don't see with your eyes, don't invent with your mouth.

Funny Quotes About Jews

- Anytime a person goes into a delicatessen and orders a pastrami on white bread, somewhere a Jew dies. - Milton Berle
- Jesus was a Jew, yes, but only on his mother's side. - Archie Bunker
- America is a place where Jewish merchants sell Zen love beads

- to agnostics for Christmas. - John Burton
- A car hit a Jewish man. The paramedic says, "Are you comfortable?" The man says, "I make a good living.

Popular Yiddish Words

In the early part of the 20th century, more than 10 million people world-wide spoke Yiddish. By the middle part of that century, the numbers had declined to around 2.5 million but it is still being spoken today.

Here are some of the common words you might want to know the meaning of:

- bubbe - Grandmother, other similar words are bobe or bobeshi
- chutzpah - extreme arrogance or nerve, another similar word is khutspe
- glitch - a slip or nosedive
- kibbitz - to chat or joke around
- kibbutz - a collective farm
- klutz - a block of wood; a clumsy of dumb person; another word is klots
- kosher - food or other things that is acceptable to Orthodox Jews
- kvetsh - to press or squeeze; complain
- Mazel Tov - good luck; congratulations; another word is mazltof
- mishegas - craziness; insanity
- mishpocheh - family; other words are mishpokhe or mishpucha
- oy vey - means dismay or grief; "oy vey iz mir" means "Oh, woe is me."

- plotz - to explode, extreme aggravation; another word is plats
- shalom - deep peace; a greeting
- shlep - to drag; unwillingly carry something
- shtick - gimmick; something you do, like a routine on stage
- spiel - very long sales pitch
- shiksa - implies that a non-Jewish woman's main traits are her good looks and youth
- shagetz - a non-Jewish boy who is unruly or bad natured
- tuches - your bottom; your rear end; other words are tuchis, tuches or tokhis
- yente - a gossip; a busybody

A fleeing Taliban terrorist, desperate for water, was plodding through the desert when he saw something in the distance.

Praying it wasn't a mirage, he hurried toward the object only to find a little old Jew standing beside his weathered display rack, selling ties.

The terrorist blurted, "Give me water!"

The old man replied, "Sorry, no water. Would you like to buy a tie? They're only $5."

The terrorist screamed, "Idiot! Infidel! I don't need an over-priced western adornment. I spit on your ties! I need water!"

"Sorry, no water, just ties. Pure silk, and only $5."

"Fah! A curse on your ties! I'd twist one around your scrawny neck and choke the life out of you but . . . I must save my strength and find water!"

"Nu," said the little old Jew, "so you don't want to buy a tie from me, and you hate me, call me infidel and threaten my life. But I'm bigger than all of that, so I'll tell you that if you go west, over that hill for about two miles, you'll find a restaurant. They serve the finest food and all the ice-cold water you could ever drink. Go in peace."

Grumbling another curse, the desperate Taliban terrorist staggered west, over the hill.

Several hours later, he crawled back, nearly dead, and gasped, "They won't let me in without a tie!"

Jewish Views on Cremation

BY MY JEWISH LEARNING

Jewish law mandates that human remains be buried after death, and this has been dominant Jewish practice for millennia.

Extensive sources from the Torah through the later rabbinic authorities attest to this requirement, and there is a powerful taboo against cremation reinforced by the millions of Jews burned in Nazi crematoria during the Holocaust. Nevertheless, as cremation becomes more common in mainstream society, the number of Jews opting for cremation appears to be increasing, forcing Jewish authorities to consider a number of related issues, including whether cremated remains may be interred in a Jewish cemetery and whether a rabbi may officiate at a funeral for someone who has been cremated.

Is cremation permitted by Jewish law?

Defenders of cremation point out that there is no explicit prohibition against cremation in Jewish legal sources. However there are prohibitions on defiling dead bodies and detailed procedures for handling them prior to burial — all of which appear inconsistent with the act of cremation. Proponents of cremation also point to biblical sources suggesting that Jews may have practiced the burning of dead bodies in ancient times.

Against that is a large body of Jewish literature that deals extensively with burial of the dead. In Genesis (3:19), God declares of man: "For dust you are, and to dust you shall return." Deuteronomy (21:23) commands in the case of an executed criminal, "You shall surely bury him." The requirement of burying the dead is explicitly codified in multiple later rabbinic sources as well, including Sanhedrin 46b, Maimonides' Sefer Hamitzvot and the Shulchan Aruch.

Moreover, there are additional historical, cultural and spiritual arguments against cremation. According to the Jewish mystical tradition, the soul does not immediately depart the body after death, and the process of decay in the earth allows a gradual separation rather than the more immediate and painful one resulting from the burning of the body. Cremation was historically associated with pagan practices that Jews are repeatedly enjoined in the Torah to reject. And because the body is traditionally considered the property of God, it is forbidden to defile it, which some regard the willful burning of human remains to be.

For all these reasons, Orthodox and Conservative rabbinic authorities maintain that cremation is prohibited. The Reform movement has adopted conflicting positions on this question over the years, but the most recent rabbinic opinion on the subject states that while cremation ought to be discouraged, the practice is not considered sinful.

Can the remains of cremated Jews be buried in a Jewish cemetery?

Generally yes. Even in traditional communities, the fact that someone may not have adhered to Jewish law in their lifetime does not constitute grounds for their exclusion from Jewish burial grounds. Individual burial societies or Jewish cemeteries might decline to inter the ashes of a cremated body, in part as a deterrent to others who might also choose cremation. But there is nothing in Jewish law that bars them from burying ashes. Many Jewish cemeteries are known to bury ashes upon request, and the Reform movement has said explicitly that cremated remains of a Jewish person should be buried in a Jewish cemetery.

Can a rabbi officiate at a funeral for someone who was cremated?

It depends on the circumstances. According to a ruling adopted by the Conservative movement's legal authorities in 1986, in a case where a family declines the advice of a rabbi not to cremate a family member's remains, the rabbi should not officiate at the interment, but may choose to officiate at a ceremony prior to the cremation. If the family did not consult a rabbi prior to cremation, the rabbi may choose to officiate at the interment. The Reform movement does not object to its rabbis presiding over a funeral at which a cremation is to take place.

Does a deceased's wish to be cremated have to be honored?

The Shulhan Arukh rules explicitly, citing Maimonides, that heirs must not respect the wishes of a deceased person not to be buried. While some rabbinic authorities differed on this point, contemporary Orthodox and Conservative authorities uphold the view that next of kin are not obliged to defer to the wishes of the deceased in such a case. The Reform movement has said that children are not forbidden from honoring a parent's request to be cremated, yet neither are they obliged to do so if it contravenes their own religious principles.

Is cremation cheaper than burial?

Yes. According to a study from the National Funeral Directors Association, the median cost of a funeral in the United States in 2014 was $7,181, while cremation cost $6,078 — and could easily be far lower if certain services were foregone. However, given the importance traditionally accorded to Jewish burial, many Jewish communities have resources, such as free burial societies, to subsidize a traditional burial in cases where the family lacks sufficient financial resources. In addition, it is traditional Jewish practice to bury someone in a simple pine casket, rather than the more expensive types of caskets that funeral homes often market.

Is embalming permissible in Jewish tradition?

Embalming is the process of preserving human remains, often to enhance presentability for public viewing. As with cremation, embalming is traditionally viewed as inconsistent with Jewish practices surrounding death and burial. Embalming a body is generally seen as a form of mutilation of the dead body, while the whole notion of preservation runs counter to the tradition that the dead be buried quickly and in as natural a state as possible. However exceptions for certain embalming procedures are occasionally made in extenuating circumstances, as when it is required by law or if a body must travel overseas for burial.

Jews and Guns

Jewish law forbids hunting, and few Jews own firearms.

BY MY JEWISH LEARNING

Jews, particularly American ones, have a longstanding aversion to guns. According to a 2005 American Jewish Committee study, Jews have the lowest rate of gun ownership of all religious groups, with just 13 percent of Jewish households owning firearms (compared to 41 percent for non-Jews) and only 10 percent of Jews personally owning a gun (compared to 26 percent).

The majority of American Jews, who overwhelmingly live in urban rather than rural communities (where gun ownership tends to be more widespread) support the Democratic party, whose platform calls for stricter gun control, and major Jewish organizations have repeatedly thrown their support behind gun control measures. A 2013 list of prominent anti-gun activists compiled by the National Rifle Association included several of the largest Jewish groups.

Jewish gun groups, meanwhile, are few and far between, with limited influence. The most visible is Jews for the Preservation of Firearms Ownership, based in Bellevue, Washington, which reported less than $100,000 in revenues in 2015 and lists only three board members on its IRS filing. Still, some Jews have long argued that the community's broad opposition to firearms is naive and dangerous given the history of Jewish oppression and the persistence of anti-Semitism, sometimes violently expressed.

Is Jewish tradition in favor of gun control?

The debate over gun control policy, like most contemporary policy issues, has sources in the Jewish tradition to support both sides.

On the pro-gun side is the famous Talmudic dictum: If someone comes to kill you, rise up and kill him first. This statement from the

Talmudic sage Rava is derived from a Mishnah passage that permits a homeowner to kill an intruder in self-defense if the trespasser arrives in the night. Some Jewish gun proponents have argued that since the Torah commands self-preservation, acquiring the means for that preservation is also a religious requirement, with some going so far as to suggest that gun control laws prevent Jews from exercising their religious obligations.

Others have made the more pragmatic argument that in an era of heightened terrorist concerns, prudence dictates that Jews acquire firearms for self-defense — especially given that Jewish institutions are routinely targeted by Islamic and white supremacist terrorist groups. (Many institutions are, as a result, protected by security guards and other defensive measures.) Rabbi Dovid Bendory, sometimes known as the "gun rabbi," has asserted that, given the history of Jewish oppression and the ongoing threats to Jewish institutions, Jews should be the first people in line to acquire defensive weaponry.

"How do Jews expect to put teeth behind the words "Never Again!" if not with the ability to apply and project personal force when righteous — and necessary — for survival?" Bendory wrote in an article on the JPFO website.

Jewish critics of the prevailing anti-gun sentiment within the Jewish community, have also noted the critical role guns and other weapons played for Jewish partisans — Jews who actively resisted the Nazis — during World War II, and later for Israelis fighting to establish and defend their state.

On the gun control side are a number of frequently cited rabbinic principles. Judaism mandates that one avoid unnecessary danger, and some studies show that gun ownership is risky. The Talmud in Avoda Zara prohibits selling weapons to idolaters, prompting one rabbinic authority to extend the ban even to Jewish bandits — a statement readily invoked to justify restricting gun sales to criminals and the mentally ill. Rabbinic groups from all three major Jewish denominations — Orthodox, Conservative and Reform — have all cited Jewish legal precedent in resolutions supporting gun control.

Finally, there's the famous saying of Isaiah, who prophesied a time when nations would beat their swords into plough shares — a vision often said to reflect Judaism's belief that the ideal society is one devoid of deadly weaponry. This dim view of weapons is cited in a Mishnah that records a disagreement over whether it is permitted to carry weapons on Shabbat. Rabbi Eliezer maintains that they are merely "ornaments," but his colleagues, citing Isaiah, disagree, saying weapons are "indignities."

The Orthodox Rabbinical Council of America, in its 2014 resolution in favor of restricting "American citizens' easy and unregulated access to weapons," cited Isaiah in support of its call for avoiding "recreational activities that desensitize participants to killing, weaponry, and violence."

Didn't gun control cause the Holocaust?

Some have suggested that if Jews had possessed guns in Nazi Germany, the Holocaust might not have occurred. Germany's move to forbid Jewish gun ownership prior to launching the Final Solution is typically cited as a key support for this belief. Republican presidential candidate Ben Carson briefly made this notion a matter of public debate after including it in his 2015 book *A More Perfect Union* and in subsequent interviews. The Anti-Defamation League responded that it was ludicrous to suggest armed Jews could have stopped the Holocaust. (Carson called the ADL statement "foolishness.")

But the argument has also surfaced in publicity materials from Jewish gun activists, including the 2010 documentary *No Guns for Jews*, which implied that gun control measures in Europe in the 1930s enabled the Nazi genocide. "When the right to self defense is denied, God's law is violated," the film intones. "Would history have been rewritten if the SS confronted thousands of armed Jews during the riots of Kristallnacht?"

Does Jewish law allow hunting?

Most authorities say it is not permissible to hunt for sport. Two sources are generally cited in this regard. The first is Rabbi Isaac Lampronri, who wrote in his work *Pahad Yitzhak* that it is forbidden to hunt animals because it's wasteful. The 18th-century rabbinic authority Ezekiel Landau added that recreational hunting is forbidden on the grounds of animal cruelty and because of the risks to the hunter. Neither of the two biblical figures known to be hunters — Esau and Nimrod — are held up as role models. All the biblical patriarchs (Abraham, Isaac and Jacob), as well as Joseph, Moses and King David were herders — nurturers of animals, not their pursuers.

Hunting for food is, in principle, not objectionable. However land animals must be ritually slaughtered by hand to render them kosher, which would make hunting them for food with a firearm impermissible.

Some American Jews do, nonetheless, hunt for sport. However, the American Jewish population is clustered in urban and suburban areas, where hunting is less pervasive than in rural areas.

Isn't everyone in Israel armed?

Guns are highly visible in Israel. Soldiers toting large automatic weapons are ubiquitous in Israeli cities, and many sites and institutions are protected by armed security guards. In addition, some civilians carry sidearms, particularly in Jewish settlements in the West Bank. Supporters of looser gun laws in the United States have pointed to Israel as an example of a society made safer by the widespread availability of guns. Following the Sandy Hook elementary school massacre in 2012, National Rifle Association chief Wayne LaPierre claimed that Israel had ended school shootings by placing armed guards at every school. Israel said that claim was false and that there is "no comparison" between massacres by the mentally ill and those by ideologically driven terrorists. While most Israelis serve in the army, where they are trained to operate firearms, private gun ownership rates (not including military-issued weapons) are far lower in Israel than they are in the United States.

In fact, Israel has extensive restrictions on guns. Unlike the United States, Israel has no right to bear arms, and only certain groups of citizens are eligible to get a gun license — among them residents of West Bank settlements. Background checks, weapons training and demonstration of a bona fide reason for needing a gun are prerequisites for obtaining one. Maintaining a license requires completing regular courses in shooting and undergoing regular psychological evaluations. As many as 80 percent of Israel's license requests are turned down annually.

What Is Idolatry?

Rejection of "foreign worship" is a primary commandment and central to the Jewish worldview.

BY MY JEWISH LEARNING

Idolatry is among the most serious sins in Judaism and its rejection is core to the Jewish worldview. Idolatry is the subject of the first three of the Ten Commandments and its practice is one of three cardinal sins which one is supposed to die rather transgress (along with murder and illicit sex). A ban on idolatry is also one of the Noahide commandments, the seven laws that Judaism teaches are incumbent on all of humanity.

While Judaism has never been a proselytizing faith, the elimination of idolatry from the world was traditionally a central Jewish objective. In the seventh chapter of Deuteronomy, God declares that the idol worshipping nations resident in the land of Israel should be wiped out, no treaties should be signed with them and no Israelite sons or daughters offered up to them in marriage: "Instead, this is what you shall do to them: you shall tear down their altars, smash their pillars, cut down their sacred posts, and consign their images to the fire." According to Maimomindes, embracing idolatry amounts to a denial of the whole of Torah and its proscription is "the outstanding commandment of them all."

In its simplest formulation, idolatry is the worship of gods (or natural phenomena) in place of the one God who created the world, redeemed the Israelites from Egyptian slavery, and revealed the Torah on Mount Sinai. The prohibition includes the worship of celestial bodies or other natural phenomena, people, inanimate objects or foreign gods, as well as worshipping God in the manner in which idols were worshipped, which according to some biblical passages featured child sacrifice and prostitution. It is likewise forbidden to make any object of divine worship, even if it's merely for decoration.

According to some sources, it was the patriarch Abraham's rejection of the idolatry widespread in his time that merited his selection by God to become the father of the Jewish nation. According to a famous Midrash (Genesis Rabbah 38), Abraham once smashed all the idols belonging to his father, who had a shop selling them. When his father returned and inquired what had happened, Abraham pointed to the largest idol in the shop, the one he had left standing, and said that idol had destroyed all the others.

In rabbinic sources, idolatry is referred to as avodah zarah (literally "foreign worship") or avodat kochavim ("worship of stars"). These terms do not appear in the Bible, which refers to elohim acheirim — literally "other gods." The Torah also prohibits the construction of any "sculpted image" or the worship of it. The epitome of idolatry in the Bible is the Golden Calf, the idol constructed by the Israelites after Moses was delayed in returning from atop Mount Sinai.

While depicting God visually in any manner is prohibited, the Bible is actually full of anthropomorphic language. God is often portrayed in the Bible as having physical form — a finger, for example, or an outstretched arm. Rabbinic sources even imagine God as praying like one of them — laying on tefillin, wrapping in a tallit, and saying words of prayer (see Berakhot 6 and Berakhot 7).

In biblical times, the term idolatry was applied to any religion other than the faith practiced by Abraham and his family. And indeed, the Mishnah uses the term *goyim*, a generic term for non-Jews, in place of the seemingly more specific "star worshippers" used later in the Talmud. In the Mishneh Torah, Maimonides offers a brief history of how idol worship came to envelop the world, beginning with veneration of the celestial bodies and proceeding to images of them until such time as the images became objects of worship in and of themselves. This changed only with Abraham's recognition that an underlying unity lay beneath the various forces of the natural world.

During Temple times, idolatrous practices were an ever-present temptation to which many ancient kings of Israel succumbed, including King Solomon. An entire tractate of the Talmud — named, appropriately enough, Avodah Zarah — deals with the laws of idolatry, which mainly focus on limiting interactions between Jews and idolaters and proscribing any benefit from idolatrous practices. Among the prohibitions are having any dealings with idolaters prior to their festivals or selling them any items that might be used in idol worship. According to one opinion recorded in the Mishnah, anyone who encounters an idol should grind it to dust and cast it to the sea. But the rabbis disagree, saying that dust would then become fertilizer and run afoul of the prohibition on deriving benefit.

By the rabbinic era, the scourge of idolatry seems to have receded, and with it the automatic linkage between non-Jews and the worship of celestial bodies. A story recorded in the Talmud describes how this happened.

In response to the indication of divine acceptance, they observed a fast for three days and three nights, and He delivered the evil inclination to them. A form of a fiery lion cub came forth from the chamber of the Holy of Holies. Zechariah the prophet said to the Jewish people: This is the evil inclination for idol worship, as it is stated in the verse that refers to this event: "And he said: This is the evil one" (Zechariah 5:8).

When they caught hold of it one of its hairs fell, and it let out a shriek of pain that was heard for four hundred parasangs. They said: What should we do to kill it? Perhaps, Heaven forfend, they will have mercy upon him from Heaven, since it cries out so much. The prophet said to them: Throw it into a container made of lead and seal the opening with lead, since lead absorbs sound. As it is stated: "And he said: This is the evil one. And he cast it down into the midst of the measure, and he cast a stone of lead upon its opening" (Zechariah 5:8). They followed this advice and were freed of the evil inclination for idol worship.

With the decline of actual idol worship, the question arose for the first time whether other early medieval religions—specifically the other monotheistic ones—were idolatrous. The consensus was that Islam was not, but Christianity—with its rich iconography, doctrine of the trinity, and elevation of Jesus as a divine being—was a thornier question. Many Jewish thinkers, both ancient and modern, regarded the worship of Jesus as divine as a clear case of idolatry, while others employed the notion of *shittuf*—the proposition that it's not forbidden for non-Jews to worship the one God in in a way that deviates from unvarnished monotheism—to allow a more liberal attitude toward Christianity. The latter view became something of a necessity as the majority of the world's Jews came to live in Christian lands, where talmudic limits on socializing and doing business with idolaters would have had catastrophic implications. Eastern religions, with their pantheons of various gods and liberal use of divine images, are more straightforward instances of idolatry.

Even so, in contemporary times, it's rare to hear Jewish leaders inveigh against other faith traditions, either Western or Eastern, as idolatrous. To the extent that idolatry is much discussed anymore at all, it is largely modern forms of worship that draw condemnation under the idolatry rubric: worship of the state, money, power and the like. As some contemporary Jewish thinkers have pointed out, the ancient rabbis didn't regard the sun and the moon as intrinsically unholy; it was the worship of them they considered idolatrous. Likewise money and power—these are not evil in of themselves, but their elevation above all else is said to be a manifestation of idolatrous behavior.

Judaism and Sex: Questions and Answers

BY MY JEWISH LEARNING

Judaism is generally very positive about sex, regarding it as a divine gift and a holy obligation — both for the purposes of procreation and for pleasure and intimacy. The Talmud specifies not merely that a husband is required to be intimate with his wife, but sources also indicate that he is obliged to sexually satisfy her. So vital is sexual activity considered to Judaism that celibacy, even for those so devoted to spiritual life that they feel they don't have energy left for marriage and children, is frowned upon.

Nonetheless, Judaism doesn't exactly take an anything goes approach to sex. Instead, sexual activity is highly circumscribed in Jewish tradition, as the rabbis of the Talmud sought to use the human libido as a tool for increasing the population and strengthening marriage. Traditional Jewish law not only prohibits many types of sexual relationships, but it also dictates specific parameters even for permitted ones. And while Judaism is broadly permissive when it comes to sex between married adults, the same is not true for sexual activity outside of a committed relationship.

Does Judaism allow extramarital sex?

Adultery — traditionally defined as sexual intercourse between a married woman and a man who is not her husband — is forbidden in the seventh of the Ten Commandments and is among the most serious infractions in Judaism. But there is no universal prohibition on men having sexual relations out of wedlock, an allowance that is believed to stem at least in part from concerns about paternity — a women with multiple partners raises doubts about a child's parentage. Indeed several of the key figures in the Bible engaged in sexual relationships and fathered children with women who were not their wives, including the patriarchs Abraham and Jacob. The Torah and later rabbinic writings also recognize the category of concubine (*pilegesh* in Hebrew). However, the practice of Jewish men having multiple sexual partners, whether multiple wives or concubines, has not been common for centuries.

What about premarital sex?

Traditionally, premarital sex has been discouraged if not taboo, and in the contemporary Orthodox world it is strictly forbidden. Many ultra-Orthodox communities are stringent about separating males and females in large part to reduce the likelihood of romantic encounters between the unmarried. Though there is no such gender separation in more liberal Jewish communities, even contemporary Reform and Conservative rabbis have upheld Judaism's traditional preference that sex be reserved for marriage. A 1979 Reform movement responsum declared "premarital and extramarital chastity to be our ideal." Even in 2001, when a committee of Reform rabbis published a report on sexual ethics that dropped references to marriage as the sole appropriate context for sexual activity, the movement continued to urge fidelity and exclusivity in sexual relations. The committee issued a separate statement on adultery that described extramarital affairs — whether conducted in secret or with a spouse's consent — as sinful and forbidden.

The Conservative movement has taken a similar line. While officially maintaining that marriage is the only appropriate context for sex and firmly rejecting adultery, incest and general promiscuity, the movement has acknowledged that "a measure of morality" can be found in non-marital sexual relationships provided they comport with Jewish sexual values, including mutual respect, honesty, health and monogamy.

Both the Reform and Conservative movements have affirmed that their attitude toward sexual ethics applies equally to heterosexual and homosexual relationships.

What is the Jewish view on masturbation?

Traditionally, masturbation is strictly prohibited for men. The source of this prohibition is sometimes attributed to the biblical figure Onan who, charged with propagating the family line by fathering children with his brother's widow Tamar, instead withdrew from her and ejaculated on the ground — a crime for which God took his life. Many commentators subsequently understood the prohibition on masturbation as a prohibition on the spilling (or wasting) of sperm. The Shulchan Aruch rules that it is forbidden to spill seed needlessly, calling it a sin more severe than any other in the Torah and tantamount to murder. The Talmud referred to male masturbation as adultery with one's hand.

Some rabbinic authorities consider Onan's sin to have been disobedience, rather than wasted sperm, and see the source of the masturbation ban in concerns about ritual purity. Maimonides, who was a physician as well as a rabbi, wrote that excessive seminal discharge causes bodily decay and diminished vitality — a common belief in the Middle Ages that is not generally accepted by modern Western medicine.

In some Orthodox communities, the prohibition on male masturbation is taken so seriously that various other acts are also barred for fear they might lead to arousal and thus to wasting seed — including touching one's own penis, another act the Talmud banned (even during urination)

The liberal denominations have taken a somewhat more accepting approach. In a 1979 paper that addressed the question directly, Reform Rabbi Walter Jacob wrote that masturbation isn't sinful or harmful, though it should still be discouraged. Elliot Dorff, a leading Conservative rabbi who has written extensively on Jewish sexual ethics, has suggested that given the tendency among Jews in the West to delay marriage, it is unreasonable to expect complete abstention from all sexual pleasure until one's wedding night. Given the choice between premarital sex and masturbation, Dorff wrote, masturbation is morally preferable. In part to avoid such choices, some Orthodox communities strongly encourage young people to marry by their early 20s, if not earlier.

Female masturbation is less problematic in Jewish tradition, as it doesn't raise concerns about spilled seed. The issue is not directly addressed in ancient sources. Indeed, some have suggested that the rabbis of the Talmud, all of them men, couldn't even conceive of female masturbation as a form of sex. While, some authorities have inferred a prohibition based on sources that are sometimes understood as barring lustful thoughts, , other contemporary rabbis see no problem with women masturbating. Rabbi Moshe Feinstein, a leading 20th century Orthodox authority, dismissed multiple grounds for objection to female masturbation, including that sexual thoughts might lead to actual transgressions.

Is pornography acceptable?

Traditional Jewish law is firmly opposed to pornography. The Shulchan Aruch prohibited even looking at a woman's finger or her clothes lest it lead to impure thoughts and actions. Various biblical sources are also routinely invoked as a basis for banning porn. Among them, the verse (Numbers 15:39) that establishes tzitzit fringes as a bulwark against following the lustful urges of the eyes. Moreover, Jewish tradition stresses the importance of modesty and privacy in the conduct of sexual relations, and early rabbinic literature voices considerable fear about the impact of impure sexual thoughts. Rabbi Danya Ruttenberg, a Conservative rabbi who has written extensively about Judaism and sexuality, raises another concern about consumer ethics and pornography, given that much sexually explicit material is produced in ways that are exploitative of the performers.

Though ancient rabbinic sources were fairly permissive with respect to sexual activity between husband and wife, some rabbis nevertheless consider the viewing of pornography as beyond the pale even when married couples use it as foreplay or as a way to improve their sex lives. Shmuley Boteach, a rabbi and author whose books include *Kosher Sex, Kosher Lust and Kosher Adultery*, has approved fellatio and sex toys, but draws the line at pornography. "They may be making love while watching the film, but in spirit and in mind they might as well be with the people in the video," *Kosher Sex* says of couples that watch pornography together.

Rabbi Jonathan Crane, writing in the Reform movement's 2014 volume on sexuality, *The Sacred Encounter*, takes a different view. "It would seem that the tonal thrust of the textual tradition favors permitting, if not encouraging, Jews to produce and consume some forms of erotic expressions for the purpose of invigorating marital relations, with perhaps more freedom in the verbal than visual arena," he writes.

In recent years, the easy availability of online pornography has prompted serious alarm, particularly in the Orthodox world. Orthodox rabbis have issued stringent edicts about internet use, and a number of organizations have sprung up to help those battling porn addiction. GuardYourEyes, an Orthodox website endorsed by a number of prominent Orthodox (mostly ultra-Orthodox) rabbis, offers a wide range of tools for those battling addiction, including support groups, daily emails and filtering software. "I doubt that at any time in our history has there been as grave a threat to the morality of our people and to the stability of the Jewish family as the plague of addiction to internet pornography," Abraham Twerski, a leading Orthodox rabbi and respected psychiatrist specializing in addiction, has written.

Is sexting permitted?

Sexting, the sending of sexually suggestive words or images by text message, has become a common practice among teenagers and has raised alarms among educators, religious and secular alike. However, the simple act of using words to sexually entice isn't a forbidden act. Indeed, a famous Talmudic story suggests that at least one ancient

Jewish rabbi talked erotically with his wife in bed prior to intercourse. In his podcast *The Joy of Text*, Orthodox Rabbi Dov Linzer suggests that sexting one's spouse could actually be a good way to build "some sense of anticipation and excitement even before the couple moves to the bedroom."

One problem with sexting is that it can also be a means of carrying on non-physical sexual relationships outside of marriage, as evidenced by the notorious case of former Congressman Anthony Weiner. Experts have also raised concerns that sexting among teens leads to bullying and risky sexual behaviors, though some have challenged these assertions. There have also been cases in which sexted photos of underage girls have wound up online. Sexting that violates someone's privacy or leads to bullying or risky behaviors would clearly run afoul of Jewish law and ethics.

Does Judaism allow oral sex?

Though some rabbis in the Talmud were highly restrictive about which sexual activities married couples could engage in, the prevailing view was that a man may do with his wife as he wishes provided he has her consent. This ruling is explicitly codified by Maimonides and by the 16th-century authority Moses Isserles (known as the Rema), whose commentary on the Shulchan Aruch is considered authoritative by Ashkenazi Jews. While some rabbinic authorities consider fellatio to run afoul of the prohibition on spilling seed, this is not universally accepted even within Orthodox circles. The Rema cites a leniency that even "unnatural" sex — a Talmudic term usually understood as referring to anal sex — is permitted even if it leads to ejaculation. From this specific allowance for non-procreative ejaculation, some extrapolate that any sexual act undertaken in the context of a permitted sexual relationship is acceptable even if it results in sperm not being used for reproductive purposes.

As with female masturbation, oral sex performed on a woman does not raise issues of spilled semen. Though some more stringent opinions consider the practice forbidden on various grounds — among them, a prohibition on staring at a woman's genitals — both Maimonides and the Rema explicitly permit a man to kiss any limb of his wife's body that he desires.

What Is Midrash?

These writings, which fill in gaps in biblical texts, falls into two categories: halacha and aggadah.

BY MY JEWISH LEARNING

Midrash is an interpretive act, seeking the answers to religious questions (both practical and theological) by plumbing the meaning of the words of the Torah. (In the Bible, the root d-r-sh is used to mean inquiring into any matter, including occasionally to seek out God's word.) Midrash responds to contemporary problems and crafts new stories, making connections between new Jewish realities and the unchanging biblical text.

Midrash falls into two categories. When the subject is law and religious practice (halacha), it is called midrash halacha. Midrash aggadah, on the other hand, interprets biblical narrative, exploring questions of ethics or theology, or creating homilies and parables based on the text. (Aggadah means "telling"; any midrash which is not halakhic falls into this category.)

Midrash Halacha

It is often difficult to determine, simply from reading the biblical text, what Jewish law would be in practice. The text of the Torah is often general or ambiguous when presenting laws. Midrash halacha attempts to clarify or extend a law beyond the conditions assumed in the Bible, and to make connections between current practice and the biblical text. It made possible the creation and acceptance of new liturgies and rituals which de facto replaced sacrificial worship after the fall of the Second Temple, and the maintenance of continuity by linking those practices to the words of the Torah.

Midrash halacha from the two centuries following the fall of the Temple was collected in three books — the Mekhilta on Exodus, the Sifra on Leviticus, and the Sifrei on Numbers and Deuteronomy —

known as the tannaitic midrashim. (The tannaim were the rabbis from the time of the Mishnah, edited in approximately 200 C.E.)

Midrash Aggadah

The type of midrash most commonly referred to (as in, "There is a midrash which says…") is from the collections of midrash aggadah, most of which were compiled between about 200 and 1000 C.E. (Many midrashim circulated orally before then). Midrash aggadah may begin its exploration with any word or verse in the Bible. There are many different methods of interpretation and exposition.

Written by rabbis both steeped in Bible and absorbed by the Jewish questions of their time, works of midrash aggadah often occupy the meeting ground between reverence and love for the wording of the fixed text of the Torah, and theological creativity. Midrashic writings thus often yield religious insights that have made Torah directly applicable to later Jewish realities, especially the concerns of its authors. Some of what midrash aggadah yields is insight into the burning, sometimes time-bound questions of those who wrote it. Still, the interpretations produced often have more universal and timeless application to our, or any, generation.

In addition to works devoted to midrashic compilations, midrash aggadah also appears throughout the two Talmuds. Midrash Rabbah, the "Great Midrash," is the name of the collections linked to the five books of the Torah and the "Five Scrolls" (Esther, Song of Songs, Ruth, Lamentations, and Ecclesiastes) read on Holidays. Some of these works read like verse-by-verse commentaries. Others may have originated in sermons linked to the weekly Torah reading.

The Noahide Laws

Seven commandments which, according to Jewish tradition, are incumbent upon all of humankind.

BY JEFFREY SPITZER

In the ninth chapter of Genesis, we read this:

God speaks to Noah and his children as they exit the ark: 'Behold, I establish my covenant with you, and with your seed after you.' (Genesis 9:9)

Although rabbinic texts preserve various traditions about the details of this covenant, the Talmud reports the following:

The children of Noah were commanded with seven commandments: [to establish] laws, and [to prohibit] cursing God, idolatry, illicit sexuality, bloodshed, robbery, and eating flesh from a living animal (Sanhedrin 56a; cf. Tosefta Avodah Zarah 8:4 and Genesis Rabbah 34:8).

The Laws

1. Do establish laws.
2. Don't curse God.
3. Do not practice idolatry.
4. Do not engage in illicit sexuality.
5. Do not participate in bloodshed.
6. Do not rob.
7. Do not eat flesh from a living animal.

The Details

The prohibition against idolatry refers specifically to idolatrous worship, and not to beliefs. In later generations, Jews had to determine whether the prevailing religious cultures in which they lived were idolatrous. Since Islam is strictly monotheistic, Muslims have always been considered Noahides. Since the later Middle Ages, Jews have acknowledged that the Christian doctrine of the Trinity was not the same as idolatry, and they were also recognized as Noahides.

The prohibition against theft includes kidnapping, cheating an employee or an employer, and a variety of similar acts.

The prohibition against illicit sexuality includes six particular prohibitions, derived from a single verse:

Noahides are prohibited from engaging in six illicit sexual relationships: with one's mother, with one's father's wife, with another man's wife, with his sister from the same mother, in a male homosexual union, and with an animal as it says, '*Therefore shall a man leave his father...*' this refers to his father's wife; '*and his mother...*" refers to the mother; '*and cling to his wife...*' and not another's wife; '*wife...*' and not a homosexual union; '*and become one flesh*' (Genesis 2:24) excluding animals... (Maimonides, Laws of Kings, 9:5)

Eating flesh from a living animal is how the rabbis understood "But flesh with its life, which is its blood, you shall not eat" (Genesis 9:4). It has been suggested that the custom of eating an amputated limb of an animal was a way to keep the rest of the meat fresh in the days before refrigeration.

The Obligation to Create a System of Laws

According to the medieval philosopher and codifier Maimonides, the legal system which Noahides are required to set up is specifically to establish punishments for infractions of the other six Noahide laws (Laws of Kings 9:14).

Nahmanides, a medieval Bible commentator, understands the obligation more broadly:

In my opinion, the laws which the Noahides were to establish according to their seven commandments is not only to establish courts in each town, but that they were also commanded concerning theft, abuse, usury, labor relations, damages, loans, business, and the like, just as Israel was commanded to set up laws in these matters (Nahmanides, Commentary to Genesis 34:13).

Later authorities, including Rabbi Moses Sofer (1763-1839), claim that Maimonides did not exclude what Nahmanides had included, but that Maimonides considered all of these laws to be included under the prohibition of "theft." Rabbi Naphtali Tzvi Yehudah Berlin (1817-1893) states that Nahmanides' approach requires non-Jews to legislate on these matters, but the details and formulation of the legislation are left to their discretion.

Natural Law

The Noahide laws bear a striking resemblance to a separate rabbinic tradition that describes the commandments that would have been derived logically even if God had not included them in the Torah:

'You must keep my rulings' (Lev. 18:4): These are the items which are written in the Torah which, had they not been written should logically have been written, such as the [prohibitions against] robbery, illicit sexuality, idolatry, cursing God, and bloodshed." (Sifra, Ahare Mot, section 140)

The overlap here of five of the seven laws enumerated for Noahides indicates that they may have been understood as a sort of universal, natural morality. This is the way some modern philosophers, such as Hermann Cohen, understood them.

Indeed, based on the Talmudic discussion, Maimonides states:

Six items were commanded to Adam: concerning idolatry, blasphemy, bloodshed, illicit sexuality, theft, and laws…God added to Noah, the law of not eating from the flesh of a live animal." (Maimonides, Laws of Kings 9:1)

The association of these laws with Adam implies that they were established as part of the creation of the natural world.

Laws for Non-Jews Under Jewish Rule

A conversation in tractate Sanhedrin assumes that Jewish courts should enforce the Noahide laws. Therefore, later authorities, most notably Maimonides, understood these laws as describing what Jews should require of non-Jews living under Jewish rule. Since Maimonides saw revelation as the clearest form of reason, it would be folly from his perspective, for non-Jews living under Jewish rule to rely upon their own inadequate reasoning powers to determine law when they have access to the superior reasoning of revelation.

Indeed, according to Maimonides, it is unacceptable for non-Jews living under a Jewish authority not to accept the Noahide laws:

If someone from the other nations wants to convert [they may] as it says '[the law is the same] for you, for a stranger' (Numbers 15:15). But if they do not want to, we do not compel them to accept the Torah and the commandments. Moses did, however, command in the name of God to compel all people to accept the Noahide laws…" (Laws of Kings 8:10)

Maimonides' approach, however, is much disputed among the classical commentators. Some interpreters of Maimonides have argued that he meant to obligate the Jewish court, but not individual Jews, to compel non-Jews to comply with the Noahide laws. Others have argued that the entire issue is irrelevant until the days of the Messiah. Nevertheless, it seems clear that Maimonides intended that whenever it was possible to compel observance, Jews should make an effort to do so.

Other medieval authorities, rather than attempting to re-interpret Maimonides' statement, simply disagreed. Rabbi Abraham ibn Daud clearly rejects any obligation to compel observance of the Noahide laws, even in a situation where Jews have subjugated non-Jews in war. This seems to be the opinion of Rashi, Tosafot, Nahmanides, and Rashba, as well. In dealing with individual non-Jews as employees or slaves, none of the legal codes, aside from Maimonides', mentions an obligation to impose Noahide laws or to punish non-Jews for violation of the Noahide laws.

By way of contrast, when Jews are likely to sin, other Jews are obligated to try and prevent that sin through intervention and education. In general, in modern times, no such obligation is mandated towards non-Jews who violate the Noahide laws. A notable and forceful exception is the opinion of the late Rabbi Menachem Mendel Schneerson, the last leader of Chabad-Lubavitch Hasidism. Schneerson wrote:

We must do everything possible to ensure that the seven Noahide laws are observed. If this can be accomplished through force or through other kinder and more peaceful means through explaining to non-Jews that they should accept God's wishes [we should do so]... Anyone who is able to influence a non-Jew in any way to keep the seven commandments is obligated to do so, since that is what God commanded Moses our teacher ("*Sheva Mitzvot Shel Benai Noach*," *Hapardes* 59:9 7-11, 5745)

Conclusion

That Jews perceive non-Jews as bound by a set of laws–even if they are not bound by the full range of Torah law–is a significant statement. The expectation that non-Jews will set up their own system of justice became the basis for peaceful interactions between Jews and non-Jews. The Noahide laws separated humanity after the flood from the lawless violence which brought God to the point of destroying the world. The Noahide laws stand as a testament to the Jewish belief in the need for the rule of law to protect all peoples.

Ask the Expert: Kosher Pig

Can a Jewish person receive a transplanted heart valve from a pig?

BY MY JEWISH LEARNING

Question: Would an observant Jew in need of the same operation be permitted to use a valve from a pig?

Answer: In modern medicine, pig skin is sometimes transplanted onto patients with severe burns, and heart valves from pigs are often transplanted into patients with damaged or diseased heart valves. This process, called xenografting or xenotransplantation, describes transplants from any non-human animal to a human.

One might assume that Jews would be prohibited from receiving xenotransplants from pigs because of the biblical prohibition against eating and touching swine in Leviticus 11:7-8: "And the swine — although it has true hoofs, with the hoofs cleft through, it does not chew the cud: it is impure for you. You shall not eat of their flesh or touch their carcasses; they are impure for Me."

However, Rashi, an 11th-century Torah commentator, explained that this prohibition against touching pigs applied only when Jews were on their way to Jerusalem to observe the three pilgrimage festivals — Passover, Shavuot and Sukkot. During those festivals the people were required to be in a heightened state of purity, so they had to avoid touching something like the flesh of a pig. Even on the way to Jerusalem, Jews were only prohibited from touching the flesh, that is, the meat of a pig. According to *halacha* (Jewish law) the skin of an animal does not transmit impurities, especially if it has been tanned.

So there is no halachic problem with pigskin and pig heart valves— on the way to Jerusalem or at any other time. Beyond that, there's a very important tenet of Judaism called *pikuach nefesh*, or, saving a life. According to Jewish law, any of the mitzvot (commandments) in the Torah (except idolatry, murder, and forbidden sexual relationships) can and in fact *should* be violated in order to save a person's life; the pikuach nefesh principle is that strong. This means that even if the use of pig parts wasn't generally allowed by halacha, when people's lives are at stake, we are commanded to do whatever is necessary to save them.

Incidentally, this exact issue was brought up on an episode of *Grey's Anatomy* a few years ago. In the episode ("Save Me" Episode 8, Season 1) an Orthodox Jewish girl refuses to have a life-saving xenotransplant from a pig because it's not kosher. The surgeons eventually do the procedure with a xenotransplant from a cow, instead. When the episode first aired, the Orthodox Jewish community responded by condemning the depiction of Jews and Jewish law. Rabbi Avi Shafran, director of public affairs for Agudath Israel of America, called the character's refusal of the pig part "silliness."

Bottom line: If it's a life-saving procedure, there's no problem using parts of a non-kosher animal — unless that part is a ham sandwich, and the procedure is not so much life-saving, such as lunchtime.

How to Acquire the Right Mental State for Prayer

The pursuit of proper kavanah, the Hebrew term for directed attention, has long concerned Jewish thinkers.

BY JOEL HECKER

One of the perennial dilemmas that confronts Jewish prayer is the challenge of achieving concentrated attention within a fixed liturgy. Jewish thinkers have long wrestled with this challenge and devised strategies, both conceptual and practical, to reconcile this binary of practice and spirit.

The problem has been resolved primarily in the domain of kavanah, the Hebrew term for a desired focus or directed attention. This heightened state of mental concentration ranges from a basic practice of mindfulness—simply attending to the words that one utters in prayer—to elaborate schemes of connecting spiritual realms, and even ascending through them.

In perhaps the first prescriptive statement in Jewish literature regarding kavanah in prayer, the Mishnah (Berachot 5:1) states:

[One] should not stand up to pray unless he is in a reverent frame of mind. The original pious ones used to wait a while and then pray, in order to direct their hearts towards the Omnipresent. [While one is reciting Shemoneh Esrei,] even if the king greets him, he should not respond to him, and even if a snake is coiled around his heel, he should not cease.

The Jerusalem Talmud relates a series of colorful methods used by different rabbis to prepare their minds for prayer. Rabbi Hiyya meditated on the Persian political hierarchy to help him concentrate. Rabbi Samuel counted birds. And Rabbi Bun bar Hiyya counted rows of bricks. These latter approaches are strikingly similar to the simple act of counting one's breaths as a means to calm the mind, a method used in mindfulness meditation as practiced today. In the Babylonian Talmud, we read about diverse kinds of legal matters that one should contemplate in order to put oneself in a reverent frame of mind for prayer.

By the medieval period, Jewish thinkers were beginning to offer more detailed prescriptions for how to attain proper kavanah. Moses Maimonides (1135–1204), the most famous medieval philosopher, wrote that any prayer that lacks proper concentration does not constitute prayer. But how to achieve that concentration?

In his legal code, the Mishneh Torah, Maimonides recommends clearing one's thoughts, and sitting for a time before beginning prayer. But in his philosophical work, the Guide of the Perplexed, Maimonides proposes an even more rigorous program for mystical contemplation during the recital of the Shema and the beginning of the daily Amidah prayer:

The first thing that you should cause your soul to hold fast onto is that while reciting the Shema you should empty your mind of everything and pray thus. You should not content yourself with being intent while reciting the first verse of Shema and saying the first blessing [of the Amidah]. When this has been carried out correctly and has been practiced consistently for years, cause your soul, whenever you read or listen to the Torah or listening to it, to be constantly directed—the whole of you and your thought—toward reflection on what you are listening to or reading… (Guide of the Perplexed 3:51).

In this remarkable passage, Maimonides reveals the depth of commitment required to develop the ideal form of kavanah. This is not for the faint of heart. Maimonides prescribes a practice that tilts decidedly toward non-verbal contemplation as the highest form of worship. In this treatment, inner religious awareness, self-effacement, and a pervasive focus upon divinity constitute the aim, rather than observance with a patina of spirituality.

In Maimonides' wake—and partially in response to his unmatched influence — came the flourishing of a new and distinctive form of Jewish mysticism, known as Kabbalah. Jewish mysticism was not a new phenomenon, but the kabbalistic literature of the 12th century and onward provided novel forms of Jewish spirituality.

The kabbalists described divinity as comprising ten aspects or rungs called *sefirot*. Since the Torah is conceived as a revelation of God's own being, every word or phrase, even its unwritten vowels and cantillation notes, signifies one of the sefirot. This approach makes space for the interpretation of a verse from the Torah as a complex string of sefirot.

Kabbalistic thinking extended the esoteric significance of the words of the Torah to the liturgy. Each word or prayer unit symbolizes a specific sefirah. Kavanah is the technique for uniting aspects of one's heart, mind and soul with these higher cosmic meanings of the prayer text.

In one passage, the Zohar, the central work of Jewish mysticism, explains that through the mental act of concentration one causes one's entire being to be constituted as a human tabernacle, prepared to receive divine overflow. Another passage explains that the 248 words of the Shema not only correspond to the 248 limbs of the human body (as per rabbinic teaching), but with the proper intent, reciting them joins together the 248 limbs of the divine body. Further, one is instructed to avoid any interruption between the blessings for the Shema and the recital of the whispered Amidah prayer in order to conjoin the masculine and feminine potencies of divinity.

In the hands of 16th-century kabbalists, and elaborated by many more subsequently, the approaches to kavanah became increasingly technically complex. At the same time, the popularization of kabbalistic attention to kavanah led to the appearance of various formulas to be recited before the recitation of particular prayers. Many of these were variations of the following: "For the sake of the unification of the blessed Holy One and His *Shechinah*, in fear and in love, in love and in fear, through unification of the name *yod* he with *vav* he [the letters of the tetragrammaton, YHVH] in the name of all of Israel."

With the rise of the Hasidic movement in Eastern Europe in the 18th century, with its emphases on joy and communion with the divine, the desire for simpler metaphors and symbols led to the marginalizing of more technical kavanot. Yet, with the advent of cheaper printing, the simple kabbalistic kavanah quoted above became widespread, particularly in Hasidic prayerbooks. Indeed, this popularizing movement made kavanah—whether as rudimentary formulas or as emotive expression—the preeminent focus of religious life.

A letter from Israel Baal Shem Tov, traditionally thought of as the founder of Hasidic Judaism, instructed his brother-in-law to sustain a particular technique of intention during prayer and Torah study. He explained that "in every single letter there are worlds and souls and divinity. These ascend and bond and unite with each other. Then, the letters bond and unite with each other, becoming a word, and they unite in true unity with divinity. Include your soul with them in each and every aspect."

One of the most basic Hasidic teachings is that the entire material world, and even more so the letters of Torah and of prayer, pulsate with divine energy and godly luminosity. Through envisioning the spirituality within each letter of one's prayer, every Hasid could unite with holiness and participate in bringing unity to the fractured reality they experienced. Ecstasy was within reach!

The story of kavanah's trajectory continues to our day. The 1960s witnessed a proliferation of Eastern and New-Age spirituality, in tandem with a popularization of the study of kabbalah. To the extent that these efforts are invested in sincere spiritual searching, they often involve the use of kavanot in prayer and contemplation. Of late, there has been great creativity in developing new kavanot adapted for new forms of prayer and spiritual practice. At the same time, a small but significant number of Jews who are trying to deepen their literacy have also turned to traditional formulas, infused with a new spirit. Indeed, kavanah may today be the subject of the greatest amount of spiritual attention in the English-speaking Jewish world.

Quick Reference For Hebrew Terms

The Talmud is the source from which the code of Jewish Halakhah (law) is derived. It is made up of the Mishnah and the Gemara. The Mishnah is the original written version of the oral law and the Gemara is the record of the rabbinic discussions following this writing down. It includes their differences of view.

Is the Talmud part of the Torah?

The Talmud is a record of the rabbinic debates in the 2nd-5th century on the teachings of the Torah, both trying to understand how they apply and seeking answers for the situations they themselves were encountering.

What is the difference between the Midrash and the Mishnah?

Only Mishnah is—like other ancient Near Eastern law—apodictic, recognizing no need for justification. But Midrash existed before Mishnah and its law served as grounding for the non-justificatory Mishnaic texts.

What is the Talmud in the Bible?

The Talmud, meaning 'teaching' is an ancient text containing Jewish sayings, ideas and stories. It includes the Mishnah (oral law) and the Gemara ('Completion'). The Mishnah is a large collection of sayings, arguments and counter-arguments that touch on virtually all areas of life.

What are the six sections of the Talmud?

The six orders of the Mishnah are:

- Zera'im ("Seeds"): 11 tractates.
- Mo'ed ("Festivals"): 12 tractates.
- Nashim ("Women"): 7 tractates.
- Neziqin ("Torts"): 10 tractates.

- Qodashim ("Sacred Things"):1 tractates.
- Tohorot ("Purity"): 12 tractates.

What are the first 5 books of the Bible called?

The Pentateuch

The five books making up the Torah are *Be-reshit*, *Shemot*, *Va-yikra*, *Be-midbar* and *Devarim*, which in the English Bible correspond to Genesis, Exodus, Leviticus, Numbers and Deuteronomy.

Shalom Aleichem

Peace be to you, ministering angels, messengers of the Most Hight, the supreme Sovereign, the Holy and Blessed One. May you come in peace, messengers of the Most High, the supreme Sovereign, the Holy and Blessed One. Bless me with peace, messengers of the Most High, the supreme Sovereign, the Holy and Blessed One. May your departure be in peace, messengers of peace, messengers of the Most High, the supreme Sovereign, the Holy and Blessed One.

THE BLESSING OVER CHILDREN

For Boys: May God make you like May God make you like Ephraim and Menashe.

For Girls: May God make you like Sarah, Rebecca, Rachel and Leah.

For Both: May God Bless you and guard you. May the light of God shine upon you, and may God be gracious to you. May the presence of God be with you and give you peace.

The blessing for the wine.

Blessed are You, Eternal our God, Sovereign of the universe, Creator of the fruit of the vine. B*aruch atah Adonai, Eloheinu Melech haolam, borei p'ri hagafen.*

Blessing for Lighting the Shabbat Candles.

Blessed are You, Eternal our God, Sovereign of the universe, who sanctifies us with mitzvot and takes delight in us.

In love and favor, God made the holy Shabbat, our heritage as a reminder of the work of Creation.

It is first among our sacred days, and a remembrance of the Exodus from Egypt.

O God, You have chosen us and set us apart from all the peoples, and in love and favor have given us the Sabbath day as a sacred inheritance.

Praise to You, Eternal, for the Sabbath and its holiness.

Shalom aleichem, malachei hashareit, malachei elyon, mimelech malchei ham'lachim, hakadosh baruch hu.

Boachem l'shalom, malachei hashalom, malachei elyon, mimelech malchei ham'lachim, hakadosh baruch hu.

Bar'chuni l'shalom, malachei hashalom, malachei elyon, mimelech malchei ham'lachim, hakadosh baruch hu.

Tzeitchem l'shalom, malachei hashalom, malachei elyon, mimelech malchei hamlachim, hakadosh baruch hu.

Lift the Havdalah Spice and say: We praise You, Eternal God, Sovereign of the universe, Creator of all spices. *Baruch atah Adonai, Eloheinu Melech haolam borei minei v'samim.*

Lift the Havdalah Candle and say: We praise You, Eternal God, Sovereign of the universe: You distinguish the commonplace from the holy; You create light and darkness, Israel and the nations, the seventh day of rest and the six days of labor. We praise You, O God: You call us to distinguish the commonplace from the holy. *Baruch atah Adonai, Eloheinu Melech haolam, hamavdil bein kodesh l'chol, bein or l'choshech, bein Yisrael laamim, bein yom hash-vi-i l'sheishet y'mei hamaaseh. Baruch atah Adonai, hamavdil bein kodesh l'chol.*

Ritual Washing of hands.

Blessed are You, Eternal our God, Sovereign *Baruch Ata Adonai Eloheinu Melech* of the universe, Who has sanctified us with *haolam, asher kid'shanu b'mitzvotav.* His commandments and commanded us *v'tzivanu al n'tilat yadayim.* concerning washing of hands.

Elijah the prophet, Elijah the Tishbite, Elijah Eliyahu hanavi. *Eliyahu hatishbi. Eliyahu*, the Giladite, quickly in our days may he come Eliyahu, Eliyahu hagil'adi. Bim'hera to us with the messiah, the son of David. *veyameinu, yavoh eleinu, im mashiach ben David, im mashiach ben David.*

7 Reasons to Observe Shabbat

The Jewish day of rest is a gift — use it wisely.

BY MJL

Shabbat, the Jewish Sabbath, is unique among world religions. On the last day of each week, from sundown to sundown, Jews everywhere pause from their ordinary routines and usher in a day of holiness. Traditionally Shabbat-observant Jews abstain from 39 categories of work (including lighting a fire, writing and spending money) and spend time with their community praying, eating large meals and singing. Other ways to observe Shabbat might include meditation, retreating into nature, and catching up on sleep.

Taking time to observe Shabbat can be difficult in our fast-paced, 24/7 workaholic world. But it can also be incredibly meaningful. Here are seven reasons Jews choose this weekly refuge.

1. To Connect with Others

Though Shabbat affords amazing opportunities for individual rest and renewal, it is very much a communal experience. Many Shabbat prayers as well as the Shabbat Torah reading can't be said in isolation, but are recited in a minyan, a quorum of ten. Traditional Shabbat meals are enjoyed around a table with friends and family. This communal experience of Shabbat is wonderful for the individual, creating a buffer against isolation and loneliness. But it also strengthens the larger community, reliably bringing members together on a regular basis.

2. To Experience Personal Renewal

It has become a commonplace observation that technology keeps us connected and "on call" at all hours of every day. Shabbat is a natural antidote to this crush of electronic connection, an opportunity to ignore those devices and slow down to connect with oneself. People who observe Shabbat frequently report that it helps them to become better people, that it makes room for more creative thinking, and that it is an opportunity to feel refreshed before diving into another work week. In addition, with its decadent meals and joyful singing, Shabbat becomes an opportunity to taste a better life. This taste, symbolized by the sweet spices that are sniffed at Havdalah (the ceremony ending Shabbat), is carried over into the rest of the week, making life richer all week long. And as a foretaste of the World to Come, Shabbat can inspire the individual to work to make the world a better place.

3. To Connect to the Natural World.

The origin story for Shabbat is found in Genesis 1-2 in which God creates the world in six days and then surveys the results—"God saw all that God had made, and found it very good"— before resting on the seventh. It doesn't make sense to all later commentators that an all-powerful deity would need to rest at all, even after so enormous a task as creating the world, and God's choice to step back to and marvel at the wonder of it all is thought to be a divine example for human beings. We, too, rest once per week, and take an opportunity to marvel at the wonder of the world. As Rabbi Arthur Waskow put it, Shabbat is "a time to live in harmony rather than achieve dominion" over nature. After all, if God was impressed by creation, how much more so should we be awed by it?

4. To Stop Feeling Like a Slave to Your Work

If work has no end, then it becomes a form of enslavement. This is particularly true in an era when technology makes it possible for a great many of us to do our work anytime, anywhere. Shabbat creates an opportunity to flip that switch, to turn off all the work, and to remind ourselves that we are not slaves to our livelihoods.

5. To Stop Searching for Life's Purpose

For some, Shabbat creates an opportunity to connect to the self and discover one's life purpose. But it can also do just the opposite — offering us an excuse to stop madly seeking a purpose. As Rabbi

Gunther Plaut has noted, long ago life's purpose was simple and clear: survival. In the premodern era, merely achieving adequate shelter, food, and clothing was an achievement to be proud of. In the modern Western world when these things are less difficult to achieve (though we are mindful that they are still difficult for many), it has become less clear what life's major challenge and purpose ought to be — and too often we cobble together some vague notions of "success," "happiness" and "fulfillment." Shabbat affords an opportunity to step back from frantically trying to achieve these amorphous goals, to just be.

6. Because It's Challenging

Unplugging, eating wonderful meals, connecting with family and community — these things require discipline and preparation. Also, calming one's mind, choosing to miss out on the hubbub of the outside world, and taking a pause. It also takes effort to learn prayers and pray with kavanah (intention). Shabbat is not simply a Holiday that happens to us, it's one we make happen, and sometimes doing so is quite difficult. One reason to make Shabbat a part of one's week is not because it is easy (though taking a nap on Shabbat might be deliciously so), but because it is hard.

7. Because It's Commanded

For many Jews, the number one reason to observe Shabbat is simply that God commands us to do so. The Torah prohibits work on the seventh day and names a few varieties (gathering sticks, lighting a fire, etc.) while rabbinic literature expands and delineates these prohibitions quite elaborately. Observing Shabbat is about fulfilling the dictates of God, and conforming to standards of observance that have bound Jews together throughout the millennia.

Translation of The Shema

Cover your eyes with your right hand and say:

Hear, O Israel, the L-rd is our Gd, the L-rd is One.

Recite the following verse in an undertone:

Blessed be the name of the glory of His kingdom forever and ever.

You shall love the L-rd your Gd with all your heart, with all your soul, and with all your might. And these words which I command you today shall be upon your heart. You shall teach them thoroughly to your children, and you shall speak of them when you sit in your house and when you walk on the road, when you lie down and when you rise. You shall bind them as a sign upon your hand, and they shall be for a reminder between your eyes. And you shall write them upon the doorposts of your house and upon your gates.

And it will be, if you will diligently obey My commandments which I enjoin upon you this day, to love the L-rd your Gd and to serve Him with all your heart and with all your soul, I will give rain for your land at the proper time, the early rain and the late rain, and you will gather in your grain, your wine and your oil. And I will give grass in your fields for your cattle, and you will eat and be sated. Take care lest your heart be lured away, and you turn astray and worship alien gods and bow down to them. For then the L-rd's wrath will flare up against you, and He will close the heavens so that there will be no rain and the earth will not yield its produce, and you will swiftly perish from the good land which the L-rd gives you. Therefore, place these words of Mine upon your heart and upon your soul, and bind them for a sign on your hand, and they shall be for a reminder between your eyes. You shall teach them to your children, to speak of them when you sit in your house and when you walk on the road, when you lie down and when you rise. And you shall inscribe them on the doorposts of your house and on your gates - so that your days and the days of your children may be prolonged on the land which the L-rd swore to your fathers to give to them for as long as the heavens are above the earth.

The L-rd spoke to Moses, saying: Speak to the children of Israel and tell them to make for themselves fringes on the corners of their garments throughout their generations, and to attach a thread of blue on the fringe of each corner. They shall be to you as tzizit, and you shall look upon them and remember all the commandments of the L-rd and fulfill them, and you will not follow after your heart and after your eyes by which you go astray - so that you may remember and fulfill all My commandments and be holy to your Gd. I am the L-rd your Gd who brought you out of the land of Egypt to be your Gd; I, the L-rd, am your Gd. True.

From Siddur Tehillat Hashem. ©Copyright Kehot Publication Society, Brooklyn NY

Published and copyright by Kehot Publication Society, all rights reserved.

The Shema in the Original Hebrew

Cover your eyes with your right hand and say:

שְׁמַע יִשְׂרָאֵל, יְיָ אֱלֹהֵינוּ, יְיָ | אֶחָד:

Recite the following verse in an undertone:

בָּרוּךְ שֵׁם כְּבוֹד מַלְכוּתוֹ לְעוֹלָם וָעֶד:
וְאָהַבְתָּ אֵת יְיָ אֱלֹהֶיךָ, בְּכָל | לְבָבְךָ, וּבְכָל נַפְשְׁךָ, וּבְכָל מְאֹדֶךָ: וְהָיוּ הַדְּבָרִים הָאֵלֶּה אֲשֶׁר אָנֹכִי מְצַוְּךָ הַיּוֹם, עַל | לְבָבֶךָ: וְשִׁנַּנְתָּם לְבָנֶיךָ וְדִבַּרְתָּ בָּם, בְּשִׁבְתְּךָ בְּבֵיתֶךָ, וּבְלֶכְתְּךָ בַדֶּרֶךְ, וּבְשָׁכְבְּךָ, וּבְקוּמֶךָ: וּקְשַׁרְתָּם לְאוֹת עַל יָדֶךָ, וְהָיוּ לְטֹטָפֹת בֵּין עֵינֶיךָ: וּכְתַבְתָּם עַל מְזֻזוֹת בֵּיתֶךָ, וּבִשְׁעָרֶיךָ:

וְהָיָה אִם שָׁמֹעַ תִּשְׁמְעוּ אֶל מִצְוֹתַי אֲשֶׁר אָנֹכִי מְצַוֶּה אֶתְכֶם הַיּוֹם, לְאַהֲבָה אֶת יְיָ אֱלֹהֵיכֶם וּלְעָבְדוֹ, בְּכָל לְבַבְכֶם וּבְכָל נַפְשְׁכֶם: וְנָתַתִּי מְטַר אַרְצְכֶם בְּעִתּוֹ יוֹרֶה וּמַלְקוֹשׁ, וְאָסַפְתָּ דְגָנֶךָ וְתִירֹשְׁךָ וְיִצְהָרֶךָ: וְנָתַתִּי עֵשֶׂב בְּשָׂדְךָ לִבְהֶמְתֶּךָ, וְאָכַלְתָּ וְשָׂבָעְתָּ: הִשָּׁמְרוּ לָכֶם פֶּן יִפְתֶּה לְבַבְכֶם, וְסַרְתֶּם וַעֲבַדְתֶּם אֱלֹהִים אֲחֵרִים וְהִשְׁתַּחֲוִיתֶם לָהֶם: וְחָרָה אַף יְיָ בָּכֶם וְעָצַר אֶת הַשָּׁמַיִם וְלֹא יִהְיֶה מָטָר וְהָאֲדָמָה לֹא תִתֵּן אֶת יְבוּלָהּ, וַאֲבַדְתֶּם מְהֵרָה מֵעַל הָאָרֶץ הַטֹּבָה אֲשֶׁר יְיָ נֹתֵן לָכֶם: וְשַׂמְתֶּם אֶת דְּבָרַי אֵלֶּה עַל לְבַבְכֶם וְעַל נַפְשְׁכֶם, וּקְשַׁרְתֶּם אֹתָם לְאוֹת עַל יֶדְכֶם וְהָיוּ לְטוֹטָפֹת בֵּין עֵינֵיכֶם: וְלִמַּדְתֶּם אֹתָם אֶת בְּנֵיכֶם לְדַבֵּר בָּם, בְּשִׁבְתְּךָ בְּבֵיתֶךָ וּבְלֶכְתְּךָ בַדֶּרֶךְ וּבְשָׁכְבְּךָ וּבְקוּמֶךָ: וּכְתַבְתָּם עַל מְזוּזוֹת בֵּיתֶךָ וּבִשְׁעָרֶיךָ: לְמַעַן יִרְבּוּ יְמֵיכֶם וִימֵי בְנֵיכֶם עַל הָאֲדָמָה אֲשֶׁר נִשְׁבַּע יְיָ לַאֲבֹתֵיכֶם לָתֵת לָהֶם, כִּימֵי הַשָּׁמַיִם עַל הָאָרֶץ:

וַיֹּאמֶר יְיָ אֶל מֹשֶׁה לֵּאמֹר: דַּבֵּר אֶל בְּנֵי יִשְׂרָאֵל וְאָמַרְתָּ אֲלֵהֶם וְעָשׂוּ לָהֶם צִיצִת עַל כַּנְפֵי בִגְדֵיהֶם לְדֹרֹתָם, וְנָתְנוּ עַל צִיצִת הַכָּנָף פְּתִיל תְּכֵלֶת: וְהָיָה לָכֶם לְצִיצִת, וּרְאִיתֶם אֹתוֹ, וּזְכַרְתֶּם אֶת כָּל מִצְוֹת יְיָ, וַעֲשִׂיתֶם אֹתָם, וְלֹא תָתוּרוּ אַחֲרֵי לְבַבְכֶם וְאַחֲרֵי עֵינֵיכֶם אֲשֶׁר אַתֶּם זֹנִים אַחֲרֵיהֶם: לְמַעַן תִּזְכְּרוּ וַעֲשִׂיתֶם אֶת כָּל מִצְוֹתָי, וִהְיִיתֶם קְדֹשִׁים לֵאלֹהֵיכֶם: אֲנִי יְיָ אֱלֹהֵיכֶם אֲשֶׁר הוֹצֵאתִי אֶתְכֶם מֵאֶרֶץ מִצְרַיִם לִהְיוֹת לָכֶם לֵאלֹהִים, אֲנִי יְיָ אֱלֹהֵיכֶם·

From Siddur Tehillat Hashem. © Copyright Kehot Publication Society, Brooklyn NY

Published and copyright by Kehot Publication Society, all rights reserved.

What is Shemini Atzeret?

Not quite Sukkot, not quite its own Holiday.

BY RABBI PAUL STEINBERG

Although Hoshanah Rabbah may technically be the "last day" of Sukkot, the Rabbis decided to treat Shemini Atzeret (and Simchat Torah) as a part of Sukkot, because its significance is unequivocally informed by Sukkot itself.

Two cryptic references in the Torah cause the confusion about the status of Shemini Atzeret. In both Leviticus and Numbers, God commands that the eighth *(shemini)* day–referring to Sukkot–is to be a "sacred occasion" and an atzeret, generally translated as "solemn gathering."

What is Atzeret?

The inherent problem is that no one really knows exactly what atzeret means. Possibly it comes from the word *atzar*, meaning "stop," and thus implies that we are to refrain from work. On the other hand, *atzeret* may also be defined by its textual context, which implies that it is some sort of deliberate extension of the prior seven days. This lack of verbal clarity is likely the reason why the rabbinic sages seemed to struggle with the precise meaning of the Holiday.

The earliest rabbinic reference to Shemini Atzeret calls it *yom tov aharon shel ha-hag*, the last day of the festival. The Talmud (Taanit 20b-31a), however, declares, "The eighth day is a festival in its own right." At the same time, the Talmud (Taanit 28b) attempts to distinguish it from Sukkot, as there are 70 temple sacrifices given throughout Sukkot, compared to only one given on Shemini Atzeret. (This distinction was only theoretical as the Temple had been destroyed five centuries prior to the redaction of the Talmud.)

Cutting through this puzzle, the most appealing depiction of the Holiday may be that of Samson Raphael Hirsch, a 19th-century

Orthodox rabbi who lived in Germany. He infers the meaning of the Holiday from the word *atzeret*, which he renders as "to gather" or "to store up." Accordingly, on this eighth day of Sukkot, the final day of celebration, we must store up the sentiments of gratitude and devotion acquired throughout the entire fall Holiday season; nearly two months will pass until we celebrate another Holiday, that of Hanukkah.

How It's Different from Sukkot

Although the observances of Shemini *Atzeret* generally share the characteristics of the rest of Sukkot, there are four significant differences. The first is that there is no more shaking of the lulav and etrog. Second is that although we have our meals and recite *Kiddush* in the sukkah (though customs vary), we no longer say the blessing to sanctify us through the commandment to dwell in it, as we did the previous seven days. The third is that in the synagogue, after the Torah reading, we recite the memorial prayer (*Yizkor*).

And finally, the special prayer for rain (*Geshem*) is added to the repetition of *Musaf* and thus begins the period of an additional call for rain in our prayers, which lasts until Passover. It is customary for the leader of the Geshem prayer to wear a kitel as was done during the divine judgment of the High Holidays. Wearing the garment indicates that this is the season of divine judgment for the future year's rainfall, the time when we pray that God's goodwill may afford us the appropriate amount.

Reprinted with permission from Celebrating the Jewish Year *(Jewish Publication Society).*

How the Sounds of the Shofar Rectify Our Psyche

Introduction

On *Rosh Hashanah*, we rectify our souls by hearing the sounds of the *Shofar*. To fulfill this *mitzvah*, the only requirement is to listen to the sound of the *Shofar*. The sound of the Shofar, which is likened to a voice, has a detailed and intimate message for the soul. This sound conveys its message to the soul's very root. The listener has no direct grasp on the meaning of the message. From the soul root, the message penetrates into the psyche of the listener, and rectifies all the powers of his soul.

How the Shofar Rectifies the Super-conscious Powers of the Soul

From the root of the soul, the voice of the Shofar first reaches the superconscious powers of the soul: faith (*emunah*), pleasure (*ta'anug*) and will (*ratzon*).

Strengthening Faith (*Emunah*)

A concept that cannot be understood intellectually is actually directed at the power of faith in the soul. For this reason, we learn from many tzaddikim that one should continue to teach Torah even to a person who does not visibly understand. His soul understands, and the Torah penetrates his being and strengthens his pure and simple faith in God. The simple sound of the Shofar reaches out to this power of faith, which is equal in all Jews.

Revealing Pleasure (*Ta'anug*)

The simple song of the Shofar – the crown and root of all musical instruments — has the power to awaken and reveal the simple pleasure of the soul. There is a constant dimension of pleasure in the soul derived from its connection to God. This unvarying dimension of pleasure allows the Jew to "float" above life's difficulties, and to serenely approach his service of God with inner joy. This pleasure is the involvement of the Jew in God's experience of pleasure in Creation, and His manifestation in Creation. It is the root of his willingness to play a role on the "stage" of Creation, to descend to reality and to actualize the will of God. The voice of the Shofar reveals this pleasure, and gives power to the soul to serve God throughout the changes and transformations of the year.

Balancing Will (*Ratzon*)

The power of will in the soul has a direct affect on one's conscious function. This power often suffers from dispersion between the person's varied and sometimes disparate goals. This dispersion of will is a negative phenomenon, even if the goals of the will are not negative. The potency of the will to achieve certain goals and the inability to actualize them completely may cause sharp mood swings and even depression. Listening (ha'azanah in Hebrew, whose root means "balance") to the Shofar should give rise to a balanced will. For a Jew, balanced will does not mean suppression of his great ambitions, but rather helps him to prioritize his goals, thus making them more accessible. The voice of the Shofar concentrates and enlightens this will. When his goals are clarified, a person can pursue his greatest initiatives and challenges in a balanced and rectified manner.

How the Shofar Rectifies the Intellectual Powers of the Soul

When the voice of the Shofar penetrates the intellectual powers of the soul – chochmah (wisdom), binah (understanding) and da'at (knowledge) — it awakens the powers that direct the person's behavior throughout the entire year.

Evaluate the Situation — Chochmah

The voice of the Shofar has the potential to enliven the listener's power of insight, associated with chochmah. This insight enables him to correctly perceive and evaluate his spiritual situation. (The insight of chochmah stems from the feeling of the pleasure of Shabbat in the soul. It is this serenity that affords one the ability to accurately perceive reality.) On a deeper level, the power of Jewish insight is the power of Israel to testify to the Truth and Unity of G-d.

Repent — Binah

One of the most simple goals of the Shofar is to awaken the listener to repentance (as a result of his proper contemplation — hitbonenut — from the same root as binah) on his sorry state of distance from God. Repentance, teshuvah, and return to a close connection with God depend on the strengthening of faith. The essential bond of the soul, bound by a covenant to God even when a person descends into sin — must be strengthened. This experience awakens one to repent and awakens hope in the soul.

Balanced Decision Making — Da'at

After proper evaluation of one's situation and the subsequent desire to repent, balanced decision making tools are necessary in order to proceed in reality. A judge of reality must be expert in deciphering the contradictory themes of a given situation or concept. The voice of the Shofar gives one this sense of proper balance, which stems from the balanced superconscious will in the soul. The first letters of the words of the blessing recited before hearing the Shofar, 'Lishmo'ah Kol Shofar' are shin, kuf, lamed, the root of the word for 'balance.'

How the Shofar Rectifies the Emotive Powers of the Soul

The voice of the Shofar penetrates the emotive powers of the soul, Chesed (lovingkindness), Gevurah (fortitude) and Tiferet (beauty), and rectifies the experience of the heart in relation to both general reality and specifically, to the Nation of Israel.

Positive Perception — Chesed

The Shofar reminds us that all that was created in the world is "very good" (Genesis 1:31) — even those things that we perceive as "bad." This positive perception of reality strengthens the listener's power of chesed, lovingkindness. (The blessing recited before the sounding of the Shofar is the square of the numerical value of "very good.")

Courage to Turn the World Upside Down — Gevurah

On a simple plane, the Shofar awakens fear. The inner dimension of Gevurah is fear of heaven. The Shofar awakens rectified fear of heaven. A person who truly fears G-d fears nothing else, and is a courageous and tireless soldier in His "army." This rectified fear of heaven provides a person with the courage and daring to turn the world upside down to bring the redemption.

The Unity of Israel — Tiferet

The simple sound of the Shofar also enlivens in the soul the sense of the love of Israel. If the mitzvah of Shofar were to understand the inner message of the sounds, this would create various levels of Jews according to their cognitive talents. However, by fulfilling the mitzvah of simply hearing the voice of the Shofar, the entire tapestry of souls of Israel shines equally.

How the Shofar Rectifies the Powers of Action in the Soul

The Shofar penetrates the behavioral powers of the soul, Netzach (victory) and Hod (acknowledgement), yesod (foundation), and malchut (kingdom) energizing them and giving them focus.

Advance — Netzach and Hod

Our Sages teach that an injury to the ear is life threatening. This points to the fact that simple hearing relates to the very life force of the person. The sound of the Shofar that penetrates the behavioral characteristics of the soul causes the listener to advance toward the very essence of God, without any prior contemplation or study. This super-rational advance toward G-d is accomplished by the "two legs" of the powers of the soul — Netzach and Hod — the powers of steadfast, simple and devoted walking.

Vitality — Yesod

Hearing the Shofar awakens in the soul the power to serve G-d with vitality and exuberance.

Reflected Light — Malchut

Rabbi Nachman of Breslov explains that when a person attempts to reproach another, and the listener does not accept his words, the words return as "reflected light" to the speaker. This creates an opportunity for the speaker to find the right words to penetrate the soul of the listener as direct and inner light. Hence, when we do not understand the deep content of the sound of the Shofar, the light of the Shofar is reflected back to Heaven. Subsequently, we merit to draw down from Heaven the inner content of what we have heard.

Ask the Expert: Slanted Mezuzah

Why does the mezuzah go on a diagonal?

BY MY JEWISH LEARNING

Question: I'm about to put a mezuzah up on the doorframe of my new apartment, and all of the articles I've read say to put it at a slant, but none of them mention why. What's the deal with slanting the mezuzah ?

–Shira, Cleveland

Answer: A slanted mezuzah is a great example of a compromise in Jewish law, Shira. It might look screwy to you, but it's actually a demonstration of two legal authorities literally meeting in the middle.

Way back in the 11th century, Rashi, a French rabbi and commentator, opined that when you put up your mezuzah, it should be hung vertically (Rashi and Tosafot on *Menahot* 33a). But then Rashi's grandson came along. He's known as Rabbenu Tam, and he wrote that a mezuzah should be affixed horizontally, because the Ten Commandments and the Torah scrolls were kept horizontally in the ark in the Temple.

A hundred and fifty years later Rabbi Jacob Ben Asher, also sometimes called the Tur, was writing his book of Jewish law, the *Arbaah Turim*. In it, Ben Asher suggests that the way to hold by the precedents of both Rashi and Rabbenu Tam was to split the difference, and affix your mezuzah at a slant (pointing into the room). (*Yoreh Deah* 289)

Three hundred years later this view was codified again by the Rema, an Ashkenazi commentator, who noted that slanting a mezuzah had become the common custom among Ashkenazi Jews. (Sephardi and Mizrahi Jews today still hang their mezuzot vertically.)

It's rare to find a Jewish custom that was so clearly developed as a compromise between two different interpretations of one commandment. When you put up your mezuzah on a slant, think of how you're acknowledging the ways multiple voices and perspectives are welcome and encouraged in Jewish life.

What Is the Talmud?

An intergenerational rabbinic conversation that is studied, not read.

BY MY JEWISH LEARNING

Talmud (literally, "study") is the generic term for the documents that comment and expand upon the Mishnah ("repeating"), the first work of rabbinic law, published around the year 200 CE by Rabbi Judah the Patriarch in the land of Israel.

About the Talmud

Although Talmud is largely about law, it should not be confused with either codes of law or with a commentary on the legal sections of the Torah. Due to its spare and laconic style, the Talmud is studied, not read. The difficulty of the intergenerational text has necessitated and fostered the development of an institutional and communal structure that supported the learning of Talmud and the establishment of special schools where each generation is apprenticed into its study by the previous generation.

Want to learn Talmud with us? Daf Yomi is a program of reading the entire Talmud one day at a time, and My Jewish Learning is offering a daily dose of Talmud in your inbox. Sign up for it here!

The Mishnah

In the second century, Rabbi Judah the Patriarch published a document in six primary sections, or orders, dealing with agriculture, sacred times, women and personal status, damages, holy things, and purity laws. By carefully laying out different opinions concerning Jewish law, the Mishnah presents itself more as a case book of law. While the Mishnah preserved the teachings of earlier rabbis, it also shows the signs of a unified editing. Part of that editing process included selecting materials; many of the traditions that did not "make it" into the Mishnah were collected in a companion volume called the Tosefta (appendix, or supplement).

The Gemara ("learning")

After the publication of the Mishnah, the sages of Israel, both in the land of Israel, and in the largest diaspora community of Babylonia (modern day Iraq), began to study the both the Mishnah and the traditional teachings. Their work consisted largely of working out the Mishnah's inner logic, trying to extract legal principles from the specific statements of case law, searching out the derivations of the legal statements from Scripture, and relating statements found in the Mishnah to traditions that were left out. Each community produced its own Gemara which have been preserved as two different multi-volume sets: the Talmud Yerushalmi includes the Mishnah and the Gemara produced by the sages of the Land of Israel, and the Talmud Bavli includes the Mishnah and the Gemara of the Babylonian Jewish sages.

Studying Jewish texts at Mechon Hadar, an educational institution in New York City working to empower Jews to create and sustain vibrant, practicing, egalitarian communities of Torah learning, prayer and service. (Emil Cohen/Mechon Hadar)

Commentaries

In some ways, the Talmud was never completed; the Tosafist commentators during the middle ages extended to the whole of the Gemara the same kinds of analysis that the sages of the Gemara had performed upon the Mishnah. Other commentators, like Rashi, sought to explain the text in a sequential manner.

Modern Study

Many modern scholars have begun applying the tools of literary and linguistic analysis to the text of the Talmud. Some have used these tools to focus on the underlying uniformity and consistency of the text, while others have done sophisticated analysis of the sources and alleged history of the text. Still others have examined the literary artistry of the Talmud. Many scholars have, with varying degrees of success, tried to use the Talmud as a source for historical inquiry.

Unetaneh Tokef: Do We Control Our Fate?

The prayer that asks us to consider our mortality is an urgent call to examine our lives.

BY CANTOR MATT AXELROD

If there's one word that is closely connected with the High Holiday season, it's *teshuvah*, repentance. It's a part of the vocabulary taught to even young religious school children: looking at one's behavior and then taking steps to make better decisions and live a life free of transgressions against God and our fellow humans.

There's one iconic prayer, recited on each of the days of Rosh Hashanah and Yom Kippur, that expresses in a clear and dramatic way our need to perform *teshuvah*. The text of Unetaneh Tokef lays it all out for us and utilizes vivid imagery: Before God lies a giant book — the Book of Life — in which we hope all of our names will be inscribed for the coming year. The Unetaneh Tokef goes on to tell us that on Rosh Hashanah, those deserving names are entered — ensuring they will live through the year, and on Yom Kippur, the Book is sealed — their fates no longer alterable. We have until the very end of Yom Kippur, during the concluding Neilah service when the liturgy tells us that the gates are closing, to sway God's decision in our favor.

To drive home the serious consequences of our actions, Unetaneh Tokef then lists all the dire ways we can meet our fate. We read the classic words "Who shall live and who shall die?" — but then the rest of the paragraph is devoted to all the ways the latter outcome could take place:

Who by fire and who by water?

Who by plague and who by famine?

Who by sword and who by wild beast?

Who by hunger and who by thirst?

At last, we're given a shred of hope, the theological carrot to these long passages of stick. We read:

Uteshuvah utefilah utzedakah ma'avirin et roa hag'zeirah

But repentance, prayer, and deeds of charity can annul the severity of the decree.

This prayer is undoubtedly the climax of the High Holiday morning service. As the hazzan of my synagogue, I see my entire congregation present for this prayer (although people start to trickle out of the sanctuary soon after). Backed up by the choir, I chant it in some of the most ornate and dramatic musical selections of the year.

Yet, at the same time, I find this prayer to be the most disturbing, confusing, and theologically questionable of the entire mahzor. A close look at the wording seems to contradict everything we're supposed to believe and do on these High Holidays. It says that on Rosh Hashanah and Yom Kippur, our names are written and then sealed for the coming year. That is, the decision is made. It's a done deal. Therefore, it is already predetermined whether we will live or die during the next year. What good then are our acts of *teshuvah*? How can we annul the severity of the decree through deeds of *tzedakah* (charity) if that decree is not only recorded but in fact sealed in a book? Should we leave the sanctuary at the end of Yom Kippur and simply hope for the best, realizing that nothing we do from that moment on has any effect on whether we will survive the year ahead?

We need a better way to relate to this prayer that is so central to our High Holiday liturgy. I have come to understand this disturbing and powerful text less as a promise of childlike reward and punishment and more as a statement of the fragility of life and our own mortality. I have literally been moved to tears (no small challenge while trying to sing with a full voice along with the choir) looking out at a full sanctuary, everyone's voices joined in the familiar refrain:

B'rosh hashanah yikateivun uv'yom tzom kippur yeichateimun

On Rosh Hashanah it is written and on Yom Kippur it is sealed

At that moment, I realize that not all of us will be here next year. These people — congregants, friends, family — it is a sad but inescapable fact that some will die over the course of the coming year. Our lives are a gift. We perform *teshuvah* not to appease a distant and invisible Deity, but rather to remind us of our value to one another and strengthen our relationships with each other. We give *tzedakah* to better the lives of those around us. And we engage in prayer to further develop the bonds of our connection to Judaism and our community.

Our job is not to temporarily put on our best behavior in order to convince God to let us live for another year. Instead, we acknowledge that our time here on earth is limited and our lives tenuous. The true and vital message of *Unetaneh Tokef* requires us to ask ourselves not who shall live, but how shall we live?

Witches & Witchcraft

Throughout much of Jewish history, witchcraft has been viewed as a vice that virtually every woman will indulge in.

BY RABBI GEOFFREY DENNIS

In most cultures across the world, a witch or wizard is generally regarded to be a nefarious practitioner of magic. In Jewish culture, in contrast to both modern culture, which has reversed most images of evil creatures (vampires are now romantic figures, for example, instead of bloodlusting killers) and Christian culture, which sees them as virtually demonic, the Jewish attitude toward witches has varied considerably over time and geography.

The German Pietists, for example, did regard them as quasi-demons. In the 17th century, Manasseh ben Israel of Holland expressed a view of witchcraft virtually indistinguishable from contemporary Christian demonologists (Nishmat Hayyim 232). The talmud ic rabbis, on the other hand, while not approving of witches, blithely assume most of their own wives engage in at least some witchcraft practices (Mishnah Sanhedrin 7:4, 7:11). These differences may well reflect the attitudes of the surrounding cultures in which Jews lived. Mediterranean societies were generally more tolerant of witches than northern European societies.

In the Bible

The formal biblical attitude toward wizards and witches is severe, witchcraft being a capital offense (Exodus 22:17; Leviticus 20:27; Sanhedrin 45b). This seems to spring from its association with idolatry. Both men and women are portrayed as engaging in witchcraft, and contrary to the modern distinction made in academic circles between socially empowered sorcerers and socially marginal witches, witches in the Bible are often shown in positions of power, notably the wizards in the employ of the kings of Babylon and Egypt and the witches in the employ of King Manasseh. Queen Jezebel herself is a witch (Exodus 7: 11; Daniel 2:2; II Kings 9:22, 21:2).

Little is known about biblical witchcraft. There is an oblique reference to "voodoo-like" practices (Ezekiel 13:19), but the Bible almost universally opts to remain silent on the particular practices of the witch. The Woman of Endor, often identified as a witch in Jewish post-biblical literature, is not designated so in the Bible itself so it is not clear whether necromancy was considered a discipline of witchcraft, or a wholly separate offense (Deuteronomy 18:10-12; Isaiah 8:19-22, 19:3).

Women's Work?

Jewish sources offer several accounts of the origins of witchcraft. According to I Enoch, witchcraft was first taught by the fallen angels to their mortal wives. This presumably explains the special association between women and witchcraft that marks subsequent Jewish literature. In the medieval text Alef-Bet ben Sira, the first woman, Lilith, transforms herself into a demon/witch by the power of using the Tetragrammaton.

While Jews were generally regarded to be exceptional magicians and even some rabbis use incantations, potions, and healing rituals, in rabbinic literature witchcraft is most associated with women. Though there is an explicit statement that both men and women can engage in witchcraft, the fact that Exodus 22:17 prohibits *mahashefah* (the feminine form of the noun) is taken as a prooftext that witchcraft is a particularly feminine activity (Sanhedrin 67a).

And this is despite the existence of magical manuals such as *The Sword of Moses* (a medieval Hebrew manual of theurgy), which is clearly written with the assumption that the adept using it will be a man. Perhaps a distinction between learned sorcery (practiced mostly by men), and folk magic (practiced mostly by women) starts to emerge here.

Several passages of Talmud make a point of linking witchcraft with women (Avot 2:7; Eruvin 64b; Yerushalmi Avodah Zarah 1:9). In one citation, none other than Simon bar Yohai, a sage who is reported to have once used the evil eye to slay a man, makes this linkage. The practice of witchcraft was considered so pervasive among women that even the children of great sages could be involved (Gittin 45a).

In general, witches in biblical and rabbinic literature are thought to be engaged mostly in malevolent activities, from interfering with fertility and healthy births (*Otzar ha-Geonim*, Sotah 11) to cursing rivals and killing the unsuspecting. This stands in contrast with beneficent sorcery, such as healing rituals and amulet making, which Jewish tradition tolerates.

While there are examples recorded of "witchcraft" that serves purely utilitarian purposes (the ability to stir a boiling pot with one's bare hand, for example), in general it is assumed witchcraft is used mostly for nefarious ends. The motivation for such behavior is rarely explicitly stated in the texts, but can be inferred. Witches seem to be a source of the evil eye, indicating they are motivated by envy and jealousy. Others use their powers for personal profit.

Punishment & Hostility

Witches are sometimes portrayed as having idiosyncratic powers: one may be able to materialize bread, another drink, etc. The Talmud recounts that Rabbi Simeon ben Shetah defeated a coven of eighty witches. First, he tricked them into demonstrating their powers, then he gained the upper hand by appealing to their lusts. He brought eighty men before them, each of whom lifted a witch from the ground, thereby robbing each of her power (a piquant detail linking ancient witchcraft with earth or, perhaps, underworld power). Enforcing the biblical penalty, ben Shetah eventually had all of them hung.

While dramatic in scale, this incident is actually the only such capital punishment of witches mentioned in the entire vast rabbinic corpus, and given its particularly legendary features, many scholars have held the historicity of the story suspect.

Aside from this one story, witches in rabbinic literature are rarely portrayed as demonic creatures, though it is not clear exactly what they are. In a virtually indecipherable tale found in the Jerusalem Talmud, Rabbi Hananiah pulls the head of a witch from flax (Sanhedrin 7:13a). In general, though, witchcraft is seen more as a vice that virtually every woman will indulge in. With few exceptions, it is regarded rather just as something inappropriate that women do.

In medieval Jewish literature of northern Europe, by contrast, the image of the witch as a purely malevolent entity comes to the forefront, perhaps reflecting the greater hostility toward witches found in Christian culture at that time (*Nishmat Hayyim* 232). In *Sefer Hasidim*, witches share attributes with werewolves and vampires: they shape-shift, fly, have bloodlust, and can become the undead (456, 465).

Yet despite this more alarming view of witches, there is no record of any large-scale witch hunts among the Jews of Europe to mirror the witch-hunting mania that seized gentile society. Perhaps the popular Christian notion of the Jew as a satanic agent made Jewish authorities leery of giving fuel to such talk with the spectacle of Jews trying other Jews on such charges.

Among the Jews of the Ottoman Empire, witches were viewed with more acceptance. Even an established kabbalist like Hayyim Vital would seek the expertise of such wise women (*Sefer ha-Hezyonot* 4,120).

If You're Worried…

The threat of a witch may be deterred by reciting the following curse (Pesahim 110a): "May boiling excrement in a sieve be forced into your mouth, (you) witches! May your head go bald and carry off your crumbs; your spices be scattered, and the wind carry off the new saffron in your hands, witches!"

Seven loops of knots (tied to the left side of the body) are also a good defense against illness caused by witchcraft (Shabbat 66b).

Reprinted with permission from The Encyclopedia of Jewish Myth, Magic and Mysticism (Llewellyn Worldwide).

The Making of a Torah Scroll

Written by hand, a sefer Torah is produced according to strict specifications.

BY MICHAL SHEKEL

Jews have often been called am *ha-sefer*, the people of the book. This designation underscores the importance of text in Judaism and the belief that God communicates with us through the written word. The central text in Judaism is the Torah. Enhancing the importance of its teachings is the fact that it is written in a special way.

A Religious Act

Writing a Torah scroll is a religious act. First and foremost, a kosher (acceptable according to Jewish law) Torah scroll must be hand-written. This is done by a sofer (*scribe*), a specially trained individual who is devout and knowledgeable in the laws governing the proper writing and assembling of a scroll. Sofer is from the Hebrew root "to count." According to the Talmud (*Kiddushin* 30a), these scholars would count each letter of the Torah. More specifically, the modern scribe is called a *sofer stam*, an acronym for *sefer torah* (Torah scroll) tefillin (phylacteries) and mezuzah. All these ritual objects must be written according to strict standards regarding size, lettering style, and layout.

The materials used for creating these sacred items are restricted as well. Parchment used for the writing must be made from the skin of a kosher animal. The scribe mixes a special ink for the writing and prepares the actual writing utensil, a quill, usually from a turkey feather. He uses a reed instrument to scratch lines into the parchment in preparation for the writing. Once all the writing has been completed, the pieces of parchment are sewn together with thread made of animal veins. The finished scroll is attached to wooden rollers. No instrument containing iron or steel may be used in the creation of a Torah scroll, because these metals are used to create instruments of war.

There is a special type of lettering that is used to write the Torah, tefillin , and mezuzah. While the writing looks like a form of Hebrew block letters, certain letters are embellished with crowns, called *tagin*. The Ashkenazi and Sephardi calligraphic styles vary somewhat, but each group may use the other's Torah. Greater variations in lettering existed a few hundred years ago. Torah scrolls written by Hasidic groups had swirls in certain letters, with each letter said to convey a mystical meaning. Today, there is greater standardization among Torah scrolls.

The scribe prepares the parchment by scratching 43 horizontal lines on it and two vertical ones at each end. This allows for a standard 42 lines of writing. Each sheet of parchment contains three to eight columns of writing. Certain letters might be stretched within a column to justify the left margin.

There are some places in the Torah where certain letters are larger or smaller than standard, or where the text is written in a different type of column. Each deviation from the norm carries a special meaning. For example, the "Song of the Sea" (Exodus 15:1-19), which describes the parting of the Sea of Reeds, consists of three interlocking columns. The two outer columns symbolize the sea parted on either side, with the middle column representing the children of Israel marching on dry ground. Visually, this sets the section apart from the surrounding columns. Such changes were instituted by the Masoretes — scribes of the 7th-9th centuries who standardized the biblical text — to highlight the importance of certain passages. All of the writing and layout must be done exactly to specification in order for the scroll to be kosher.

Writing a Torah

Writing a Torah scroll is a holy task. In preparation, the scribe immerses in a *mikvah* (ritual bath). Before beginning a new scroll, he recites a formula declaring his intent to write the scroll for a holy purpose. To make sure all his tools are fit for the task, he tests the quill and ink by writing the word "Amalek" on a piece of parchment. He then crosses it out with a number of strokes in order to fulfill the commandment of blotting out the name of Amalek, a biblical enemy of the Jewish people (Deuteronomy 25:17-19).

The scribe cannot write a Torah scroll from memory, and must refer to a written book called a *tikkun* (correction guide). Memorization is permitted for the writing of other ritual items. Whenever he writes the name of God, the scribe focuses on the task by declaring out loud his intention to honor God by writing the holy name.

One other ritual item written by a scribe is the megillah (Book of Esther), which is read on Purim. However, in addition to ritual items, scribes also write legal documents such as a get (bill of divorce) or ketubah (marriage contract). The writing of all these items requires strict adherence to traditionally established form. The only place where the scribe has artistic license is in doing calligraphy for and decorating the ketubah. In this instance, creativity fulfills the precept of hiddur mitzvah, enhancing the joyous commandment by beautifying the item associated with fulfilling it.

Who Can Be a Scribe?

The Talmud (*Gittin* 45b) states that scrolls written by certain groups of people, such as women or minors, cannot be used. The argument is based on an interpretation of Deuteronomy 6:8-9, where instructions are given regarding God's teachings that you shall bind them on your hand and write them. The traditional understanding of this passage is that only those obligated to bind the teachings on their hand — that is, to wear tefillin — may write a Torah. In other words, being a sofer is restricted to adult Jewish males.

Later commentators relate the obligation to study Torah with the writing of one. This raises the question: since women are not traditionally obligated to study, does this fully prohibit them from writing a Torah, or merely exempt them from it? Today, there is recognition that women do study Torah and so there are those who argue that this permits women to write a Torah scroll. In addition, supporters of this position argue that numerous commentators in the past never put women on the list of those prohibited from fulfilling this sacred task.

The majority of scribes today are Orthodox men, though there are a few female and liberal scribes. It is only in the past few years that a traditionalist woman, Aviel Barclay, has become a scribe, and has been commissioned to write a Torah scroll. This is not without controversy as indicated perhaps by the fact that her teacher chooses to remain anonymous.

A Nascent Movement

The Bible mentions "families of scribes" (I Chronicles 2:5), which were probably schools and guilds where an individual learned through apprenticeship. Modern scribes also learn through individual apprenticeship and receive certification through a professional organization. Interestingly, this is mirrored today in a nascent informal movement of traditionalist women learning this sacred craft secretly and teaching it to each other. This widening of the circle of scribes indicates its central importance for modern Judaism.

Yom Kippur Info/Services

Welcome to the Yom Kippur services. If this is your first time, or if you have not been to synagogue too often, no need to worry; many other people in the room are in the same boat.1 Plus, most of the natives are friendly and will be more than happy to help you out.

As you enter, make sure that you are appropriately dressed. For women, this means wearing a longish skirt and a conservative top. If you are married, you will want to cover your hair as well.

For men, make sure that you have your head covered. Most synagogues have a basket with *kippahs* at the door. As you look around the room, you will notice that most of the men are wearing a prayer shawl called a tallit (or *tallis*) draped over their shoulders. In most Ashkenazic communities, we start wearing them only after marriage. On Yom Kippur we wear our *tallit* for the entire duration of the services, so now is the right time to put yours on. In all likelihood, the synagogue has a rack with some spares that you can use.

You may also notice that many people are wearing white clothing, and some are even wearing a white robe called a *kittel*. This is because on Yom Kippur we are likened to angels. The angels do not eat, and neither do we. The angels devote themselves to praising Gd, and so do we. The shroud-like *kittel* also reminds us that all life on earth comes to an end. If you do not have a *kittel*, don't worry.

Now that you are all dressed up, you need a book. The Yom Kippur prayerbook—called a *machzor*—contains all the prayers and Torah readings for the entire day. If you are attending services at Chabad, chances are that the congregation will be using the red-bound *machzor* published by *Kehot* Publication Society. It has Hebrew and English texts, Hebrew on the right and the English translation on the left. Pick one up and make your way to your seat. Remember, in traditional Jewish services men and women sit separately.

Now that we are sitting, let me tell you what you can expect tonight. For your convenience, I will be pointing out the prayers as they appear in the Chabad *machzor*. If you are using another edition, don't worry; the pages may be different, but most of the prayers are the same.

In the front of the sanctuary, you will notice a large cabinet with a curtain draped over the front. Called an ark (or *aron hakodesh*), it contains the Torah scrolls, which are read during the services. We will be opening and closing it quite a lot during the next 25 hours. It is customary for people to stand whenever the ark is open. However, if you are not feeling up to it, you may sit as long as the Torahs have not been removed.

The prayers will be led by the cantor, also known as the *chazzan*. He will begin and end each paragraph in Hebrew out loud. There will be some parts of the services that only he will say, with everyone else responding as indicated in the *machzor*. The rabbi will also be speaking from time to time (exactly how much varies). In some congregations, the rabbi will announce the pages. In others, there will be a board with page numbers that will be updated as we go along.

If you are more comfortable in English, do say the prayers in that language. After all, prayer is a conversation between you and Gd, and you need to know what you are saying.

Yom Kippur Eve

The evening service on Yom Kippur is divided into three parts:

Kol Nidrei

Maariv

Selichot

Kol Nidrei (page 35): "Kol Nidrei" means "all vows," and is a formal declaration stating that any vows that we make unintentionally during the coming year should be considered null and void. The ark in the front of the synagogue is opened, and three Torahs are removed. Three men hold the Torahs near the *chazzan*, while he repeats the Kol Nidrei prayer three times.

In addition to its technical function of ensuring that we do not accidentally break our word, this sacred declaration is also our way of saying that we are coming to Yom Kippur with no strings attached. As we approach this special day, we tell ourselves and Gd that we regret and distance ourselves from the wrong decisions that we humans inevitably make. The ancient, haunting melody of Kol Nidrei is one of the most memorable parts of the Yom Kippur service.

Maariv (page 43): Maariv is the evening prayer, which we recite on a daily basis. However, in honor of Yom Kippur there are several important additions and modifications (and on Friday night we start with special hymns to usher in the Sabbath, page 37).

Shema (page 44): As usual, the Maariv service begins with the Shema and its accompanying blessings. The Shema, in which we declare Gd's unity and our fidelity to Him, is perhaps the most central of all Jewish prayers. The next line, "*Baruch shem*" ("Blessed be the name"), is normally whispered, because it is a pronouncement so holy that it really belongs to angels. But since today we are like angels, we make a point of saying it out loud for all to hear.

Amidah (page 47): The Shema is followed by the silent standing prayer, known as the Amidah. We stand facing the front of the synagogue with our feet together, and say the words quietly, in a whisper that only we can hear.

We'll say the Amidah a record five times over the next 25 hours. Every time we say the Amidah on Yom Kippur, we conclude with an extensive confession. The confession lists the sins that we (may) have done this year, starting with each letter of the Hebrew alphabet. As a tangible expression of regret, we strike our heart with our right fist for each sin. More important, however, is the personal, unscripted confession that we each say at this time, listing and regretting any misdeeds during the past year. (Remember: if we actually harmed someone, confession alone is not enough; we need to actually make amends by righting the wrong and asking the offended party for forgiveness.)

Selichot (page 57): Literally, "forgivenesses," Selichot is a collection of poetically written prayers asking Gd to forgive us on this day. The central theme of Selichot is the Thirteen Attributes of Mercy (p. 62), which Gd shared with Moses at Mount Sinai. We will repeat these attributes dozens of times during the Yom Kippur service. Many of the Selichot are very intricate poetry, with quotations from many parts of the Bible woven together with Midrashic motifs in rhyming verses, often arranged according to the Hebrew alphabet. The Selichot conclude with another round of confessions, but this time we read them together, with the chazzan leading the way.

One last highlight is the Avinu Malkeinu (page 80), in which we address Gd in a series of verses, each one beginning with "Our Father our King." (This is omitted on Shabbat.)

Morning Services

Good morning and welcome back. The morning service (called Shacharit) starts off pretty much the way it does every Sabbath, and can be divided as follows:

Introductory Hymns

The Shema and Its Blessings

Amidah and Repetition

Torah Reading and Haftorah

Yizkor

Introductory Hymns (page 115): A selection of Psalms and other praises to Gd, you can think of these as a "warmup" for the long run ahead. Look out for the words "*Hamelech yoshev*" ("The King sits," page 135). The chazzan introduces these words with an ancient melody, and chants them loudly with a touch of trepidation.

Shema (page 141): Like last night, we say the angelic proclamation of "*Baruch shem*" out loud.

Amidah and Chazzan's Repetition (page 145): Unlike last night, after we say the silent prayer during the daytime, the chazzan will repeat it out loud. The *chazzan's* repetition is peppered with many additions. You will notice that for certain selections, those deemed especially powerful, we open the ark. Many of the additions are meant to be said responsively, as a joint effort between the *chazzan* and the congregation.

Last night, following the prayers, we said Selichot. During the day, the Selichot are incorporated into the *chazzan's* repetition of the Amidah. Thus, our ten-page Amidah triples in size, and lasts from page 156 to page 190. And again, like last night, the Selichot are followed by the Avinu Malkeinu on page 190.

Torah Reading (page 198): All stand as two Torah scrolls are removed from the ark and brought to the bimah (raised table) in the middle of the sanctuary to be read. The bulk of the reading (page 202) tells of Gd's instructions to Israel on how to conduct the Yom Kippur service in the Holy Temple, where animal sacrifices were the focus of the day's devotion. During the reading, a series of men are called up to say blessings over the Torah. This honor is known as having an aliyah. When the reading is over, the Torah is hoisted high in the air for all to see. We then take out a second scroll and read another small section of the Torah, where the day's sacrificial order is mandated.

Haftorah (page 207): The Torah reading is followed by the haftorah, a selection from the Prophets. This morning it is a portion of the book of Isaiah which discusses returning to Gd sincerely.

Yizkor (page 210): People are exiting the sanctuary, but it is not over yet. Rather, they are leaving because Yizkor is about to begin. Four times a year, a special memorial prayer is recited by those who have lost one or both of their parents. It is customary for all those whose parents are alive to leave the synagogue for the duration of this service. Many congregations also add memorials for the victims of the Holocaust. If you are fortunate enough to be among those who do not stay in for this prayer, do not wander too far, because it lasts only a few minutes.

Musaf (Page 215): We are now about to start the second silent prayer of the day. By now, you know the drill. We face the front with our feet together, and read from pages 215–226. The prayer is again followed by the alphabetical confession known as the Al Cheit. (By now your stomach is probably starting to rumble. The best way to stave off hunger is by focusing on the prayers and their meaning. After Musaf, most synagogues break for a few hours, so hang in there.)

Again, the reader will repeat the silent prayer with significant additions. Here are three major landmarks that you will notice:

- **Unetaneh Tokef** (page 238) is one of the best-known prayers of the day. It contains the chilling description of Gd's decrees for those who will not survive the year: who will perish by "water, who by fire, who by sword, who by hunger…" After those sobering pronouncements, we declare loudly (and, as you can imagine, with great sincerity) that teshuvah, *tefillah and tzedakah* (commonly translated as "repentance," "prayer" and "charity") avert the worst decree.

- **Bowing:** You will notice that people are getting down on their hands and knees and prostrating themselves on the ground. No, they did not lose anything, and sorry, there are no snacks stashed down there. Rather, we bow down when we read the words "We bend the knee, bow down and offer praise before the Supreme King..." on page 245, and a few more during the Avodah.

  What is the Avodah? Starting from page 246, we begin a blow-by-blow account of what actually took place in the Holy Temple on this day. The central figure in this narrative is the *kohen gadol*, the high priest, who performs much of the day's service. This included bringing incense into the Holy of Holies, the inner sanctum, which even he would dare enter but one day a year. Another highlight was the two goats upon which he would draw lots. One goat would be sacrificed on the altar, and the other was sent out to the desert. Where does the bowing come into the picture? Well, in addition to slaughtering and burning the animals, the high priest would also say a confession upon each one. And when he would make that confession he would do so addressing Gd with His sacred name, the one that no one else ever said. And when people would hear that, they would bow down in deference. When we read about that, we bow as well.
- The Ten Martyrs (page 266): We just read all about the sacrifices, which have been defunct for the past 2,000 years. But are there truly no more sacrifices? How about the millions of Jews who have been killed throughout the ages simply because they were Jews? Are they not sacrifices? Indeed they are. The description of the Ten Martyrs graphically depicts the horrific death of ten sages at the hand of an evil king 2,000 years ago.

Once again, the repetition of the Amidah is followed by the Al Cheit alphabetical confession, page 275.

Priestly Blessing (page 284): Congratulations! You've made it through the morning service. As a reward for your endurance, you will now receive a very special blessing. Known as Birkat Kohanim, this blessing can be given only by descendants of Aaron, the high priest. They bless the congregation with prosperity, divine favor and peace, using an ancient formula written in the Torah. You will notice the *kohanim* exit the synagogue to wash their hands before performing the blessing. During the actual blessing, they cover their upper bodies with their prayer shawls. It's customary for men to cover their heads with their prayer shawls, and for small children to stand underneath their father's *tallit* during the blessing.

Nap Time! Now is the time when most synagogues have a break. Get some fresh air and stretch your legs. If you can, take a little nap and build up some energy for the final stretch.

Minchah—Afternoon Service (page 299)

The afternoon service can be broken up into two parts:

Torah Reading and Haftorah

Amidah

Torah Reading (page 304): This reading includes some of the most fundamental laws of the Torah: whom we are allowed to marry according to Jewish law. Judaism is all about action. And even on this most sacred day, when we feel and act like angels, we cannot forget the nuts and bolts of Torah life.

Haftorah (page 306): After the Torah is lifted high and set aside, we read the *haftorah*: the Book of Jonah. One of the smallest but best-known books of the Bible, the story of Jonah is a great read, complete with a swashbuckling hero who gets swallowed by a fish. Don't miss it. While it will be chanted in Hebrew, feel free to read it in English.

Amidah (page 310): This one follows the same pattern of those before it, as does the (somewhat shorter) repetition (pages 320–342) and the confessions that follow them both. Again, if it is not Shabbat, we say the Avinu Malkeinu.

Neilah—Final Prayer (page 347)

Neilah, literally "closing," was thus named as it is said in the closing moments of the holy day, as the sun is setting and the gates of heaven are clanging shut. The Rebbe was wont to say that while the gates of heaven are closing, we are on the inside. Right now, each and every one of us is as close to Gd as we get during our lifetime. Savor the moment, and think deeply into what you have done this past year, and what you want the coming year to look like.

This fifth and final Amidah of Yom Kippur (pages 350–357) is smaller than the others, with a truncated confession. The repetition, which begins on page 358, is unique in that the Thirteen Attributes of Mercy are repeated time and time again, as we cling to the last moments of the day when the windows of heaven are open.

By now, if you take a peek out the window, you will notice that the sun has set and the stars are peeking through the clouds. At this moment, the apex of our devotion, we all cry out together, "*Shema Yisrael...*": "Hear O Israel, the Lrd is our Gd, the Lrd is One." We recite "Baruch Shem..." three times, and "*Hashem Hu HaElokim*" ("The Lrd is Gd") seven times. As you say the words that thousands of Jewish martyrs have uttered before being killed for their steadfast devotion to Gd and the Torah, imagine yourself literally giving your life for Gd. Afterward, one long triumphant blast is sounded on the Shofar, announcing the end of Yom Kippur.

It's Not Over Yet

People may be making a mass exit toward the door to hit the break-fast, and if you're feeling weak, feel free to join them. You'll probably notice that some will remain in the synagogue to pray the evening service (Maariv), which consists of the Shema and its accompanying blessings, and the silent prayer. Afterwards, you will see people going outside to recite Kiddush Levanah, a blessing we say during the first half of each month recognizing the new moon.

You did it! You just spent the past 25 hours in total oneness with Gd. Enjoy your break-fast, and savor this feeling of accomplishment.

Many have the custom to start working on their *sukkah* tonight, in order to go "from one mitzvah to the next." Whatever you do, don't let the inspiration of Yom Kippur go to waste. Resolve to do another mitzvah: perhaps you can start putting on *tefillin* every day, lighting Shabbat candles on Friday night, or attending synagogue services more regularly. Take Yom Kippur and bring it into the rest of your life.

Glossary

A

ABBA: Father; connected to DMT.

AGGADATA: Nonlegal aspects of the Talmud

AIN SOF: Without end; God-Mind.

ANAHA: Grief.

APROCRYPHA: Books removed from the Bible.

ARON HA BRIT: Ark of the Covenant.

ASIYAH: Action; lower world.

B

BEIT HA MIKDASH: Holy Temple.

BINAH: Understanding.

B'NAI: Children.

BOHU: Void.

C

CHAIYEH: Highest level of the Soul, followed by Neshamah, Ruach, and Nefesh/Lowest level of the Soul.

CHOCHMAH: Wisdom.

Choshech: Darkness.

Chutzpah: Arrogance.

Codex: Levels of symbolic meanings and numerical values.

D

Da'at: Pineal gland/knowing and knowledge; middle brain.

Davon: Act of praying.

Derech Aitz Chaym: Road to Tree of Life ; Spiritual Path.

Drash: Ethics.

Dybbuk: Bad spirit; astral.

E

Ebion: Poverty.

Even Shetiya: Foundation Stone all reality created, connected to Stonehenge and Macchu Picchu; weaving stone.

G

Gehinnom: Hell.

Gemara: Amplification and commentary of the Mishnah.

Geonim: Geniuses.

Gilgul: Transmigration of Souls; reincarnation.

Golem: Artificial Intelligence.

Goral/Lots: Divination (Urim V'Tumim); using scripture as oracle in Holy Temple on breast plate of Priest.

H

Halachah: Jewish Law.

Halal: Void.

Hasadim/RT; Gevurot/LT: Divine Masculine/Divine Feminine.

Haskalah: Enlightenment.

Histavut: Balance.

Hitzotzot: Fractal sparks; encoded in Torah.

I

Imma: Mother; connected to wine.

K

Kaballah: Receiving.

Kavanot: Mystical intentions.

Keruvim: Cherubs

Keter: Crown

Kishufim: Magic; high technology.

Klal Yisrael: Collective Soul of Israel; Oversoul.

Klipah: Dome.

Klipot: Shells; covering; reference to foreskin.

Kodesh Ha Kedoshim: Holy of Holies; Temple.

Kol Ha Tor: Voice of the Turtle Dove; analysis of Zohar.

Kotel Ha Ma'aravi: Western Wall; Mt. Moriah.

Kudlah/Kudalin: Straight serpent reuniting with self; Kundalini.

Kush: Ethiopia.

L

Levels of Creation: Atzilut, sparkling white, emanation, Spirit; Beriah, white, creation, thought; Yetzirah, red, formation, feeling; Asiyah, black, corporeal world, action.

Luz: Hazelnut; Pineal Gland (1st Temple, Brainstem, Sod; 2nd Temple Coccyx Bone, Yesod; 3rd Temple Pineal Gland, Pen); connection to Foundation Stone and Lhasa Tibet.

M

Magid: Spiritual guide.

Makom: The Place; reference to God and Pineal.

Malakh: Angel; messengers.

Malchut: Kingdom.

Mashiach: Mesiah/Twins; Oversoul of ben Yosef/ben David.

Mayim Chayim: Living liquid; water.

Mazal: Angel species.

Mazikin: Demon; causes harm to humans.

Merkava: Chariot; energy field of the body.

Midrash: Ancient commentary on Hebrew Scriptures.

Mishnah: Body and codex of the Oral Torah + Gemara.

Mispar: Numbers; root is Sefer-book.

Mitzvah: Good deed.

N

Nachash: Serpent; king over every other Being.

Nefilim: Giants; hybrids.

Nogah: Glow; spiritual state.

O

Ohr Ha Ganuz: Hidden light of God-Mind.

Olam Ha Bah: Next world; meet at Pineal.

Olam Ha Zeh: This world; meet at Pineal.

O'rlah: Foreskin.

P

Pardes: Four dimensions of Torah (Pshat, Remez, Drush, Sod).

Peniel: Face of God.

Prophecy: Kedusha, holiness; Perishah, separation; Hitbo'dedut, isolation.

Pseudepigrapha: Letters, books of Biblical references but never included in the Bible and not verified.

Pshat: Simple narrative.

R

Rav, Rebbe, Rabbi: Teacher and spiritual leader.

Remez: Intellectual.

Ruach Ha Kodesh: Holy Spirit.

S

Sar ha Panim: Prince of the face; Metatron.

Sasson, M, Joy/Simcha, F, Happiness: At end of the world they struggle.

Sefer, Book/Sapar, Storyteller/Sippur, The Story: How God Created.

Segulot: Ritual spiritual remedies.

Sekhelim Nivdalim: Separate intelligences; angels.

Serafom: Reptilians.

Shadai: Name of God/Sexual; #214 = Metatron.

Shechinah: God's Presence; female.

Shedim: Demons.

Sod: Significant meaning; opposite of Pshat.

T

Tehom: Abyss.

Talmud: Jewish civil/Mishruh and Ceremonial Law/Gemara.

Talmud: Represents the six orders of Mishnah.

Tefilah: Prayer.

Tefillin: Prayer box; used on forehead.

Teli: Dragon/astral; the Watchers.

Teshuva: Redemption.

Tikun Olam: Rectify/correct personal world.

Tohu: Chaos.

TORAH: Instructions; teachings.

TZEDAKA: Righteousness; charity.

TZELEM: Aura

TZIM TZUM: Contraction that precedes expansion in creation.

Y

YAGON: Sorrow.

YERUSHALAYIM: Jerusalem, city of peace.

YESHIVA: Seminary; religious school.

YESHUA: Jesus/Salvation; not a name.

YESOD: Spinal column

YHVH, CALLED HAVAYA: Active Being; Being in action; Total Consciousness.

Z

ZION: Location of Foundation Stone; from which all Existence emanates.

ZOHAR: Splendor, brilliance, radiance.

Index

Symbols

3 Holy Fathers 163
4th Reich 180, 190
5 books of Moses 139
5 Books of Moses 176, 210
7 Lower Sephirot 47
7 Noahide Laws 129
10 Commandments 152
12 Tribes 199
12 Tribes of Israel 182
72 Names of God 13, 15, 22, 27, 33, 39, 45, 49, 58, 59, 63, 74, 108, 143, 145, 146, 165, 176, 192, 196, 198, 220
72 Names of God Frequency #1 Time Travel 59
72 Names of God Frequency #5 Healing 58
400 Gates of Impurity 166

A

Abel 147, 148
Absolute Infinity 52
Adam Kadmon 51, 105
Age of Aquarius 47, 141
Alternative Medical Apocrypha 207, 218
Amalek 152
Ana B'koach Prayer 199
Anakim 153
Angelic Frequency 141
Angel of Death 65, 67
Antifa 153
Antimatter 24, 70, 163, 165

Aramaic 19
Aravah 92
Archangel Michael 221
Aries 65
Ark of the Covenant 220, 256
As Above, So Below 197

B

Bar Mitzvah 84
Benjamin Netanyahu 118
Bible 16, 21, 36, 56, 69, 70, 80, 89, 97, 116, 120, 121, 122, 123, 127
Biblical Scholars 48
Black Lives Matter 153
Blue 226
Book of Deuteronomy 96, 130
Book of Ester 56
Book of Formation 119
Book of Genesis 164
Book of Kings 70
Book of Life 83
Book of Psalms 96
Book of Revelation 48
Book of Ruth 212
Book of the Maccabees 36
Book of Yetzirah 119
Books of Leviticus 103
Brain of God 220
B'rich Sh'mei 15
Bris 159, 160
Brown 43
Brown Merger 67

Butterfly People 169
Butterfly People of Joplin 192

C

Cain 147, 148
Cancer 106
Cave of Machpelah 165, 166
Chakra Bands 149
Cheshvan 32
Christ Consciousness 141
Christopher Columbus 133
Coat of Many Colors 198
Covid-19 18
Crown Chakra 226

D

Dark Lord 145
Dark to Light 34
Decoding Your Life 209
Deep State 227
Deuteronomy 24, 202
Divine Essence 70
Divine Intervention 145
Divine Monologue 81
Dreidel 38

E

Elohim 82
Emanuel 177
End of Days 48, 151, 179, 198
End Times 48, 156
Essence of God 82
Etrog 92

F

Feast of Saturnalia 34
Federal Reserve 190
Fertility 65
Festival of Lights 35
First Book of Enoch 123
Flame of God 226
Frequency #1 Time Travel 176

G

Garden of Eden 122, 159, 165
Gedaliah 91
Gemini 104
Generation of Knowledge 48
Golden Calf 152
Golden Menorah 36

Great Challenge 154, 156, 191
Great Flood 127
Green Spiral Staircase 125
Guinness Book of Records 38

H

Hadassim 92
Heart Chakra 78, 143
Heart Chakra Band 185
Heights of Health 207
Hell 144
High Holy Days 55
Hillary Clinton 123
Hindu 52
Holy Mother 39
Holy Temple 15, 67, 69, 70, 77, 89, 95, 109
Hyperspace 11, 28, 67, 79, 104, 141, 147, 149, 162, 166

I

Infertility 56
Infinity Archetype 150
inner consciousness 65

J

Jewish New Year 20, 78
Joseph Stalin 213
Jupiter 39, 55, 58

K

Kaparot Ceremony 21
King David 162
King Solomon 18, 70, 82, 115, 135
Kol Nidre 85

L

Lamentations and Ecclesiastes 212
Learn to Read Hebrew in 6 Weeks 173
Light of Justice 100
Light of Mercy 163
Light of the Torah 106
Lilith 123
Lulav 92

M

Ma'ariv 85
Mars 66
Megillat 56
Mikvah 33

Milky Way 167
Mind of Creation 66
Mind of God 24
Miracles 55
Miracles in Motion 215
Montauk Project 116
Moon 59, 107, 109, 110, 111, 112
Moses 82, 104, 107, 121, 139, 145, 152, 186
Mother Energy Intelligence 36
Mother Matrix of all Creativity 81
Mount Eival 94
Mount Grizim 94
Mount Sina 152
Mount Sinai 93
Move: The Forces Uprooting Us 169
Mt. Sinai 105

N

Namaste 52
Name Frequency #1 Time Travel 22, 198
Name Frequency #5 Healing 22, 39, 145
Name Frequency #46 Absolute Certainty 146, 212
Name Frequency #54 Correct Death 220
Name Frequency #58 Letting Go 216
Name of God 123
Name of God Frequency #1 Time Travel 13
Name of God Frequency #5 Healing 14
NASA 167, 170, 179, 207, 208
Nazi 4th Reich 207
New Testament 145, 183
Noah 32
Numerical Gem of the Torah 69

O

Old Testament 24
Orion Belt 179
Oversoul 11, 28, 41, 61, 62, 67, 73, 79, 100, 104, 112, 141, 149, 157, 162

P

Passover 32, 65, 66, 67, 68, 93, 104, 106
Pisces 55
President Trump 118
Purim 55

Q

Queen of Persia 56

R

Red Sea 49, 145, 152, 186
Revelations of Time & Space, History and God 165
Rosh Hashanah 19
Royal Blue 136, 166
Royal Blue Chakra 226

S

Sagittarius 39, 55
Saturn 127
Scorpio constellation 32
Self-Integration Archetype 67
Sephirot 46
Shalom 69
Shavuot 93, 104, 105, 106
Shield of David 197
Shield of Protection 46
Shofar 17
Simchat Torah 32
Sodom and Gomorrah 162
Soldiers of Light 228
Solomon's Temple 94
Song of Psalms 212
Stage of Creation 79
Star of David 46, 53, 92, 185, 207
Strings of the Universe 141
String Theory 24, 141
Superconsciousness 51
Sword of Moses 47

T

Talmud 103
Taurus 68
T-Bar Archetype 79, 196
Tel Aviv 59
Tetragrammaton 123
The Bible Code 296
The Book of Enoch 152
The Name of God 45
The Plains of Mamre 165
The Rudiments of Hebrew Grammar 132
The Tribe of Levi 199
Totality of Creation 161
Totality of Existence 105
Tower of Babel 199
Tree of God 137
Tree of Knowledge 137, 185
Tree of Life 57, 96, 137, 143, 165

Triangle Archetype 162
Tribe of Dan 141, 222
Tribe of Levi 221
Tribe of Naphtali 222
True Reality 146

U

Ultimate Protection 47
Unetanah Tokef 83

V

Venus 19, 68
Violet 123, 226
Violet Ultimate Protection Archetype 46
Violet Ultimate Protection Technique 53

W

White House 189
White Star of David 53
Witchcraft 123
World War II 131

Y

YHVH 45, 49, 82, 92, 128
Yiddish Scientific Institute 213
Yom Kippur 21, 22, 52, 55, 78, 83, 84, 85, 86, 88, 89, 92, 93, 95, 96, 144, 221

Z

Zhe Shalom Torah 50
Zodiac 19